Atheistic Humanism

Atheistic. Humanism

Antony Flew

THE PROMETHEUS LECTURES

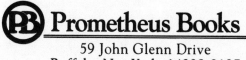 **Prometheus Books**

59 John Glenn Drive
Buffalo, New York 14228-2197

Published 1993 by Prometheus Books

97 96 95 94 93   5 4 3 2 1

Library of Congress Cataloging-in-Publication Data

Flew, Antony, 1923–
    Atheistic humanism / Antony Flew.
        p.   cm. — (The Prometheus lectures)
    Includes bibliographical references.
    ISBN 0-87975-847-3
    1. Atheism. 2. Humanism. 3. Humanistic ethics. I. Title. II. Series.
BL2747.3.F54   1993
211′.8—dc20   93-36215
                                                                    CIP

Printed in the United States of America on acid-free paper.

Contents

PART TWO: DEFENDING KNOWLEDGE AND RESPONSIBILITY

Introduction

If you will, man's situation is left bleaker. . . . Compared with a situation where the human mind . . . had higher mind and higher personality . . . to lean on and to take counsel from, this other situation where it has no appeal and no resort for help beyond itself, has . . . an element of tragedy and pathos. To set against that, it is a situation which transforms the human . . . task . . . to one of loftier responsibility. . . . We have, because human, an inalienable prerogative of responsibility which we cannot devolve, no, not as once was thought, even upon the stars. We can share it only with each other.

Sir Charles Sherrington, O.M., F.R.S.

These sobering words are drawn from the final paragraph of one of the great sets of Gifford Lectures, *Man on His Nature* (Cambridge, England: Cambridge University Press, 1940). All the essays included in the present volume connect more or less closely with the contentions of that paragraph. Those of part one, "The Fundamentals of Unbelief," which were developed from the first set of Prometheus Lectures delivered at the State University of New York at Buffalo in November 1991, combine to sustain its atheist presuppositions. If this atheism is correct then—unless there is some similar or superior kind of organisms to be found elsewhere in the universe—members of our species are indeed the only beings which, because we can and therefore cannot but make choices, are endowed with that inalienable prerogative of responsibility. For it is precisely because we always and necessarily could choose, and could have chosen, to act otherwise than we do choose, and have chosen, that we become capable of responsibility, and therefore also of irresponsibility.

The folly, and still more the sheer evil, of so many of the choices actually made by human choosers provide a most creditable and sympathetic reason for longing to discover a God as—in Matthew Arnold's famous phrase—"something, not ourselves, which makes for righteousness." But when we recognize the lack of sufficient, not to say any, good evidencing as opposed to motivating reasons for believing in the existence of such a Being, we ought to be consoled by the realistic remarks of Albert Einstein in *Out of My Later Years* (London: Thames and Hudson, 1950):

> Nobody, certainly, will deny that the idea of the existence of an omnipotent, just and omnibeneficent personal God is able to accord man solace, help and guidance. . . . But, on the other hand, there are decisive weaknesses attached to this idea in itself, which have been painfully felt since the beginning . . .
> . . . if this being is omnipotent then every occurrence, including every human feeling and aspiration, is also his work. How is it possible to think of holding men responsible for their deeds and thoughts before such an almighty Being? In giving out punishments and rewards he would be . . . passing judgement on himself (pp. 26–27).

The connection between part two, "Defending Knowledge and Responsibility," and the contentions of Sherrington's final paragraph is less direct. Chapters 5 and 6 are both primarily concerned to argue that the discovery of the nonevidencing causes of believing some proposition to be true does not necessarily foreclose the possibility of believers having, and knowing that they have, sufficient evidencing reasons to justify their claims to know. But, in the course of establishing that prime contention, chapter 5 also shows that the potential for rationality and hence also for irrationality, like the potential for responsibility and thence for irresponsibility, is necessarily dependent upon the capacity to make choices. For, if we were so inexorably necessitated to hold whatever beliefs we do actually hold that we could not alter or abandon any of these beliefs, regardless of any discoveries of good evidencing reasons for so doing, then we could not be said, strictly and properly, to know anything; that is, to hold a belief having sufficient reason for so doing.

These conclusions about rationality, responsibility, and choice are essentially connected with the topic of chapter 7, "Mental Health, Mental Disease, Mental Illness: 'The Medical Model'." For the thesis there is that the "medical model" requires that for a condition to be properly rated as a mental illness it must be either a psychological, or a psychologically caused, kind of incapacitation. And the obvious implication is that those put down as mentally ill must be, to some greater or lesser extent, not responsible agents but helpless patients.

Part one attacks the assumption that we can find in "the idea of the existence of an omnipotent, just, and omnibeneficent personal God" the longed for "something, not ourselves, which makes for righteousness." Part three, "*Scientific* Socialism?", examines what has for many constituted a satisfactorily secular alternative. For in our century many of those unable to believe that a supernatural and unlimited Power will eventually ensure the realization of their ideals have nevertheless persuaded themselves that History, and its putative naturally necessitating laws of development, guarantees the establishment of Utopia, "an association in which," in the words of the *Communist Manifesto,* "the free development of each is the condition for the free development of all."

The final section, part four, "Applied Philosophy," engages with some more obviously and immediately practical issues. For instance, Hamlet famously wished that "the Everlasting had not fix'd/ His canon 'gainst self-slaughter!" In the perspective of part I there can no longer be so absolute a ban upon any exercise of "the right to death"; a right which, chapter 11 argues, is implicit in the right to life proclaimed by the American Declaration of Independence. Again, chapter 12 applies, to charges and countercharges of "brainwashing" and "deprogramming" arising from conversions to various disfavored so-called cult religions, ideas developed in chapter 7, "Mental Health."

With the exceptions of chapters 1, 2, 4, and 13, all the essays in the present collection draw more or less heavily upon previous publications. Chapter 3, "Evidencing Naturally Impossible Occurrences," reemploys materials both from "Historical Credentials and Particular Revelation" in R. J. Hoffmann and Gerald A. Larue, eds., *Jesus in History and Myth* (Buffalo, N.Y.: Prometheus, 1986) and from "Parapsychology, Miracles and Repeatability," in Kendrick Frazier, ed., *The Hundredth Monkey and Other Paradigms of the Paranormal* (Buffalo, N.Y.: Prometheus, 1991).

In part two, chapter 5, "Must Naturalism Self-Destruct?", and chapter 6, "Sociology of or against Knowledge?", are both extensively revised versions of papers originally published as, respectively, "Must Naturalism Discredit Naturalism?" and "A Strong Programme for the Sociology of Belief." The former was included as chapter 17 of Gerard Radnitzky and W. W. Bartley III, eds., *Evolutionary Epistemology, Rationality and the Sociology of Knowledge* (La Salle, Ill.: Open Court, 1987), whereas the latter appeared as a "Critical Notice" in *Inquiry* 25 (1982) published by Universitetsforlaget A/S of Oslo. Chapter 7, "Mental Health," is a slightly revised version of what originally appeared under the same title as chapter 6 of Philip Bean, ed., *Mental Illness: Changes and Trends* (New York: John Wiley and Sons, 1983).

In part three, *"Scientific* Socialism?", chapters 8 and 10 are substantially unaltered reprints of articles that originally appeared under the same titles in, respectively, *Philosophy* (April 1991) and the *Public Affairs Quarterly* (January 1991). Chapter 9 is an extensively revised version of an article first published in the *International Journal of the Unity of the Sciences* (Fall 1991).

In part four, chapter 11, "The Right to Death," is a conflation of articles that originally appeared in *Reason Papers* (1980) and in G. Lesnoff-Caravaglia, ed., *Aging and the Human Condition* (New York: Human Sciences Press, 1982). Chapter 12, "Brainwashing," is an only very slightly revised version of an article originally published under the same title in *Reason Papers* (1988). Chapter 13, "Three Concepts of Racism," is, as was said earlier, one of four originally written for the present volume. But mention should perhaps be made, if only by way of an obituary tribute to that ever-embattled journal of political and cultural freedom, of the fact that a much shorter article under the same title appeared in what regrettably turned out to be the penultimate issue of *Encounter*. Chapter 14, "Freedom and Human Nature," draws heavily upon materials first published in chapter 1 of my *Equality in Liberty and Justice* (London and New York: Routledge, 1989) and in an article under the same title in *Philosophy* (January 1991).

My thanks are due, and most gladly given, to all the editors and publishers of the various books and journals from which previously published materials have been taken for granting their permission to reemploy those materials in the present volume.

Antony Flew
Reading, England
October 1992

Part One

Fundamentals of Unbelief

1

A Defeasible Atheism

Great and terrible systems of divinity and philosophy lie round about
us, which, if true, might drive a wise man mad.

Walter Bagehot, 1879

Before accepting any belief one ought first to follow reason as a guide,
for credulity without enquiry is a sure way to deceive oneself.

Celsus, about 170 A.D.

Those two motto quotations are borrowed from John Gaskin's excellent
collection of readings *Varieties of Unbelief: From Epicurus to Sartre*
(New York and London: Macmillan and Collier Macmillan). After
insisting in his preface that Epicurus and his poetic prophet Lucretius
are the founding fathers—"the philosophical archetypes for looking at
the world as a single natural system in which supernatural agents and
bodiless spirits play no part"—Gaskin proceeds in the introduction to
distinguish three elements in their comprehensive unbelief. First comes
"lack of belief in supernatural agents—God, gods, demons, or any
abstraction intended as a substitute for these, for example, Tillich's
'ground of our being.' " Next is "lack of belief in miracles, interventions
in the natural order by supernatural agents." And the third is "lack
of belief in a future state, in the continuance of any individual person

17

after that person's real bodily death."

The person privileged to deliver the first set in a series of Prometheus Lectures was, surely, duty bound to treat at least one or two if not all of these three topics. The lectures actually given in Buffalo during November 1991 concentrated upon the first and the third, the two that together cover the field of Natural Theology, and their material was drawn from drafts for what now appear as chapters 1, 2, and 4 of the present book. Natural Theology consists, or some would be tempted to say consisted, in the study of what can or could be known about God and about our personal immortality absent any divine revelation. Since any such self-revelation would necessarily be supernatural, it is customary to speak here of the possibilities and limitations of unaided natural reason.

While concentrating, however, on Gaskin's first and third elements of a comprehensive unbelief, it is necessary also to indicate the relevance of Natural Theology to the second. For it is often thought, or at any rate confidently assumed, that it is rational, or would be, to accept something as a revelation without appealing for support to any actual or alleged prior knowledge of the putative revealer. Such support, it might be argued, is unnecessary. It could be sufficient for the authentically revelatory teachings to be either independently identifiable through the occurrence of endorsing miracles or else to be somehow unmistakably self-certifying.

But now, even suppose that we waive Humian and Neo-Humian objections concerning the difficulty if not the sheer impossibility of establishing, by the methods of secular as opposed to sacred history, that a genuine miracle did actually occur (objections, that is to say, of the kind deployed in chapter 3 below); still we have to press the question how, if at all, those without prior knowledge of that God would be able to assure themselves that any particular teachings thus miraculously endorsed did indeed constitute a true self-revelation of God, rather than the deceivings of some much less than unique and omnipotent evil spirit. For the New Testament itself provides more than one warning against the dangers of such pseudorevelations.

That first set of Prometheus Lectures was not directly concerned with any tradition other than that of Western Christianity. But it is very much to be hoped that some future Prometheus lecturer will examine rival claims to possess authentic divine revelations, and, in particular, with those of Islam.[1] For in today's world that—especially in the fiercely militant form usually characterized as fundamentalist[2]—is by far the most politically formidable of those "Great and terrible systems of divinity . . . which, if true, might drive a wise man mad." It is also one that appears to have been almost totally neglected by rationalists in those countries where it could be challenged safely. Yet the very fact that it would be scarcely possible to make and to publish a direct challenge to the revelation claims of Islam in any of the Islamic countries is a reason why we who are more fortunately placed should accept an obligation to provide the missing materials.

1. An attempt to see with fresh eyes

In lecturing in what seemed to be the inevitable area for the first series of Prometheus Lectures, I had a peculiar problem. For in the more than forty years since the first publication of a much reprinted squib mischievously yet not ineptly entitled "Theology and Falsification" I had already covered the ground fairly thoroughly; and most of this work is either still in print—some indeed from Prometheus Books[3]—or otherwise readily available in libraries. So I needed to find some new twist, some gimmick.

(i) What I eventually found was suggested by a visit in 1990—on account of the massacre in Tienanmen Square a visit one year deferred—to the Institute of Foreign Philosophy in Beijing. The hopefully sufficient innovation is to try to approach questions about the Mosaic God— the God of what Islam knows as "the peoples of the Book"—as if we, fully grown, were meeting the concept of that God, also fully developed, for the first time, and as if we were now, also for the first time, wondering whether that concept does in fact have actual application. For it is, surely, significant that almost everyone who has ever given sustained attention to this question has treated it as being about the concept of the logically presupposed source of a putative self-revelation, and that accounts of those putative self-revelations have been handed down and made familiar to these questioners through generations of parents and pedagogues, of priests and rabbis, of imams and ayatollahs.

The radically fresh and open-minded approach to be attempted here is that required by the extremely able young philosopher who served so considerately and so efficiently as my "minder" during my visit to Beijing. Certainly Tsu Chi, through his readings of "Foreign Philosophy," had met the Mosaic concept of God. But he had met it only as today anyone anywhere might happen to come upon the notions of Aphrodite or Poseidon. He had never had occasion to confront it as what William James called a "live option"[4]—any more than, for any of our contemporaries anywhere, belief in the real existence of the Olympians constitutes such an option.

If today any of the Olympians are thought of at all, they are thought of as personifications of particular kinds of phenomena, personifications wholly definable in terms of those phenomena, and having no independent existence. Such personifications necessarily cannot in any way control or influence the phenomena personified. Nor can the corresponding concepts possess explanatory power, since an explanation has to do more than restate some or all of the facts to be explained. About such degenerate and innocuous conceptions of divinity everyone can afford to let Lucretius have the last word:

> If anyone decides to call the sea Neptune, and corn Ceres, and to misapply the name of Bacchus rather than to give liquor its right name, so be it; and let him dub the round world "Mother of the Gods" so long as he is careful not really to infest his mind with base superstition.[5]

(ii) Of course, for example in his reading of Descartes, Tsu Chi had come across the concept of the Mosaic God. But for him the Cartesian arguments for the actual existence of a "good God who is no deceiver" were and could only be no more than curiosities in the history of ideas. If anyone offered them to him as evidencing reasons why he or any other scientifically informed contemporary should accept the existence of that God, and should proceed to make appropriate adjustments to his life style, then that person would simply be laughed at. "The Ontological Argument? The Trademark Argument?[6] You must be joking"; or, employing a vulgar idiom learnt from me, "Pull the other one!"

For consider how the arguments of *A Discourse on the Method* must appear to someone from a background such as that of Tsu Chi rather than to someone made familiar with that concept of God through the teachings of "generations of parents and pedagogues, of priests and rabbis, of imams and ayatollahs." In part I Descartes begins by expressing reverent and studiously uncritical acceptance of the particular teachings to which he had himself been exposed:

> I revered our theology, and hoped as much as anyone else to get to heaven, but having learned on great authority that the . . . truths of revelation which lead thereto are beyond our understanding, I would not have dared to submit them to the weakness of my reasonings.

A little later in the same part I he proceeds to remark that, "It seemed to me that I might find much more truth in the reasonings which someone makes in matters that affect him closely, the results of which must be detrimental to him if his judgment is faulty, than from the speculations of a man of letters in his study." The moral would seem to be that everyday, perceptually grounded and perceptually checkable practical judgments are much more to be relied upon than any theological teachings. For whereas with judgments of the former kind the penalties of error can be both immediate and severe, the incomparably more terrible penalty of eternal damnation is both relatively remote and typically felt to be—understandably even if falsely—ultimately escapable. Notice too, by way of further powerful reinforcement to that moral, that in the latter area to all appearance equally rational people are committed to a variety of often mutually incompatible beliefs. As Descartes shrewdly observed in part II:

> Having learned from the time I was at school that there is nothing one can imagine so strange or so unbelievable that it has not been said by one or other of the philosophers; and since then, while travelling, having recognized that those who hold opinions quite opposed to ours

are not on that account barbarians or savages, but that many exercise as much reason as we do, or more; and having considered how a given man, with his given mind, being brought up from childhood among the French or Germans becomes different from what he would be if he had always lived among the Chinese or among cannibals . . . I was convinced that our beliefs are based much more on custom and example than on any certain knowledge.

Yet when, having said all this, Descartes launches what is surely the most shattering single-sentence salvo in the entire philosophical literature his prime target is precisely those everyday perceptual judgments upon which he really has the strongest reasons to rely:

So, on the grounds that our senses sometimes deceive us, I wanted to suppose that there was not anything corresponding to what they make us imagine . . . [and] taking account of the fact that all the same experiences which we have when we are awake can also come to us when we are asleep without there being one of them which is then veridical, I resolved to pretend that everything which had ever entered into my mind was no more veridical than the illusions of my dreams.

So how does Descartes propose to put this wholesale and systematic doubt to rest? It is, as has just been said, by arguing "for the existence of a 'good God who is no deceiver.' " And the premises of the arguments offered are that our Maker has imprinted upon every human soul—as his trademark, as it were—the (authentic) idea of God, a concept that supposedly is too splendid to have been shaped by merely human agency, and from which it is allegedly possible immediately to infer the existence of the corresponding object, God.

The most elegant way of disposing of these premises is by referring to the seventeenth-century Jesuit mission to China. For at first, wisely seeking as far as possible to sinicize their message, these missionaries attempted to identify the Christian God with the Confucian Heaven (Ti'en[7]). But once this expedient was reported back to Rome it was forthwith forbidden, for the simple yet abundantly sufficient reason that Heaven possesses few if any of the defining characteristics of that God.

The appropriate starting point for us, therefore, modelling ourselves on Tsu Chi, is a negative rather than a positive atheism; the prefix in the term "atheism" here being construed as it regularly is in words such as "amoral" or "atypical."[8] In this understanding negative atheists, even if they do not entirely lack the relevant concept of God, must never have entertained the idea of the existence of that God as a "live option" for their own belief. But they are certainly not any kind of bigoted dogmatists. Their atheism constitutes no more than a defeasible presumption. They are, as rational people, ready and willing to examine and, for sufficient evidencing reason given, to accept what Hume in apt yet also mischievous words characterized as "the religious hypothesis."[9] They insist, however, upon examining it in the light of the findings of both the natural and the human sciences, and upon approaching the question with, as far as can be, unprejudiced eyes, as if the key concept had just now been presented to them for the first time.

2. Traditional definitions as incongruent constructs

Were we proceeding to investigate the question of the existence of some controversial creature such as Bigfoot, or the Loch Ness Monster, or the Abominable Snowperson, then there would be little if any need for preliminary discussion of the concept before proceeding to the substantive dispute. For if any of these legendary beings do in fact exist, then they must be—they are indeed implicitly defined as being—ordinary or perhaps rather extraordinary creatures of flesh and blood. Any of them if caught could in principle be confined and put on show in either a cage or an aquarium. Nor is there any doubt or difficulty over what would constitute acceptable, decisive evidence of existence.

(i) Definition is, therefore, essential here. But we need now to try to look at the long familiar words of standard definitions with fresh and very foreign eyes, ready to notice any incongruities in the combination of the various elements that are there combined. One temptation, to which even the greatest seem to have succumbed, is to assume that all the several characteristics proposed as defining are already known to characterize a single, unitary, existent Being, and hence to assume that what might be good evidence for the existence of something with some of these defining characteristics must be equally good evidence for the existence of a Being having them all. But, as we shall soon be seeing, the various characteristics customarily attributed to the Christian God do not all mutually entail one another, and some are such as no one would a priori expect to be attributes of a Being characterized by the others. Another temptation, to which again some of the greatest have succumbed, is to make the mistake of assuming that some characteristic which could be known only, if at all, through revelation is knowable and known to natural reason.

The first sentence of the first of the Thirty-Nine Articles of Religion, a foundation document of what is in my own country still "the church by law established," provides a minimum account of the "one living and true God, everlasting, without body, parts, or passions; of infinite power, wisdom and goodness, the Maker, and Preserver of all things both visible and invisible." (Since the other two main varieties of Mosaic theism emphatically reject it, we can here ignore the doctrine of the Trinity, stated in the following sentence.) Richard Swinburne, in the first of his three major contributions, offers a somewhat fuller definition, one that bids fair to become the agreed starting point for all future philosophical discussion:

> A person without a body (i.e., a spirit), present everywhere, the creator and sustainer of the universe, able to do everything (i.e., omnipotent), knowing all things, perfectly good, a source of moral obligation, immutable, eternal, a necessary being, holy, and worthy of worship.[10]

(ii) Both these definitions raise problems, the second even more than the first. What, for instance, are the criteria to be employed in judging worthiness of worship and what are we to understand by "a source of moral obligation"?[11] Again, since "incorporeal person" would appear to be a self-contradictory expression,[12] the Being here defined could presumably be identified, if at all, only as the hypothesized Cause of the supposedly created universe.

In the present perspective, however, two things stand out. First, that we have been given no hints—unless these are somehow implicit in the attribution of interventionist value characteristics—as to how to set about testing a claim that there is indeed "one living and true God" as here described. Second, and equally fundamental, is the difficulty of reconciling the contention that there is a "creator and sustainer of the universe, able to do everything (i.e., omnipotent), knowing all things" with the contention that that Creator does as it were take sides in conflicts within His creation, approving of some things which happen or are done and disapproving of others. For the second of these two ideas is not, to put it very mildly, one certain to occur immediately to anyone entertaining the first for the first time.

Since the actual condition of the observable universe has always, and very reasonably, been seen not as supporting but rather as the main objection to the contention that there is a "Maker, and Preserver of all things" who is at the same time "of infinite power, wisdom and goodness," the ideally fair and systematic heuristic method would seem to be—following the natural order of progress from the lesser to the greater—to begin with the question whether there is any kind of initiating and sustaining cause of all things. After that we might proceed successively to the questions whether that hypothesized Cause is somehow personal and whether, if so, it is endowed with infinite power and wisdom. Only in a final stage should we pursue the question whether this Creator is "perfectly good" in any human understanding of goodness.

That properly final question is often taken, indeed taken for granted, first. This matters because it is only and precisely in so far as a Creator is believed to be in some way an actual or potential partisan within the created universe that the question of the existence of that Creator becomes one of supreme human interest. Compare and contrast the gods of Epicurus who existed in "complete tranquillity, aloof and detached from our affairs . . . exempt from any need of us, indifferent to our merits and immune from anger."[13]

The step from the existence of a Creator to the conclusion that that Creator is indeed any sort of partisan in the created universe is as big as it is crucial. Because they have taken their concept of God to be one and indivisible, assuming that anything possessing any of the defining characteristics must possess them all, many even of the greatest thinkers have made this step without noticing, and in consequence without anxiously seeking some justification for, the making of it.

Joseph Butler, who held the senior see of Durham in days when a Christian commitment was still a precondition for securing such appointments, was certainly one of the two finest philosophical minds ever to adorn the Church of England's bench of bishops. Yet even he could argue:

> There is no need of abstruse reasonings and distinctions, to convince an unprejudiced understanding, that there is a God who made and governs the world, and will judge it in righteousness . . . to an un-prejudiced mind ten thousand instances of design cannot but prove a designer.[14]

To Butler it thus seemed utterly obvious that a proof of a designer and maker of the universe must at the same time be a proof that that designer and maker will also be a righteous judge, rewarding and punishing. Yet earlier Butler had himself maintained that:

> Upon supposition that God exercises a moral government over the world, the analogy of this natural government suggests and makes it credible that this moral government must be a scheme quite beyond our comprehension; and this affords a general answer to all objections against the justice and goodness of it.[15]

(iii) Of course to say this is to make your claims about the goodness and justice of your God, at least in this life and in this universe, in principle unfalsifiable, and hence to make your theism, in that understanding, not only indefeasible but also insupportable. For, in so far as a scheme is "quite beyond our comprehension," we cannot pick out and identify evidence that that scheme either is or is not in fact realized. So Butler's kamikaze tactic has costs as well as benefits. For Butler the benefit is that his contention about God's moral government becomes humanly irrefutable. The cost is that that contention is simultaneously and with an equal necessity emptied of any humanly intelligible substance. Butler is thus in effect, though certainly not in intention, abandoning the claim that his "God exercises a moral government over the world."

Since it is apparently impossible to reconcile all the various characteristics definitionally attributed to God both with each other and with the admitted facts of a far from perfect world, something simply has to give. That was and remains the burden of the falsification challenge, as I stated in "Theology and Falsification":

> Someone tells us that God loves us as a father loves his children. We are reassured. But then something awful happens. Some qualification is made. . . . We are reassured again. But then perhaps we ask: what is this assurance of God's (appropriately qualified) love worth, what is this apparent guarantee really a guarantee against? Just what would have to happen not merely (morally and wrongly) to tempt but also (logically and rightly) to entitle us to say "God does not love us" or even "God does not exist"?

All this ought to be recognized as a sufficient reason for the peremptory dismissal of moral arguments for the existence of the Mosaic God. It is one thing to maintain that a God has supernaturally revealed that that God[16] somehow authorizes and endorses some value system. But it is quite another to argue from the actual existence and acceptance of such systems to the existence and activity of some supernatural originator, sustainer, or enforcer of those systems. We ought to know and not to forget that, a century or more before Darwin first published *The Origin of Species* (1859), the Scottish founding fathers of the social sciences had begun to develop a naturalistic account of the evolution of norms.[17]

The difficulties pointed out in the present section 2 arise, surely, as consequences and costs of the historical development of a finite, one-among-many, this-worldly, tribal god into the unique, omnipotent, omniscient creator God of "the peoples of the Book." For it is entirely natural to think of tribal gods as devoted to the best interests of the tribe, endorsing its established norms, and providing support in its wars. That, after all, is what such gods are for. But would anyone who was not prejudiced by influences from that book and who was open-mindedly and for the first time entertaining the idea of an omnipotent, omniscient

Creator ever think of such a Being as possibly intervening as a partisan in conflicts within (his, or her, or its?) creation?

It would, surely, appear obvious to such a person that everything which occurs or does not occur within a created universe must, by the hypothesis, be precisely and only what its Creator wants either to occur or not to occur. What scope is there for creatures to defy the will of their Creator? What room even for a concept of such defiance? For a Creator to punish creatures for what by the hypothesis he necessarily and as such (ultimately) causes them to do would be the most monstrous, perverse, and sadistic of performances. Absent revelation to the contrary, the expectations of natural reason must surely be that such a Creator God would be as detached and uninvolved as the gods of Epicurus. Indeed some Indian religious thinkers not prejudiced by any present or previous Mosaic commitments are said to describe a Creator as being, essentially and in the nature of the case, "beyond good and evil."

3. The argument from personal experience

Encouraged by the suggestion that our definitions appear to offer no hints on "how to set about testing a claim that there is indeed 'one living and true God,' " some believers will want to protest—in defiance of the dogmatic ruling from the First Vatican Council[18]—that everyone now knows that it is impossible either to prove or to disprove the existence of God. But even if that is true and even if everyone knew it, the consequent moral would not be what it is so often mistaken to be, that we should feel free to plump for either of the two alternative truth values, just as the fancy takes us. For it is similarly impossible, indeed, all too similarly, either to prove or to disprove the existence of the Olympians. Yet no one, surely, wants to maintain that people maintaining any pretensions to rationality are entitled either to believe or to disbelieve in the real existence of those gods, just as the fancy takes them.

Aquinas was absolutely right to rebuke as "frivolous" (levis) the suggestion that faith should simply plump for one particular world system over all possible rivals, without the support of any good evidencing reasons for that preference.[19] It is, of course, because the objective is truth that the reasons have to be evidencing rather than motivating: arguments in the tradition of Pascal's Wager abandon the quest for evidences in favor of a search for motives to self-persuasion.[20] And, furthermore, if it really is the case that there is no good evidencing reason for believing in the existence of the Being characterized by these definitions, then we perhaps ought to remember what most of us consider to be the reasonable response in less elevated but otherwise parallel cases; cases, that is, of other hypothetical beings in principle elusive to observation and identification. It is not, surely, an agnostic suspension of belief but more or less contemptuous dismissal.

(i) To a challenge to meet and attempt to defeat the presumption of atheism perhaps the most presently popular response is to refer to the compelling personal experience of believers. Certainly this is the move most favored by "born again" Christians. The most formidable spokesperson here is John Hick, who argues:

> The right question is whether it is rational for the religious man himself, given that his religious experience is coherent, persistent, and compelling, to affirm the reality of God. What is in question is not the rationality of an inference from certain psychological events to God as their cause; for the religious man no more infers the existence of God than we infer the existence of the visible world around us. What is in question is the rationality of the one who has the religious experiences. If we regard him as a rational person we must acknowledge that he is rational in believing what, given his experiences, he cannot help believing.[21]

Certainly we can and must concede at once that it is one thing to say that a belief is unfounded or well-founded, and quite another to say that to hold to or to reject that belief is irrational or rational for some particular people, in their particular times and circumstances, and with their particular experiences and lack of experiences. But this granted, gladly and immediately, we have to insist upon the fundamental distinction that is in this case crucial.[22] In the ordinary, everyday, layperson's sense of "experience" to say that someone has had experience of cows or computers is to say that they have had dealings with flesh

and blood cows or chip and wire computers. In this sense such statements entail the actual, mind-independent existence of the objects
supposedly experienced.

In the second sense—call it the philosophers' sense—experience is
essentially subjective or, as Berkeley would have said, "in the mind."
I could truly claim to have enjoyed the experience of cows or computers
or whatever else, in this sense of "experience," notwithstanding that that
experience had consisted exclusively of dreams, nightmares, waking
visions, and hallucinations, and even though I had had no dealings
whatsoever with actual cows or computers or whatever else. I could
even make a claim to such experience of some kind of objects of which
there are in fact no actual specimens. Yet still that claim could be denied
only at the cost of calling me a liar.

The confidence of Hick's religious man in the rationality of proceeding to "affirm the reality of God" must be based upon the conviction that his "coherent, persistent and compelling" experience is experience in the ordinary, everyday sense of the word. For how else,
if at all, could it warrant affirmations of "the reality of God"? And,
in default of any obvious alternative, it seems that that "religious man"
would have to rate this religious experience as, if not the same as, then
at any rate crucially similar to, perception.

Certainly the man who can see something with his own eyes and
feel it in his own hands is in a perfect position to know that it exists.
His position is indeed so perfect that, as Hick says, it is wrong to speak
here of evidence and inference. If, for instance, you had a grandstand
view of a crime then you have no need to infer from bits and pieces
of evidence that and by whom it was committed, although for the judge
and jury, who were in no position to see it as it happened, your testimony
will be the decisive evidence in the case. (The idiomatic expression "the
evidence of my own eyes" derives its paradoxical piquancy from the
fact that to see for oneself is better than to have what is necessarily
less direct evidence.[23])

If this religious experience was indeed a kind of perception, then
it would be quite correct to argue that "what is in question is not the
rationality of an inference from certain psychological events to God
as their cause." But God as just now defined cannot, surely, be an object

of perception in anything remotely like any ordinary understanding of the word "perception." How could one become and know that one was immediately aware, either through the senses or in any other natural way, of a Being defined as both incorporeal and endowed with those transcendent defining characteristics?

So in the end it is a question of precisely the kind that Hick maintains it is not. It is, that is to say, a question of the rationality of an inference: "from certain psychological events"—religious believers having, in the second sense of "experience," experiences of God—to God as the cause of those events, and, of course, as the cause causing them in the way that (other) objects of perception cause perceivers to perceive them. And about inferences of that kind the incorrigible Thomas Hobbes wrote what ought to have been the last word:

> If any man pretend to me that God hath spoken to him . . . immediately, and I make doubt of it, I cannot easily perceive what argument he can produce to oblige me to believe it. . . . For to say that God . . . hath spoken to him in a dream is no more than to say he dreamed that God spoke to him.[24]

(ii) Hobbes, however, goes on to allow that, "God Almighty can speak to a man, by Dreams, Visions, Voice, and Inspiration," adding, characteristically, "yet he obliges no man to believe he has so done to him that pretends it; who (being a man) may err, and (which is more) may lie." It is with that final possibility in mind that many people approach the claims made by Bernadette Soubirois at Lourdes or, more recently, the reports of similar apparitions from Medjogorje in the former Yugoslavia. But there may well be, and so far as I know there is, no good reason to doubt any of the testimony—so long, that is, as it is construed merely as testimony to having had such and such experiences, in the second sense of "experience." It is, however, another matter altogether to attempt to establish that these witnesses were privileged to assist at appearances of the Blessed Virgin—in that quite different sense of "appearances" in which actors and actresses make personal appearances. To establish that, if it ever could be established, it would presumably be necessary to appeal to criteria provided by revelation rather than natural reason.

Finally, in considering these and all similar questions of the veridicality of visions we must never forget that adherents of other and often incompatible systems of religion are also persuaded that they too have had, in the everyday sense, experience of the very different objects of their own religious devotions—experience, that is, of Apollo and Athena, of Shiva and Ganesh, just as much as of Jesus bar Joseph and of his supposedly virgin mother. So how can it be reasonable of Hick's cobelievers to rest so confidently upon their conviction that they alone have been privileged to enjoy genuinely informative religious experience? How can it be reasonable, that is, until and unless they have, by first meeting and defeating the presumption of atheism, manoeuvered themselves into a position to maintain that it is through some prior knowledge of the existence and normal activities of its ostensible objects that they have become qualified to pick out their own brand of religious experiences as uniquely revelatory? (A parallel difficulty confronts those who claim that their particular preferred system of putative Revelation is proved to be uniquely authentic by the occurrence of endorsing miracles. For to make out their case they need not only to demonstrate that the miracles supposedly constituting authoritative endorsement of that particular system did actually occur, but also to discredit the claims to have received any similar endorsement of all rival systems. For discussion of the problems of establishing by natural reason that any such endorsing miracles have ever actually occurred, see chapter 3.)

4. A conserving and/or initiating cause?

So we return at last, after what may be seen as a long digression, to what it was earlier argued ought to be the first question. Is it possible or necessary to infer an external cause for the existence of the universe, either an initiating cause, if the universe in fact did have a beginning, or in any case a sustaining cause, a cause without which—in the memorable words of the memorable Archbishop William Temple—"it would collapse into nonexistence"?[25] It cannot be from the start assumed that there must be or is such a cause, much less that, if there is, it is or must be personal, "a Maker, and Preserver of all things."

Since it cannot be taken for granted that the universe had a beginning, any more than it can be taken for granted that it will have an end, the question of a sustaining cause comes first. If the universe did have a beginning, then the economical presumption would be that any sustaining cause will also have caused that beginning. But on that hypothesis, and prior to all knowledge of the nature of the cause of that beginning, or even that it had a cause, there would seem to be no reason to believe that, the universe once given, there is need of any sustaining cause for its continuance.

It is usual to argue to the existence and nature of a sustaining cause on the basis of some general characteristics possessed by our universe but which another might conceivably not have had. But there are also those, including some who on other counts merit intellectual respect, who reach a similar conclusion on the basis of the mere existence of anything at all, altogether regardless of the number and qualities of these existents.

Apparently the distinguished Jesuit father who was one of the original respondents to "Theology and Falsification" was of their number. For to the question "What would have to occur or to have occurred to constitute for you a disproof of the love of, or of the existence of, God?" he responded that for him the only decisive disproof would be the nonexistence of anything at all. It is difficult to see how an answer of this kind can avoid a pantheistic, Spinozistic, and hence heretical identification of God with the universe—*Deus sive natura*—an identification through which the universe becomes itself its own producing and sustaining Cause.

Such an answer connects with the question "Why is there anything, rather than nothing at all?" It is a question that sounds profound. Certainly it is puzzling. The appearance of profundity perhaps arises, somewhat paradoxically, from the height of the abstraction—talk about an existent or existents with no specified characteristics whatsoever. The puzzlement, at least in my own case, is not perplexity about the true answer to a well understood question, but bafflement about the nature of the explanation sought in the uttering of that interrogative sentence, and about why it is thought that such an explanation must be available.

I recall that Gertrude Stein, a literary friend and early promoter of Picasso, is said on her deathbed to have asked, in an appropriately solemn manner: "What are the answers?" She then answered herself with the question: "What are the questions?" and forthwith died.

In the everyday cases in which people ask why there is something—perhaps some particular thing or collection of things—in some particular place, rather than nothing, or at any rate nothing of the such, questions of this form expect answers telling of what, or much more usually who, caused this perplexing or distressing or otherwise untoward situation to obtain. So the question "Why is there anything, rather than nothing at all?" seems to have been custom built—Anglice, tailormade—to require "Because God created it" as the sole acceptable answer. For "the simplest and most psychologically satisfying explanation of any observed phenomenon is that it happened that way because someone wanted it to happen that way."[26]

Yet the whole progress first of the natural and later of the social sciences has gone to show that comparatively little in this universe does in fact occur "because someone wanted it to happen that way." Nor, even before Darwin, should a straightforward, supposedly empirical Argument to Design have appeared well founded. For, of all the sorts of objects known to us, by far the most complicated and sophisticated are in fact not products of human industry but the producers of those products. Furthermore, as we were beginning to suggest towards the end of section 2 above, many of the fundamental social institutions—institutions including those extraordinarily subtle and sophisticated instruments of communication, the natural languages—must have been produced originally through the shortsighted interactions of people incapable either individually or collectively of such feats of creative design. "Mankind," as Adam Ferguson famously maintained, "in striving to remove inconveniences, or to gain apparent and contiguous advantages, arrive at ends which even their imagination could not anticipate . . . and . . . stumble upon establishments, which are indeed the result of human action but not the execution of human design."[27]

Some lines from *Uncle Tom's Cabin* are more revealing here than perhaps the authoress herself recognized. For, unlike the Yankee Miss Ophelia, poor Topsy had never been theologically indoctrinated by either parent or preacher. But she had had abundant opportunity to learn from rural observation what in my young day urban fathers used to reveal to schoolbound sons as "the facts of life." So, when Miss Ophelia asked the question calculated to reveal the latter's lamentably uninstructed ignorance, it was Topsy who could answer for unprejudiced common sense and common experience:

> "Do you know who made you?"
> "Nobody, as I knows on," said the child with a short laugh. The idea appeared to amuse her considerably; for her eyes twinkled, and she added: "I s'pect I grow'd. Don't think nobody never made me."[28]

5. Traditional Arguments to Design

What we can learn from Topsy, even if Miss Ophelia did not, is that all the phenomena that have traditionally served as foundations for Arguments to Design ought instead to be seen—absent revelation to the contrary—as information about what actually occurs, and hence what is naturally possible, without supernatural contrivance. It is high time and overtime to take a fresh, open-minded, skeptical look at Arguments to Design. It has to be not *from* design but *to* design because such arguments—which have been and remain the most widely employed and effectively persuasive of all arguments for the existence and activities of a creator God—are supposed to be arguments from experience. Given agreement that something is in truth an artifact, then the inference to a designer or designers becomes immediate and altogether compelling. It is precisely and only in so far as there is dispute as to whether objects of some kind are indeed artifacts that there is need for argument to settle the question, and in particular, for argument from experience.

Consider, for example, the classic statement from William Paley's *Natural Theology*, a treatise that Charles Darwin read during his time at the University of Cambridge, and by which he was at that time entirely persuaded:

Suppose I had found a watch upon the ground, and it should be inquired how the watch happened to be in that place, I should hardly answer that, for anything I knew, the watch might always have been there. The watch must have had a maker, who comprehended its construction and designed its use. Every indication of contrivance, every manifestation of design which existed in the watch, exists in nature, with the difference on the side of nature of being greater or more, and that in a degree which exceeds all computation.

If while walking in the Scottish hills I were to spot a watch under the heather then I should certainly at once recognize it as an artifact, just as Robinson Crusoe, if he had found a watch lying on the beach of his island, would also at once have recognized that as an artifact. But we could both have also recognized as artifacts objects requiring far less skill and knowledge for their manufacture than watches; archaeologists, for instance, are doing it all the time. For what makes an artifact an artifact is the fact that it was made; not that it is something of mind-boggling complexity, but that it is something of a kind that does not grow on trees, and is not to be found in untrodden territories.

In the fifth of the Five Ways presented as proofs of the existence of God in the second question of part 1 of the *Summa Theologica* Aquinas develops a significantly different Argument to Design. Whereas Paley would seemingly have us conclude that the Design is temporally prior to the facts in which it is supposedly manifested, Aquinas wants to establish a Design continuously controlling and sustaining. He therefore starts from what he alleges to be "the guidelines of nature. An orderedness of actions to an end is observed in all bodies obeying natural laws." He proceeds immediately, without any further reason offered, to assert, "Nothing, however, that lacks awareness tends to a goal, except under the direction of someone with awareness and understanding; the arrow, for instance, requires an archer." From this Aquinas leaps in one bound to his desired conclusion: "Everything in nature, therefore, is directed to its goal by someone with understanding, and this we call 'God.' "

One shudders to imagine Topsy's reaction to this argument. For Aquinas is here confidently offering all those apparently teleological phenomena that to all appearance proceed without "the direction of someone with awareness and with understanding" as among the bases of the contradictory conclusion that "everything in nature . . . is directed to its goal by someone with understanding." (Had Topsy been a child of our time she might have found in this scandalous argument some justification for speaking disrespectfully of "dead white males"!)

Certainly an arrow requires an archer if it is to be shot. But what about all those other teleological phenomena which can be observed in the progress of organisms through their life cycles? At any rate to all appearance, as Topsy would have insisted, living things just grow. Certainly there are not observable archer substitutes. So to conclude from the premises presented by Aquinas—"Everything in nature . . . is directed to its goal by someone with understanding, and this we call God"—is to conclude, on the basis of evidence largely albeit not exclusively contrary, that in all these biological cases where there seems to be no human or other natural direction, all development is nevertheless completely subordinate to and dependent upon supernatural control. This argument really does constitute a most gigantic begging of the question, and a begging of it in defiance of the available evidence actually offered in support of the conclusion thus illicitly attained.

Presumably it is in part by equivocating in the employment of such terms as "teleological" and "goal-directed" that Aquinas and others have reached it: in one understanding these entail conscious direction, and in another they do not. Those outside a Thomist tradition are perhaps more likely to reach the same conclusion—that such teleological phenomena must be the products of conscious direction—in another way. For to many people it has seemed and still seems indisputably obvious, as it did to Descartes, not only that nothing can possibly come about without some kind of cause, but also that that cause necessarily has to be somehow proportionate and adequate to its effect.[29]

Descartes himself spoke of perfection, rather than of adequacy or proportion. But our contemporaries are more inclined to urge that consciousness, self-consciousness, the capacity for reasoning discourse, and various other characteristics, most of which so far as we know are the prerogatives of human beings, simply could not have emerged as the unplanned and unintended byproducts of interactions between entities that could not themselves be significantly described as possessing any such characteristics. Such characteristics, it is sometimes added, cannot conceivably characterize anything purely and simply material.

But now remember Hume's fundamental insight, that we do not and cannot know a priori that any particular thing or sort of thing either must be or cannot be the cause of any other particular thing or sort of thing, or indeed that everything must have any sort of cause at all much less one that is somehow proportionate to its effect. For anyone maintaining either that these characteristics cannot result from interactions between entities not themselves possessed of them, or that they cannot correctly be attributed to anything through and through material, the crucial question—as always, absent special revelation— is how this is supposed to be known. For our only natural knowledge of such characteristics is obtained because, and in as much as, they are characteristics possessed by ourselves and by other members of that very special class of creatures of too, too solid flesh to which all of us belong: "Many are the wonders of the world, but none more wonderful than man."[30]

Notes

1. Such a lecturer might like to be reminded of a point made against Christianity and by implication in favor of Islam by Thomas Paine in *The Rights of Man:* "Had it been the object or the intention of Jesus Christ to establish a new religion, he would undoubtedly have written the system himself, or *procured it to be written,* in his lifetime" (p. 100 in the Penguin Books edition of 1984, emphasis added).

2. This is, I suggest, a misleading description. For the term "fundamentalism" is derived from the title of a series of tracts—*The Fundamentals*— published in the United States in 1909, and it is defined as the belief that the Bible, as the Word of God, is wholly, literally, and infallibly true. But whereas, in order to rate as a Christian it is fully sufficient to hold to the Apostles' and other Creeds, and not necessary to be in this understanding fundamentalist, in order to be accepted as a Muslim isn't it, surely, absolutely essential to be fundamentalist with regard not to the Bible but the Koran?

3. See, for instance, either *God and Philosophy,* reissued as *God: A*

Philosophical Critique (La Salle, Ill.: Open Court, 1984), or *The Presumption of Atheism*, reissued as *God, Freedom, and Immortality* (Buffalo, N.Y.: Prometheus Books, 1984). The latter work is one of the thirty and more publications to include a reprinting of "Theology and Falsification." These include translations into Danish, Welsh, German, Italian, and Spanish.

4. See the title essay in his *The Will to Believe and Other Essays* (London: Longmans Green, 1897), section 1.

5. *On the Nature of Things*, 2.652–57.

6. For an examination of these two arguments in context compare, for instance, my *Introduction to Western Philosophy* (London: Thames and Hudson, revised edition, 1989), chapter 8.

7. This is, of course, the Ti'en of Tienanmen Square.

8. John Gaskin draws our attention to the fact that this usage was anticipated by some nineteenth-century thinkers. Thus Sir John Lubbock in his much reprinted *The Origins of Civilization* (London: Bohn, 1870) speaks of *"Atheism;* understanding by this term not a denial of the existence of a Deity, but an absence of any definite ideas on the subject" (p. 136). A little later, in Charles Bradlaugh, Annie Besant, and Charles Watts, eds., *The Freethinkers' Text Book* (London: Charles Watts, 1876), Bradlaugh wrote:

> The Atheist does not say "There is no God," but he says "I know not what you mean by God; the word 'God' is to me a sound conveying no clear or distinct affirmation. I do not deny God, because I cannot deny that of which I have no conception, and the conception of which, by its affirmer, is so imperfect that he is unable to define it to me." (p. 118).

9. *An Enquiry concerning Human Understanding*, section 2.

10. *The Coherence of Theism* (Oxford: Clarendon, 1977), p. 2. This was the first volume in a trilogy, its successors being *The Existence of God* (Oxford: Clarendon, 1979) and *Faith and Reason* (Oxford: Clarendon, 1981).

11. Notoriously, if things are to be defined as good simply because God wills them, then praise of God for his goodness must become empty and unfounded. But if God wills whatever he does will because those things are good independently of his willing them, then how can God be "a source of moral obligation"? Compare Flew, *Western Philosophy*, chapter 1, section 2, *ad fin.*

12. See chapter 4.

13. Lucretius, *On the Nature of Things*, 2.646–51.

14. *Works*, edited by W. E. Gladstone (Oxford: Oxford University Press,

1896), vol. 1, p. 371 (2[10]2 of *The Analogy of Religion, Natural and Revealed*).

15. Ibid., p. 162 (1[6] of the *Analogy*). I cannot recommend too strongly Sir Leslie Stephen's treatment of Butler in his classic study of *English Thought in the Eighteenth Century* (New York: P. Smith, reproduction of the third edition of 1902, 1949).

16. The here awkward employment of the noun springs from recognition that all personal and impersonal pronouns must be equally inapplicable to a Being defined as both a person and incorporeal. For how could an incorporeal entity have a sex or—as among those ignorant of grammar it is now fashionable to say—a gender?

17. See, for instance, book 3 of David Hume, *A Treatise of Human Nature* (1740), and Adam Smith, *A Theory of the Moral Sentiments* (1759), and, on the evolution of law prior to the invention of legislation, compare F. A. Hayek, *Law, Legislation and Liberty, Vol. 1: Rules and Order* (London: Routledge and Kegan Paul, 1973).

18. H. Denzinger, ed., *Enchiridion symbolorum* (Herder: Frieburg i. Breisgau, 29th revised edition, 1953), section 1806. The "known for certain" (*certo cognosci*) of this definition replaced the more drastic "demonstrated" (*demonstrari*) of an earlier draft.

19. *Summa contra Gentiles*, 1.6. More will be made of this in chapter 3.

20. For an exposition and critique of Pascal's argument, see either *God, Freedom and Immortality*, chapter 5, or *An Introduction to Western Philosophy*, chapter 6, section 7.

21. *Theology Today* (1967): 86–87.

22. It is remarkable, and scandalous, that even professional philosophers can contrive to produce lengthy discussions of "our experience of" this and that without ever recognizing this fundamental distinction and the difference that it makes. Compare, for instance, H. D. Lewis, *Our Experience of God* (London: Allen and Unwin, 1959).

23. Compare J. L. Austin, *Sense and Sensibilia* (Oxford: Clarendon, 1962): "I have, it will be said, 'the evidence of my own eyes.' But the point of this trope is exactly that it does *not* illustrate the ordinary use of 'evidence'—that I *don't* have evidence in the ordinary sense" (pp. 115–16).

24. *Leviathan*, chapter 23.

25. I do not know where he put this into print. But once, as my father's son, I heard it from his own lips.

26. Thomas Sowell, *Knowledge and Decisions* (New York: Basic Books, 1980), p. 97.

27. *An Essay on the History of Civil Society,* D. Forbes, ed. (Edinburgh: Edinburgh University Press, 1966), p. 123. For more on Ferguson and his associates see "Making Visible the Invisible Hands" in my *Thinking about Social Thinking* (London: Harper-Collins, 1992), and, for their influence on Darwin, compare my *Darwinian Evolution* (London: Granada Paladin, 1984), pp. 85-92.

28. Harriet Beecher Stowe, *Uncle Tom's Cable* (New York: Books, Inc., undated), p. 206.

29. These principles appear—as Axioms 3 and 4, respectively—in a very characteristic exercise included in Descartes' replies to the second set of solicited objections to his *Meditations:* "Reasons which prove the existence of God and the distinction between the mind and the human body, arranged as geometry."

30. Sophocles, *Antigone,* 332. And compare David Stove, *The Plato Cult and Other Philosophical Follies* (Oxford: Blackwell, 1991), pp. 84ff., 119, and 173-74.

2

Theism Indefeasible and Insupportable

God can either take away evil from the world and will not, or being
willing to do so cannot. If he is willing and cannot, then he is not
omnipotent. If he can but will not, then he is not benevolent. If he
is neither willing nor able, then he is neither benevolent nor omnipotent.
If he is both willing and able, whence then evil?

Epicurus, quoted by Lactantius

Aquinas was raised and lived his whole life within a culture accepting
as revealed truth, "In the beginning God created the heaven and the
earth."[1] It is, therefore, remarkable that he should have recognized, and
against murmured charges of heresy insisted, that there was no natural
reason for believing in such a beginning.[2] For, absent available scientific
evidence to the contrary, the always defeasible presumption should surely
be that the universe had no beginning and will have no end.

1. Five blind alleys

The classic arguments for the existence of God as the creative, controlling,
sustaining Cause of the universe are those presented by Aquinas in the
second question of part 1 of the *Summa Theologica*. We should never

42

forget what has already been emphasized in the treatment of the fifth of these so-called Five Ways in section 5 of chapter 1, above—that these arguments are not supposed to be leading us to the first term in a temporal succession. Aquinas was not propounding any form of the egregiously unsound argument that there must have been, in the beginning, a (capitalized) First Cause, because every event has a cause, and the precession of causes supposedly could not go back forever.[3]

On the contrary: the First Mover, First Cause, and other prime destinations to which these Five Ways are supposed to lead are all at the apex of hierarchies, rather than at the beginning of temporal series. The argument is not that a process must have a start, but that a hierarchy must have a summit. Once this is understood, there are two related questions that need to be pressed. First, why is it thought that the universe needs a sustaining cause, without the support of which it would supposedly "collapse into non-existence"? Second, why is it thought that every actual hierarchy of every kind must have not just a top term that happens to be, as things actually are, the top term, but an actual realization of the conceivable "mostest"?

(i) Let us take the second and more difficult notion first. Aquinas says: "The fourth way is based on the gradation observed in things. Some things are found to be more good, more true, more noble, and so on, and other things less, but such comparative terms describe varying approximations to a superlative; for example, things are hotter and hotter the nearer they approach what is hottest." Clearly Aquinas is asserting the truth of a general proposition, of which he then proceeds to provide, as a particular application, another proposition that is now known to be false. For there simply is not an absolute hottest as there is an absolute zero. Given therefore that the second premise of this argument is false we are not licensed to draw even the interim conclusion: "Something therefore is the truest and best and most noble of things . . ." But Aquinas continues immediately:

> and hence the most fully in being; for Aristotle says that the truest things are the things most fully in being. Now when many things possess some property in common, the one most fully possessing it

causes it in the others: "fire," to use Aristotle's example, "the hottest of all things, causes all other things to be hot." [*Metaphysics* 2 (1) 993 B30 and B25]. There is something therefore which causes in all other things their being, their goodness, and whatever other perfection they have. And this we call "God."

Aquinas is thus adding to the initial argument, with its to us manifestly false second premise, two further most remarkable assertions. The significance of the first of these—"that the truest things are the things most fully in being"—is that it must involve some sort of identification of existence and excellence. To this we shall return. Those accepting this metaphysical identification thus make "goodness" and "reality" convertible terms and so ensure that for them any Supreme Being becomes as such and necessarily supremely good. They thus spare themselves the theist's Problem of Evil, albeit at the cost of making empty tautological claims that their God is supremely good.

The second assertion—that "when many things possess some property in common, the one most fully possessing it causes it in the others"—is remarkable most for its Platonizing. For it can be understood only by reference to the Theory of Forms or Ideas. The Form or Idea of So-and-Soness is taken both to possess that characteristic in preeminent degree and to be the cause of all those particular things that are so characterizable being so characterizable. If only in the light of nearly two and a half millennia of hindsight it should be obvious that this involves a confusion between criterial and causal senses of the word "make": satisfying the criteria for the application of the predicate "just" is what, in one sense, makes whatever is properly so describable properly so describable, but the criteria do not and could not by themselves cause anyone to be just.[4] So Aquinas reaches his final conclusion here by way of a further false premise.

(ii) Proceeding next to the question "why it is thought that the universe needs a sustaining cause," the first thing to notice is that, as always in the *Summa Theologica,* all that Aquinas acknowledges as his own thought is presented in the form of answers to objections: "I reply that we must say that God can be proved in five ways." Of the two objections from which the present article begins, the first is a characteristically crisp formulation of the Mosaic theist's Problem of Evil, to which we shall return. The second is an equally crisp formulation of the presumption of what, in deference to Strato of Lampsacus, Hume called "the Stratonician atheism" (Strato was next but one in succession to Aristotle as president of the world's second university foundation, the Lyceum):

> If a few causes fully account for some effect, one does not seek more. Now it seems that everything we observe in this world can be fully accounted for by other causes, without assuming a God. . . . Thus natural effects are explained by natural causes, and contrived effects by human reasoning and will. There is therefore no need to suppose that a God exists.

The first three of the Five Ways, urging the need for a sustaining cause, are directed to the defeat of that presumption. They all employ and depend upon and must in the end stand or fall with Aristotle's physics, which was of course the best available either to Aquinas or to any contemporary opponent. This dependence is most manifest in the first, the argument from motion or change, the argument Aquinas himself describes as the most manifest.[5] He takes it as obvious and universally agreed that "anything in process of change is being changed by something else," offering as his illustration of the causing of a movement a man waving a stick. Hence he argues:

> It is only when acted upon by the first cause that the intermediate causes will produce the change: if the hand does not move the stick, the stick will not move anything else. Hence one is bound to arrive at some first cause of change not itself being changed by anything, and this is what everybody understands by God.

But the premise of that argument is grounded upon what is only a part of our ordinary, everyday experience. For Topsy, while allowing that if a man is waving a stick then that stick will continue to move only so long as he continues to move it, could have told us that, if the man hits a ball with that stick then that ball may continue to move through the air with no visible intermediate causes to explain that continuation. That other and by Aquinas here unnoticed element in our experience must have been one of the things that encouraged Newton to formulate the modern First Law of Motion. It is this law that enables us to dispense with the invisible and unbelievable atmospheric movements hypothesized by Aristotle to account for the continuing movement of missiles after being loosed by their projectors. And it also removes the premise upon which Aquinas based what seemed to him the most manifest of his arguments.

If and in so far as it is correct to construe the First Way as an argument to a sustaining rather than an initiating First Mover, and it surely is, then it must also be correct to construe the Second Way as—despite appearances—an argument to a sustaining rather than an initiating First Cause, a First Cause which is, so to speak, always at the head of a causal hierarchy. But since the sustaining First Mover as head of the motion hierarchy is redundant, so too is a First Cause operating in a similarly elevated capacity.

(iii) About the Third Way there are only two things that need to be said here: first, that it ought not to be construed, as it so often has been, as a form of that Leibnizian Cosmological Argument famously refuted by Kant;[6] and second, that it can have little force with anyone whose thinking has not been shaped, as was that of Aquinas, by Aristotle's *Physics* and *Metaphysics*.

This provides an occasion for pointing out that the Principle of Sufficient Reason, from which Leibniz developed his Cosmological Argument, is, so far from being necessarily true, necessarily false.[7] For Leibniz that "great principle" was "that 'Nothing happens without sufficient reason,' "[8] But the truth is that every explanation of why things happen as they do is, and cannot but be, in terms of explanatory principles (*explicantes*) that explain but which, at least at that stage, are not themselves explained (are not things needing to be explained—*explicanda*). So, however far the process proceeds—particular happenings explained in terms of general laws, general laws in terms of still more general theories, and so on—there must always be something, or perhaps some things, that will have to be accepted as the ultimate and inexplicable brute facts; the ultimate *explicantes* in terms of which all the *explicanda* which can be explained have to be.

If theists do have a competitive edge over Stratonician or any other kind of atheists, then it is not because they, unlike opponents, can explain absolutely everything. For the existence of their own preferred ultimate *Explicans* could itself be explained only if the Ontological Argument was valid, which it is not. Their competitive edge, if they had one— and this would, surely, be more than sufficient?—would be in the simple truth of their beliefs about the existence and activities of their God.

2. God and the Big Bang

Unlike Aquinas, we do now have excellent natural scientific reasons for believing that the Universe did in fact have an explosive beginning. This has led some physicists and others to say that the further cosmological investigations are pressed, the nearer the investigators approach to God. As a psychological fact about contemporary cosmologists that may well be true. Perhaps they are indeed tending to "get religion." It may also, and more likely, be true that they are in these investigations rapidly approaching a point beyond which it becomes physically impossible to press physical enquiries. But these are both very different things from saying that the Big Bang must have been touched off by the agency of God—God as defined by Richard Swinburne or in the Thirty-Nine Articles.

(i) To say that is to go much too far and too fast. For whatever basis have physicists got for postulating agency as the initiating cause, to say nothing of endowing that postulated agent with the other attributes for which those definitions provide? The very most that is warranted by the news that it all started with a Big Bang is conceding that altogether indeterminate "cause of the universe" of which Philo speaks in part 2 of Hume's *Dialogues concerning Natural Religion*. That concession enabled the author to deny the dangerous charge of atheism, but without committing himself to belief in an omnipotent Judge who is expected to punish some of his human creatures for one kind of conduct while rewarding others for another, and/or to take in some other way an intervening interest in human life. What Philo was there scripted to say was:

> Where reasonable men treat these subjects, the question can never be concerning the being, but only the nature of the Deity. The former truth, as you well observe, is unquestionable and self-evident. Nothing exists without a cause; and the original cause of this universe (whatever it be) we call God.[9]

So what might justify the move from that indeterminate Philonian cause to a willing Agent? Here we need to reformulate the Stratonician atheism. This is a presumption about the ultimates of explanation. However far we may go in the process of explaining why the facts are what in fact they are, there will always have to be some facts by reference to which whatever is explained is explained, but which themselves, at least at that stage, have to be left as unexplained brute facts. The always in principle defeasible presumption of the Stratonician atheist is that the explanatory ultimates are the sheer existence of the universe, a universe subject to whatever laws of nature science discovers to be most fundamental. (For the theist the explaining but not themselves explained ultimates must be the existence and the will of God.)

The introduction of a " 'Cosmos-Explaining-Being,' or 'CEB' for short,"[10] constitutes an attempt to defeat this presumption. Against the counter that, "The CEB might not have existed; it needs explaining too," the reply is that, "What we must remember is that the object of an explanation is to produce a gain in intelligibility."[11] And this, it is suggested, is achieved by making the hypothesized CEB an agent.

Certainly the object of the search for explanations is to produce a gain in intelligibility. But that is a gain that ought not to be produced at the price of making otherwise arbitrary and unevidenced assertions. Certainly too what social scientists call, in deference to Max Weber, *verstehen* explanations are in a way more intelligible than explanations in terms of natural laws. We are indeed able to understand our fellow human beings as we cannot understand anything else. For we can understand what they did or felt by appreciating that, after their upbringing and in their situation, we ourselves might have felt or done the same. This is, of course, all part of the reason why "the simplest and most psychologically satisfying explanation of any observed phenomenon is that it happened that way because someone wanted it to happen that way."

But that itself is an excellent methodological reason not for rushing to attribute agency and will to the postulated CEB, but for being extremely cautious about any such anthropomorphizing attribution. For, as was stressed previously, the whole progress first of the natural and later of the social sciences has gone to show that comparatively little in this universe does in fact occur "because someone wanted it to happen that way." Absent excellent evidencing reasons—and it appears that such reasons are indeed absent—it becomes preposterous to postulate an anthropomorphic, animistic initiating Cause at the perceived end of the scientific road. Have we really come all that way, both from popular superstitions about spirit causes and from Aristotelian Intelligences moving the astronomical spheres,[12] only to bring it all back in a form infinitely more formidable?

(ii) It is, however, argued that such a postulation provides an explanation that is, because both simple and unifying, scientifically respectable.[13] These certainly are traditional scientific objectives—*Simplex sigillum veri*, simplicity is a sign of truth—while perhaps the greatest of scientific achievements is to produce a theory that unifies what previously were two separate areas of enquiry.

The contention that it is because a personal creator wants things to have been and to be as they were, are, and will be (and that the universe is governed by whatever natural laws are in fact found to obtain) certainly constitutes a theory at once both simple and unifying. It is indeed the ultimate in both simplicity and unification. Unfortunately it has a fatal fault that must discredit any claim to scientific respectability. That fatal fault is that, until and unless we become able to attribute to this universal and comprehensive *Explanans* some characteristics not deducible from a conjunction of its *explananda*, it cannot possess any additional predictive power, that is to say, predictive power additional to that of those *explananda*. Without that this pretended explanation is no more useful than the all-too-universally apt comment: "Kismet, it was fated." In order to be of any use as an explanation, indeed even perhaps to deserve to be accounted an explanation at all, a candidate must explain why it is that the actually obtaining *explananda* do in fact obtain, and not any conceivable alternatives.

If we hypothesize for the universe a personal or any other kind of cause to which we cannot legitimately attribute any characteristics licensing inferences that could not more directly and with equal validity be drawn from the universe itself, then, at least for explanatory purposes, this hypothesized cause remains substantially the same as the Philonian God without qualities, that is, the God upon whose existence, but not upon whose nature, all are agreed, and about the existence of which or whom most of us could not care less. The contention that the Cause, the "God," thus hypothesized exists becomes—at least in this world and this life—in principle and not only in practice, indefeasible.

(iii) Suppose, for example, that we attribute to that hypothesized Cause all the transcendent characteristics of the God defined in the Mosaic tradition. Then it becomes impossible validly to draw any inferences the falsification of which would falsify the hypothesis. As Hume observed in section 11 of an *Enquiry concerning Human Understanding,* this Deity would be known to natural reason only through "his productions, and is a single being . . . not comprehended under any species or genus, from whose experienced attributes or qualities, we can, by analogy, infer any attribute or quality in him":

> The great source of our mistake in this subject . . . is that we tacitly consider ourselves as in the place of the Supreme Being. . . . But . . . it must evidently appear contrary to all rules of analogy to reason for the intentions and projects of men, to those of a Being so different, and so much superior.

Here we may recall how Butler, having satisfied himself that Arguments to Design are more than sufficient to establish that "There is a God who made and governs the world, and will judge it in righteousness," proceeded to offer the proposition "This moral government must be a scheme quite beyond our comprehension" as, what it all too truly is, "a general answer to all objections against the justice and goodness of it."[14]

3. The Argument to Design *redivivus*

Any consideration of the possible attributes of a hypothesized initiating cause for the Big Bang now needs to take note of various fundamental physical calculations, the results of which appear to provide a fresh basis for an Argument to Design. These calculations, made on the assumption that the fundamental laws and constants of physics are what physicists today believe them to be, show that, had the values of some or perhaps any of those constants been appreciably different from what they now appear to be, then intelligent life, or perhaps any life at all, could not have evolved. The upshot, in a nutshell, is that, as the great Duke of Wellington said of his victory over Napoleon in the decisive Battle of Waterloo, "It was a damned nice, closerun thing." Since, on these assumptions, the differences required to prevent the origin and development of any living organisms at all are in the case of some of these values quite fabulously small,[15] there is a strong temptation to argue that it is inordinately improbable that these constants would, without any conscious intention or design, just have happened to have the precise values that they do in fact have.

(i) To any such suggestion about the probability or improbability of universes the stock Humian response is to argue that, since the actual universe is, by definition, unique—"Universes," as C. S. Pierce happily put it, "are not as plentiful as blackberries"—therefore we can never have any basis for saying anything about the a posteriori probability or improbability of any suggested external and supernatural origin or support for the universe. I must confess to some uncertainty about what force to allow here to a dissenting argument which in its original context was altogether compelling. So let us concede, even if only provisionally, that the results of these calculations do point to some sort of intending agency.

Certainly, for the reasons just now cited from Hume, only a very little ingenuity is needed to show that these results, like any other actual or possible facts about the universe, are not necessarily inconsistent with the hypothesis that its initiating cause was the transcendent God of Mosaic theism. But this fresh Argument to Design, like all its predecessors, is, and in the nature of the case must be, much too weak to prove the existence of such an infinite, omniscient, and omnipotent God. For design is necessarily the intelligent employment of means to achieve an end which the designer is not achieving and presumably cannot achieve by direct fiat. It is, to put it very mildly, at the very least egregiously odd to suggest that a hypothesized Almighty who by the hypothesis presumably determines both the content of the physical laws and the values of all the physical constants, and who, again by the hypothesis, supposedly saw or sees the production of intelligent life as a or the main object of the whole exercise, nevertheless went or goes about it in such an extraordinarily indirect and chancy way. Given omniscience and omnipotence, why bother with means at all, whether indirect or direct? Why not, in the forthright fashion of the God of Genesis, create whatever you want immediately and without any intervening means or otherwise redundant accessories?

(ii) It would perhaps be wrong to conclude this consideration of the supposed theological implications of cosmological discoveries without any mention of J. D. Barrow and F. J. Tipler, *The Anthropic Cosmological Principle* (Oxford: Oxford University Press, 1988), although the authors themselves remain staunchly secular in their speculation.[16] They offer not one but three anthropic principles, a weak, a strong, and a final. Strictly speaking, none of the formulations provided is anthropic. For none actually mentions our particular species. Much more serious is the failure of all three to make absolutely clear what are the warrants for accepting the principles thus formulated.

The weak anthropic principle (WAP) runs: "The observed values of all physical and cosmological quantities are not equally probable but they take on values restricted by the requirement that there exist sites where carbon-based life can evolve and by the requirement that the Universe be old enough for it to have already done so." The strong version (SAP) is: "The Universe must have those properties which allow life to develop within it at some stage in its history." The final version (FAP) becomes: "Intelligent information-processing must come into existence in the Universe, and once it comes into existence, it will never die out."

What so urgently needs to be, yet surely is not, made clear, and kept clear, is the authority for these restrictive demands, the meanings of these musts. The heart of the matter is that all three principles demand that all physical and cosmological theorizing should be consistent with certain biological facts, or, in the case of the FAP, certain way-out biological speculations.

In this appeal WAP and SAP are correctly construed as insisting only that, to be true, all our theories must consist within certain known and altogether indisputable facts. Yet even such sophisticated theorizers as Barrow and Tipler sometimes seem to be making the mistake that their anthropic principles are members of a kind of Kantian synthetic a priori truths about the actual organization of any Universe. Nor are they always completely masters even of the distinction between logical and physical necessity, being inclined to confound the logical necessity with which some proposition validly deduced follows from a premise or premises with a physical necessity supposedly asserted by that deduced proposition.

4. God as perfectly good?

The "natural light of human reason" is, it would seem, insufficient to reveal "the one and true God our creator and lord." Even if it were, that would certainly not be enough to establish either that "God our creator" is, at least in any ordinary understanding, perfectly good or that the Creator acts within the creation as a partisan, calling for and rewarding some kinds of conduct while denouncing and punishing others. Neither of these two are assertions which anyone would be at all inclined to make were they meeting the concept of agent creation for the first time.

The first is at first sight so implausible that, in the article of the *Summa Theologica* in which he deploys his five putative proofs, Aquinas makes the familiar and apparently decisive evidence for its falsity the basis for the first Objection:

> It seems that there is no God. For if, of two mutually exclusive things, one were to exist without limit, the other would cease to exist. But by the word "God" is implied some limitless good. If God then existed, nobody would ever encounter evil. But evil is encountered in the world. God therefore does not exist.

(i) To this challenge Aquinas himself responds in two quite different and surely irreconcilable ways. These two responses together constitute one of several cruces at which the Angelic Doctor succumbs to the besetting temptation of the synthesizer—that of trying to have it both ways. One response, as we have already noticed,[17] is straight out to identify being or reality with goodness.

The objection, to repeat, is an objection to the claim that a Creator of the known universe is, in an "ordinary understanding, perfectly good." But that first response scarcely engages at all with the objection, so understood. This bizarre identification of the good with the real is a trophy drawn from Greek philosophy, something very far removed from pre-Hellenic Jewish religion. The subsequent marriage of these two traditions, as is most clearly brought out in one of the classics of the history of ideas,[18] was a bizarre miscegenation. It gave birth to a cross between the initially creating, perennially intervening, agent God of Abraham, Isaac, and Israel, and a timelessly eternal, abstract, remote, theoretically ideal God intellectually descended from Plato's Form of the Good or the Real. In effect, the two were merged and identified one with the other. By thus taking for granted an equation between goodness and existence or reality Aquinas ensures that his Supreme Being, in virtue simply of existing as such, must also be supremely good. But, where that is given, to say that the Supreme Being is supremely, perfectly good is to praise a supreme goodness that simply is no more, nor less, nor other than supreme, absolute, total power.

The equation upon which this apologetic is based is one of those outrageous philosophical moves that demands a robust, authentically Australian dismissal. Like Berkeley's insistence that if I am not in my study and I say that there is a table there, I "mean thereby" that I would enjoy tablish sense data if I were there, "it is so astoundingly false that it defies criticism, at first, by the simple method of taking the reader's breath away. . . . Say, or imply, for example, that in English 'value' means the same as 'individuality.' You can be miles down the track of your argument before they get their breath back."[19]

In so far as he insists upon this outrageous identification Aquinas in effect simply accepts manifestations of God's power, God's glory, as constituting their own sufficient justification. We do well here to recall how Hobbes treated the notorious Problem of Evil. He had been a young man when the Authorized Version was first published, and had a very thorough knowledge of the Bible:

> And Job, how earnestly does he expostulate with God, for the many afflictions that he suffered, notwithstanding his righteousness. This question in the case of Job is decided by God himself, not by arguments derived from Job's sin, but his own power.[20]

Quite true, and very much to the point. For Job chapter 38 begins: "Then the Lord answered Job out of the whirlwind, and said 'Who is this that darkeneth counsel by words without knowledge? Where wast thou when I laid the foundations of the earth? Declare, if thou hast understanding.' " So it goes on, for two whole chapters, a magnificently eloquent hymn to the creative omnipotence and omniscience of God, but all without another word of justification, or, at any rate, not of justification in the narrower sense in which justification amounts to showing to be just. In the end Job is induced to shut up. Who is he or any other creature to question or challenge the absolute, infinite power of the despot? Hear and obey! Job chapter 40 thus begins:

> Moreover the Lord answered Job, and said, "Shall he that contendeth with the Almighty instruct him? he that reproveth God, let him answer it."
>
> Then Job answered the Lord and said, "Behold I am vile; what shall I answer thee? I will lay mine hand upon my mouth. . . . I will proceed no further."

(ii) Among what are offered as answers to the original objections, after the main body of the article in which Aquinas presents his Five Ways, he gives an alternative supposed solution to the Problem of Evil:

> As Augustine says, "Since God is supremely good, he would not permit any evil at all in his works, unless he were sufficiently almighty and good to bring good even from evil." It is therefore a mark of the limitless goodness of God that he permits evils to exist, and draws from them good.

As it stands this simply will not do. For, unless the evils cited are specified as logically (as opposed to causally) necessary conditions of the subsequent goods, the subsequent manifestations of divine power and goodness will provide absolutely no justification for the antecedent evils. For example: injury is the logically necessary precondition of forgiveness. Absent any antecedent injury there is nothing to forgive. If the evils supposedly being justified by reference to subsequent goods are only the causally, not the logically, necessary preconditions of those goods, then the supposed justification is irrelevant. For in that case an almighty God could have, while a perfect God would have, produced the subsequent goods without permitting or producing the antecedent evils. Even where that specification can be and is satisfied the remaining challenge to justification is formidable. For how are the logically higher-order goods—the goods, that is, that logically cannot be had save at the cost of some antecedent evil—to be shown to be so much superior in their goodness as to be worth having even at the price of the occurrence of the logically lower-order evils that are their logically necessary preconditions?

5. A Creator as interventionist?

The claim that a Creator is, in an "ordinary understanding, perfectly good" needs to be distinguished from, what it is usually taken at least to imply, the claim that that Creator somehow intervenes as a partisan within the creation, whether that intervention is thought to be partly or wholly direct and immediate in this present life or whether it is only or additionally indirect and ultimate in the form of promised rewards and threatened punishments in a future life.

(i) That first claim itself—the claim that the hypothesized Creator is, in an "ordinary understanding, perfectly good"—is not of course universally made by believers, and even where it has been it may in the end, under the pressure of falsifying evidence, have to be abandoned.[21] Judaism, as we have just been reminded, has its Job. And is there in Islam any tradition of theodicy, of laboring to show how the assertions that Allah is "the compassionate, the merciful" can consist with the assertion that the disobedient and the unbelieving will be tortured forever? Allah would in fact seem to be presented, and be seen, as the quintessential oriental despot—the cosmic, omnipotent, omniscient, everlasting Saddam Hussein! In discussing divine perfection we should recall a characteristically Hobbist observation: "In the attributes which we give to God we are not to consider the signification of philosophical truth, but the signification of pious intention, to do him the greatest honour we are able."[22]

(ii) The assertion that a definitionally all-powerful Creator intervenes as a partisan within the creation is, as was said before, not one "which anyone would be at all inclined to make were they meeting the concept of agent Creation for the first time." For the immediate response of such persons would surely be to insist that, since everything that occurs or does not occur within a created universe must, by the hypothesis, be precisely and only what its Creator wants either to occur or not to occur, then for that Creator to punish his creatures for what he necessarily and as such makes them do or fail to do would be the most monstrous as well as the most perverse and sadistic of performances.

Absent as always revelation to the contrary, the expectations of natural reason must surely be that such a Creator God would be as detached and uninvolved as the gods of Epicurus. In the historical development of that particular conception of God that our contemporaries are inclined to accept or reject as a packaged deal, the assertion that God is perfectly good—when, meant in any ordinary understanding of supremely or perfectly good, it has been made at all—seems to have come second, whereas the monotheistic idea of a single (capitalized) "God our creator" certainly postdates that of numerous interventionist (lowercase) gods.

Interventions in favor of the tribe or the city were, after all, what nonomnipotent, noncreating, but nevertheless superhumanly powerful tribal or city gods were for. Whatever would have been the point of building the Parthenon on the Acropolis as a residence for the goddess Athena if she could not by such properly attentive and respectful treatment be induced to do her bit to protect and promote Athens? There are traces of the survival of such lesser gods even in the Pentateuch. Surely it is significant that the "other gods" mentioned at the beginning of Exodus chapter 20 are not said not to exist:

> I am the Lord thy God, which have brought thee out of the land of Egypt, out of the house of bondage. Thou shalt have no other gods before me. . . . Thou shalt not bow down thyself to them, nor serve them: for I the Lord thy God am a jealous God.

Even without the addition of any doctrine of human immortality the apparent implications for us of the teaching that the universe is a creation might seem too uncomfortable to contemplate continuously. That it was intended to happen may be the "simplest and most psychologically satisfying explanation of any observed phenomenon." But that is not to say that all its consequences are equally agreeable. For a start it is natural to feel much worse about afflictions that are perceived to be intentionally imposed than about those that fall upon us through no one else's fault. And how could anyone tolerate the constant awareness that their own every action, intention, and experience is ultimately and inescapably intended by their Creator? If now we add to the doctrine of, so to speak, basic creation that most inconceivably appalling of revelations—the revelation that the Creator creates some if not most of us knowing, and hence intending, that we shall for all eternity be preserved in extremes of torment—then we do indeed have the greatest and most terrible of those "systems of divinity and philosophy . . . which, if true, might drive a wise man mad."[23]

6. The Free Will Defense

That in fact it has not always done so may be most decisively discovered by contemplating the *Theodicy*.[24] For, notoriously, that book, which was the only one Leibniz published during his lifetime, argued that a universe of which that "damnable doctrine"[25] is true would be, indeed is, "the best of all possible worlds."

(i) The least unpromising way of attempting to justify the ways of God to man, whether or not those ways are taken to include eternally tormenting some or most of his creatures, starts from what is now standardly described as the Free Will Defense.[26] Its first move is to point out: "Nothing which implies contradiction falls under the omnipotence of God,"[27] or, better, a self-contradictory utterance does not miraculously become sense just because you chose to make the word "God" its grammatical subject.[28]

The second move is to assert that "God gave us free will," and that this necessarily implies the possibility of doing evil as well as good, that is to say, that there would be a contradiction in speaking of creatures with freedom to choose good or evil but not able to choose evil—which, no blame to God, is what God's human creatures so often do.

A third, slightly more sophisticated move is to add that some goods, and in particular some virtuous actions such as forgiving, logically presuppose antecedent evils, which, in that case, are the injuries forgiven.

Although the Free Will Defense certainly constitutes the least unpromising apologetic strategy, it is scarcely promising. For a start it is absolutely out of the question to justify—in the strong sense in which "to justify" is construed as meaning to show to be just—the infliction of an eternal and very far from trifling penalty for any offense or series of offenses, however serious, which is or are nevertheless finite. Whatever the often different psychological truth, charity requires us to treat attempts by believers to justify the altogether unjustifiable as the forced and desperate labors of wretched creatures intimidated by irresistible threats. For what, after all, would we ourselves not be prepared to do if we believed what they believe about their God?

Yet even given the jettisoning of any doctrine of Hell, and the consequent release from the need to defend that "damnable doctrine," the apologetic task surely remains impossible. For the apologist, proceeding on the assumptions of the second move of the Free Will Defense has to show all actual nonmoral evils to be logically necessary preconditions of actually resulting logically higher order moral goods. Even all that would still be insufficient. For it would also be necessary to show that it was worth having these logically higher order moral goods at the price of the logically necessary antecedent evils.

(ii) Even if, given all the assumptions of the second move of the Free Will Defense, all this could be done, still that defense cannot be effectively maintained. For those assumptions themselves cannot all be granted. The mistake is to assume that by "giving us free will" God could and does ensure that the ultimate responsibility for choosing to act in whatever ways we do choose to act is not God's but ours. This, we have to insist, is simply, and it ought to be obviously, not true. For such a Creator is, by the hypothesis, the ultimate yet everpresent sustaining cause of every thought and every action of all creatures.

Within the universe there neither is nor could be any adequate analogue to this relationship. One that might be offered as a first approach is that of puppets to their puppeteer. Apparent conflicts between individual puppets or puppet factions are always and necessarily bogus, their course and outcomes being totally determined by the (offstage) puppeteer rather than by the pretendedly independent (onstage) puppets. For a puppeteer to hold the puppets whose every move he himself manipulates responsible for those moves would be absurd. He would escape further condemnation as a moral outrage only because objects of wood and cloth are necessarily insentient and impassible. There is another analogue that embraces both sentience and passibility: the relationship between an all-powerful hypnotist and a subject acting out that hypnotist's posthypnotic suggestions.

The introduction of such unlovely pictures is bound to provoke indignation and protest. It constitutes, it will be said, the most monstrous misrepresentation of the way in which Christians think. For Christians, we will be told, believe that the Creator "gave free will" to those creatures who are made in His image. So, typically, Christians think of the relations between the Creator and that Creator's human creatures on the model of those between a human father and his children. And, of course, it is only in certain scandalous and extremely exceptional cases that parents can properly be held responsible for the misdeeds of their grown-up children, and then, even in those rare cases, only partially and very remotely.

But what is presently at issue is not the question of how Christians typically do in fact think, but the question of how, in consistency with the fundamental doctrines to which they are explicitly and categorically committed, they ought to think. Certainly no one has any business to deny the manifest truths that human beings are members of a peculiar kind of organism that can and cannot but make choices, and that, wherever there are choices, there must necessarily be alternative possibilities between which the choosers choose. But if we are indeed creatures of a Creator in any Mosaic understanding, then that Creator must necessarily make us the individual people who, confronted with choices to be made, do in fact choose to act in whatever ways we in fact do individually choose to act.

(iii) Although by now unavoidable, the label "Free Will Defense" is misleading. For the crucial questions are not about people acting of their own free will, as opposed to acting under compulsion. They are about the presuppositions and implications of agency and choice. Both people who act of their own free will and people who act only under compulsion are as such agents choosing to act as they do, and not otherwise. When before the Diet of Worms Luther said, "Here I stand. I can no other. So help me God," he was not pretending that he was not in this case an agent at all, that he had been struck by a sudden paralysis that made it physically impossible for him to retreat even had he so chosen. Or again, when a businessman is so unfortunate as to receive "an offer which he cannot refuse," he acts under intolerable compulsion. But he does act. He could have chosen an alternative; his brains rather than his signature on the deed which transferred his business to the Godfather.

These examples—developed further in a more secular treatment in section 5 of chapter 5—should here be sufficient to suggest that it is misguided and perverse to launch a discussion such as that in *Free Will and the Christian Faith* by constructing an elaborate nonostensive definition of "libertarian freewill,"[29] a definition that, heavy as it is with technical symbolism, most philosophical and theological laypersons could scarcely begin to understand. For by erecting this difficult and unfamiliar conception of a sort of free will—a sort that supposedly must be available to us if we ourselves, rather than the apologist's God, are to be ultimately responsible for our faults—the apologist leaves himself with the formidable further problem of showing that free will, in that esoteric understanding, actually is a universal human endowment.

The truth is, surely, that what people ordinarily mean when they say that God gave us free will is that the Creator made us creatures who can and cannot but make choices. Since it is obvious and known to all—whether or not we are in the strict, theological sense creatures— that we can and cannot but make choices, all the words and expressions essential to the discussion of choices and responsibility for choices must be explicable by reference to experience that is universally and indeed distinctively human and, hence, as such and inescapably available to us all.

Perhaps the best way to explicate the crucial "notions" is by taking a hint from Locke's great chapter "Of Power."[30] The hint is to start by ostensively defining two kinds of bodily movements: movings which can, and motions which cannot, be initiated or inhibited at will. From there we can go on to define "doing" and "being able to do other than we do do" in terms of movings and refraining from movings, while the ideas of physical necessity and physical impossibility are derivable from the experience of trying but failing to control motions. How indeed could any of these key ideas, or the further fundamental concept of contrary-to-fact conditionality, be acquired by or explained to creatures lacking either our own or similar experience of limited and nonomnipotent agency?

So what are the implications? Does the fact that we are creatures who can and cannot but make choices, and who, in the understanding just now explicated, could always act in ways other than those in which we do act, license apologists to maintain that a Creator can, indeed does, justly call us to account, since the ultimate responsibility for our conduct is ours, rather than that of our Creator? It should be obvious that it does not. For nothing has been said to suggest, much less to show that, even though in the present understanding we always could have done other than we did do, there were not physically necessitating causes for our being the people who made just the choices that we did make—and, of course, that there are such ultimate supernatural if not immediate natural causes, for our choices as for everything else, is the manifest implication of the doctrine that the universe is indeed a creation.

(iv) The most persuasive way to enforce this devastating conclusion is by authoritative quotation. Perhaps most surprising, at any rate to those aware of the present condition of that organization, is the 1922 Commission Report on *Doctrine in the Church of England.* This admitted that, "The whole course of events is under the control of God . . . logically this involves the affirmation that there is no event, and no aspect of any event, even those due to sin and so contrary to the Divine will, which falls outside the scope of his purposive activity."[31]

Almost equally surprising to those who have been taught that the doctrine of predestination was a Calvinist peculiarity is the question "Of Predestination" in which Aquinas writes: "As men are ordained to eternal life through the providence of God, it likewise is part of that providence to permit some to fall away from that end; this is called reprobation . . . Reprobation implies not only foreknowledge but also something more." Aquinas here shrinks from saying that God is the cause of sin, notwithstanding that his premises imperatively dictate this conclusion. But he has at least to allow that although reprobation "is not the cause of what is in the present—namely, sin, nevertheless it is the cause of abandonment by God. It is the cause . . . of what is assigned in the future—namely, eternal punishment."[32] Elsewhere Aquinas is more forthcoming:

> Just as God not only gave being to things when they first began, but is also—as the conserving cause of being—the cause of their being as long as they last . . .; so he also not only gave things their operative powers when they were first created, but is also always the cause of

these in things. Hence, if this divine influence stopped every operation would stop. Every operation, therefore, of anything is traced back to him as its cause.[33]

Aquinas goes on to spell out the relevant and extremely uncomfortable implications of that final sentence in two later chapters:

> God alone can move the will, as an agent, without doing violence to it. . . . Some people . . . not understanding how God can cause a movement of our will in us without prejudicing the freedom of the will, have tried to explain . . . authoritative texts wrongly; that is, they would say that God "works in us, to wish and to accomplish" means that he causes in us the power of willing, but not in such a way that he makes us will this or that. . . . These people are, of course, opposed quite plainly by authoritative texts of Holy Writ. For it says in Isaiah (26, 2)[34] "Lord, you have worked all our work in us." Hence we receive from God not only the power of willing but its employment also.[35]

Presumably "God alone can move the will, as an agent, without doing violence to it" because only God is able to cause me to be a person who freely chooses whatever God wants me to choose. But now, if these are indeed the implications of creation, in the theologians' sense, as they most surely are, then it becomes inescapably obvious that to describe a Creator as perfectly just must be, if that Creator is also said in any way to punish any creatures for any of their perceived deficiencies, morally outrageous. And, furthermore, if the punishments are in their duration or intensity themselves infinite, the case is—in the strictest and most literal understanding—infinitely worse.

It can be salutary to compare and contrast Luther's treatment of the same questions. Noticing that he wrote *de Servo Arbitrio* and St. Augustine *de Libero Arbitrio,* but then forgetting that Luther was an Augustinian friar, some have falsely assumed that their doctrines here were as contrary as the titles of these books. We may begin to suspect the truth when we find the Reformer saying:

Now, by "necessarily" I do not mean "compulsorily" . . . a man without
the Spirit of God does not do evil against his will, under pressure,
as though he were taken by the scruff of his neck and dragged into
it, like a thief or a footpad being dragged off against his will to
punishment; but he does it spontaneously and voluntarily.[36]

Certainly not compulsorily, for the necessity that Luther meant was
that imposed by the Creator's total and constantly exercised manipulative
power. Yet to reconcile that with ultimate human responsibility before
Divine justice admittedly exceeds all the capacities of reason. So Luther
points his alternative:

The highest degree of faith is to believe He is just, though of His
own will he makes us . . . proper subjects for damnation, and seems
(in the words of Erasmus) "to delight in the torments of poor wretches
and to be a fitter object for hate than for love." If I could by any
means understand how this same God . . . can yet be merciful and
just, there would be no need for faith.[37]

Later, Luther addresses himself to the question: "Why then does
He not alter those evil wills which He moves?" Understandably, if
unsatisfactorily, Erasmus receives no answer here:

It is not for us to inquire into these mysteries, but to adore them.
If flesh and blood take offence here and grumble, well, let them grumble;
they will achieve nothing; grumbling will not change God! And however
many of the ungodly stumble and depart, the elect will remain.[38]

But the Reformer, unlike the Angelic Doctor, was not so completely
the complacent apparatchik as to proceed to a cool summary of the
reasons why—very properly—"the blessed in glory will have no pity
for the damned." The relevant passage in *Summa Theologica* (III Supp.
[xciv] 1–3) reads:

In order that the happiness of the saints may be more delightful to
them and that they may render more copious thanks to God first,
they are allowed to see perfectly the sufferings of the damned . . . the

Divine justice and their own deliverance will be the direct cause of the joy of the blessed, while the pains of the damned will cause it indirectly . . . the blessed in glory will have no pity for the damned.

As used to be said in the unhallowed ranks of the Royal Air Force, "F--- you Jack, I'm fireproof!"

Notes

1. Genesis 1:1.

2. See his *de Aeternitate Mundi contra Murmurantes.*

3. This disgraceful argument is outstanding among fallacies: not merely does the conclusion not follow from the premises; it actually contradicts one of them, while they each contradict the other.

4. For a fuller exposition and discussion of these matters. compare, for instance, Antony Flew, *An Introduction to Western Philosophy* (London: Thames and Hudson, revised edition, 1989), chapter 2.

5. Although all translators seem to translate the Latin thus, the form *manifestior* would usually be rendered as "more manifest" or "more obvious."

6. This hermeneutic thesis is argued in Antony Flew, *God, Freedom, and Immortality* (Buffalo, N.Y.: Prometheus Books, 1984), chapter 4.

7. See Terence Penelhum, "Divine Necessity," in *Mind* (1960).

8. "The Principles of nature and Grace founded on Reason," sections 6 and 7.

9. The sentence concludes, "and piously ascribe to him every species of perfection." Concerning such pious ascriptions compare the text to note 22, below.

10. R. N. Smart, *Philosophers and Religious Truth* (London: SCM Press, 1964), pp. 103–104.

11. Ibid., p. 104.

12. See, for instance, Herbert Butterfield, *The Origins of Modern Science: 1300–1800* (London: G. Bell, 1949), chapter 1.

13. See, for instance, Richard Swinburne, "The Justification of Theism," in *Truth: A Journal of Modern Thought* (Dallas, Tex.) for Fall 1990, pp. 69–77.

14. See subsections 2(ii)–(iii) of chapter 1, above.

15. See, for instance, John Leslie, *Universes* (London and New York: Routledge, 1989).

16. Indeed they are so kind as to commend the present writer as "the most profound of contemporary critics of theism" (p. 104)!

17. Compare subsection 1(i), above.

18. A. O. Lovejoy, *The Great Chain of Being* (New York: Harper Torchbooks reprint of 1936 first edition, 1960).

19. David Stove, *The Plato Cult and Other Philosophical Follies* (Oxford: Blackwell, 1991), p. 142.

20. *Leviathan,* chapter 31.

21. For a sympathetic yet critical account of how C. S. Lewis—surely the most widely read of all Christian apologists in the second half of the present century—was eventually forced to this conclusion, see John Beversluis, *C. S. Lewis and the Search for Rational Religion* (Grand Rapids, Mich.: Eerdman, 1985).

22. *Leviathan,* chapter 31.

23. I still treasure my now ancient copy of the *Eternal Punishment* pamphlet in a Roman Catholic series entitled "The Treasury of the Faith." What a treasure!

24. G. W. Leibniz, *Theodicy,* translated by E. M. Huggard (London: Routledge and Kegan Paul, 1951).

25. See Norah Barlow, ed., *The Autobiography of Charles Darwin* (London: Collins, 1968), p. 87.

26. I believe that I am ultimately responsible, since I certainly introduced the expressioon, in the present context, in my "Divine Omnipotence and Human Freedom," an article first published in 1955 in the long since defunct *Hibbert Journal,* and later revised and reprinted in Antony Flew and Alasdair MacIntrye, eds., *New Essays in Philosophical Theology* (London: SCM Press, 1956).

27. Thomas Aquinas, *Summa Theologica,* 1.25.4.

28. Compare Antony Flew, *God: A Critical Enquiry* (La Salle, Ill.: Open Court, 1984), Section 2.50.

29. W .S. Anglin, *Free Will and the Christian Faith* (Oxford: Clarendon, 1990).

30. John Locke, *An Essay concerning Human Understanding,* edited by P. H. Nidditch (Oxford: Clarendon, 1975), 2 (21). Relevant passages are quoted, and the present suggestion is further developed, in section 5 of chapter 5.

31. (London: Church Publishing House, 1922), p. 47. Anyone doubting that that church is, in more than one sense, in secular decline might profitably refer to Antony Flew, *Self-Improvement and Social Action* (London: Social Affairs Unit, 1989).

32. *Summa Theologica,* 1.23.3. Jonathan Edwards (1703-1750) was the

first major philosopher-theologian to be born and raised within what were to become the territories of the United States. In his treatise on *The Freedom of the Will* (New Haven, Conn.: Yale University Press, 1957)—volume 1 of *The Works of Jonathan Edwards,* under the general editorship of Perry Miller—Edwards is forced to admit that God must be the author of sin. He dislikes the phrase. Yet he cannot in honest deny that, in a sense, it does apply. For God is "the permitter, or not hinderer of sin; and at the same time a disposer of the state of events in such a manner . . . that sin . . . will most certainly and infallibly follow" (p. 399).

33. *Summa contra Gentiles,* 3.87.

34. For a rich collection of further biblical texts to the same effect, see Jonathan Edwards, *The Freedom of the Will.*

35. *Summa contra Gentiles,* 3.88–89.

36. Martin Luther, "The Bondage of the Will," in E. G. Rupp, A. N. Marlow, P. S. Watwon, and B. Drewery, eds. and trans., *Luther and Erasmus: Freewill and Salvation* (Philadelphia, Pa.: Westminster, 1969), p. 139.

37. Ibid., 2.7 (p. 138). No doubt Luther had vividly before his mind a never too often to be pondered passage from Romans (9, 18–34):

> Therefore hath he mercy on whom he will have mercy, and whom he will he hardeneth. Thou wilt say unto me, "Why doth he yet find fault? For who hath resisted his will?" Nay but, O man, who art thou that repliest against God? Shall the thing formed say to him that formed it, "Why hast thou made me thus?" . . . What if God, willing to show his wrath, and to make his power known, endured with much long suffering the vessels of wrath fitted to destruction; and that he might make known the riches of his glory on the vessels of mercy, which he had afore prepared unto glory, even us, whom he hath called . . . ?

Compare also the passages from *Leviathan* quoted in subsections 4(i) and 5(i), above.

38. Luther, "The Bondage of the Will," 2.6 (p. 139).

3

Evidencing Naturally
Impossible Occurrences

Nothing is so convenient as a decisive argument . . . which must at
least *silence* the most arrogant bigotry and superstition, and free us
from their impertinent solicitations. I flatter myself, that I have discovered an argument . . . which, if just, will, with the wise and learned,
be an everlasting check to all kinds of superstitious delusion, and
consequently, will be useful as long as the world endures. For so long,
I presume, will the accounts of miracles and prodigies be found in
all history, sacred and profane.

David Hume
An Enquiry Concerning Human Understanding, 10(1)

Hume, the first of the two great philosophers of the eighteenth century
Age of Enlightenment, was also the first thinker of the modern period
to develop systematically a world outlook that was through and through
skeptical, this-worldly, and human-centred. A friend and admirer of
Benjamin Franklin, living just long enough to hear of and to welcome
the American Declaration of Independence, Hume was the philosophical
founding father of what is in the United States today so widely and
so fiercely denounced as "secular humanism."

Our immediate concern, however, is with only twenty or so pages of all Hume's writings. These pages, the treatment "Of Miracles" in *An Enquiry Concerning Human Understanding,* provoked in his own lifetime more protest and controversy than all the rest of those writings put together. Hume himself, like his contemporary critics, was most interested in "the accounts of miracles and prodigies" found in what in those days people still distinguished as "sacred history." Both he and they were above all concerned with the application of his supposed "everlasting check" to accounts of what was believed to be the supremely significant prodigy—the physical resurrection of Jesus bar Joseph.

All were agreed that, if this alleged occurrence had actually happened, and could be known to have happened, then that would constitute a decisive verification of the claim that Christianity is the one true religion. But Hume's argument has a much wider reference. It not only concerns and, "if just," threatens to undermine the rational foundations of "a system of religion." It can, for instance, and should, also be employed to throw light upon the phenomena, or putative phenomena, of parapsychology as these appear, or appear to appear, in an entirely secular context.

1. Miracles and the rationality of faith

During the lifetime of Hume and for a century and more thereafter there was a standard, two-stage, systematic program of rational apologetic for Christianity.[1] Apologists began by essaying to establish, while appealing only to natural reason and secular experience, the existence and certain minimal characteristics of God. From that first conclusion they proceeded to argue that this somewhat sketchy "religion of nature" can and should be supplanted and enriched by a more abundant revelation. This second part of the case for Christianity rested upon the contention that there is ample historical evidence to show that the New Testament miracles, including crucially the physical resurrection of Jesus bar Joseph, did actually occur. Since miracles necessarily constitute achievements by exercises of supernatural power of what is naturally impossible, it was argued that these New Testament miracles constitute divine endorsements of the teachings thus enforced.

*   *   *

(i) In 1870, during the third session of the First Vatican Council, the beliefs that both parts of this program of rational apologetic can indeed be accomplished became defined dogmata of the Roman Catholic Church, and hence essential elements of its faith. The canon defining the first part reads: "If anyone shall say, that the one and true God, our creator and Lord, cannot be known for certain through the creation by the natural light of human reason: let them be cast out [*anathema*]."[2] The canon defining the second part reads: "If anyone shall say, that miracles cannot happen, and hence that all accounts of them, even those contained in holy Scriptures, should be relegated to the category of fables or myths; or that miracles can never be known for certain nor the divine origin of the Christian religion be proved thereby: let them be cast out [*anathema*]."[3]

It is important to recognize—credit where credit is due—the fundamental rationality of this traditional apologetic project, and to contrast it, if only perhaps implicitly and by implication, with some of its degenerate and irrationalist successors. For it is not here proposed to demand faith either against all reason or without sufficient reason both for making any leap of faith at all and for making one particular, approved leap as opposed to all the other available alternatives. Thus, if we turn to chapter 6 of book 1 of the *Summa contra Gentiles,* we find St. Thomas arguing in section 1 that:

> Those who place their faith in this truth . . . "for which the human reason offers no experiential evidence" . . . do not believe foolishly, as though following artificial fables (II Peter, 1, 16). For these "secrets of divine Wisdom" (Job, 11, 6) the divine Wisdom itself, which knows all things to the full, has deigned to reveal to men. It reveals its own presence, as well as the truth of its teaching and inspiration, by fitting arguments; and in order to confirm those truths that exceed natural knowledge, it gives visible manifestation to works which surpass the ability of all nature.

After concluding section 3 with the claim that, "Even in our own time, God does not cease to work miracles through his saints for the confirmation of the faith," St. Thomas goes on in a final section 4 to dispose of rival candidate revelations, and in particular the most formidable contemporary competitor, Islam. Simply plumping for a faith that has not been endorsed by miracles is dismissed as frivolous (*levis*):

> On the other hand, those who founded sects committed to erroneous doctrines proceeded in a way that is opposite to this. The point is clear in the case of Mohammed. He seduced the people with promises of carnal pleasure to which the concupiscence of the flesh goads us. . . . He did not bring forth any signs produced in a supernatural way, by which alone divine inspiration is appropriately evidenced; since a visible action which can only be divine reveals an invisibly inspired teacher of truth. . . . It is thus clear that those who place any faith in his words believe frivolously.

(ii) Such appeals to accounts of miraculous occurrences as evidences for the authenticity of an allegedly divine revelation have long since gone out of fashion. Thus, for instance, the 1922 Commission Report on *Doctrine in the Church of England* proclaimed, "It has to be recognized that legends involving abnormal events have tended to grow very easily in regard to great religious leaders, and that in consequence it is impossible in the present state of knowledge to make the same evidential use of the narratives of miracles in the Gospels that appeared possible in the past" (p. 51).

The commission's contention was both right and rational. But it was also, on two counts, rash. In the first place, and more generally, if a candidate is not identifiable as an authentic divine revelation by reference to the occurrence of endorsing miracles, then how else, if at all, is decisive identification to become possible? St. Thomas, it should be recalled, in the paragraph from which the immediately previous quotation was drawn, dismissed the claims of Islam on the grounds that its Prophet:

did not bring forth any signs produced in a supernatural way. . . . On the contrary, Mohammed said that he was sent in the power of his arms—which are signs not lacking to robbers and tyrants. . . . Those who believed in him were brutal men and desert wanderers . . . through whose numbers Mohammed forced others to become his followers by the violence of his arms.

The second reason for accounting that commission contention rash is more particular. It is what used to be called the scandal of particularity. This consists in the fact that Christianity, alone among the great world religions, centers on what is supposed to have happened during a particular period, in a particular country, and upon this particular planet, Earth. The Christian is, in the words of the Apostles' Creed, defined as one who believes "in God the Father Almighty, Maker of heaven and earth: and in Jesus Christ his only Son our Lord, who was conceived by the Holy Ghost, born of the Virgin Mary, suffered under Pontius Pilate, was crucified, died, and buried," and who on "the third day . . . rose again from the dead."

The scandalous particularity consists here in the fact that one particular alleged miracle, occurring at one particular time and place on one particular planet, is not just one part of the evidence for identifying Christianity as a revelation of, and from God, but is itself the crucial element in the essential content of that putative revelation. For, absent that resurrection, there remains no sufficient reason for accepting either that the man Jesus is to be incomprehensibly identified with "God the Father Almighty, Maker of heaven and earth," or that his actual teachings, whatever they may have been, are thereby revealed to be supremely authoritative. As was so incisively and correctly argued by St. Paul, "If Christ be not risen then is our preaching vain, your faith is also vain."[4]

It is illuminating to contrast Islam with Christianity on this count. For, although the providing of a revelation of Allah by the Prophet was equally particular, its content was not. To the Muslim, indeed, any suggestion of an identification of Mohammed with Allah has to be supremely blasphemous. It is this Earth-centered particularity which has made the possibility of rational agents elsewhere in the universe embarrassing for Christians in a way in which for adherents of other religions it is not.

2. The presuppositions of critical history

The argument about to be presented is epistemological rather than ontological. It is, that is to say, an argument directed not at the question of whether miracles occur but at the question of whether—and, if so, how—we could know that they do, and when and where they have. This argument is fundamentally the same as that first published in section 10 of Hume's first *Enquiry*. But it has for present purposes been substantially strengthened.[5] (Such strengthening is needed mainly but not only because, by denying earlier in that *Enquiry* that we either do or even can have experience of physical necessity and physical impossibility, Hume disqualified himself from distinguishing the merely marvellous from the genuinely miraculous.)

(i) The heart of the matter is that the criteria by which we must assess historical testimony, and the general presumptions that alone make it possible for us to construe the detritus of the past as historical evidence, must inevitably rule out any possibility of establishing, upon purely historical grounds, that some genuinely miraculous event has indeed occurred. Hume himself concentrated on testimonial evidence because his own conception of the historian, later illustrated in his own bestselling *History of England*,[6] was of a judge assessing, with judicious impartiality, the testimony set before him. But, in the present context, this limitation is not immediately important.

The basic propositions are: first, that the present relics of the past cannot be interpreted as historical evidence at all unless we presume that the same fundamental regularities obtained then as still obtain today; second, that in trying as best they may to determine what actually happened, historians must employ as criteria all their present knowledge, or presumed knowledge, of what is probable or improbable, possible or impossible; and, third, that, since the word "miracle" has to be defined in terms of physical necessity and physical impossibility, the application of these criteria inevitably precludes proof of the actual occurrence of a miracle.

Hume illustrated the first proposition in his *Treatise,* urging that it is only upon such presumptions of regularity that we can justify the conclusion that ink marks on old pieces of paper constitute testimonial evidence. Earlier in the first *Enquiry* he had urged the inescapable importance of the criteria demanded by the second. Without such criteria there can be no critical discrimination, and hence no history worthy of the name. The application of both the second and the third contention can be seen most sharply in the footnote in which Hume quotes with approval the reasoning of the famous physician De Sylva in the case of Mlle. Thibaut: "It was impossible that she could have been so ill as was 'proved' by witnesses, because it was impossible that she could, in so short a time, have recovered so perfectly as he found her."[7]

(ii) We need at this point to ask and to answer a question that Hume was in no position to press. What, if anything, justified De Sylva in his rejection of a proposition apparently proved true by the testimony of eyewitnesses? What, if anything, justified him in thus stubbornly continuing to maintain that the miraculous cure did not in fact occur, because it could not have done?

It is a matter of what evidence there is or can be, a matter of verification and of verifiability. The two crucial and conflicting propositions are of very different and quite disproportionate orders of logical strength, of confirmation and confirmability. For the proposition or propositions asserted by the putative witnesses were singular, and in the past tense. They were of the form "Once upon a time," on one particular occasion, this or that actually happened. The days are, therefore, long past when these claims could be directly confirmed or disconfirmed. But the proposition or propositions that rule out the alleged miraculous occurrences as physically impossible must be open and general. They are of the forms "Either it is physically necessary for every, or it is physically impossible for any, so-and-so to be such-and-such." Nomological propositions, as these are called, propositions asserting the subsistence of laws of nature and/or of causal connections, can in principle therefore, if not necessarily and always in practice, be tested and retested anywhere and at any time.

Historical reasoning of the form here exemplified by the physician De Sylva, like reasoning in all other valid forms, will sometimes, if its premises are false, lead to false conclusions. Hume himself, by dismissing reports of phenomena that the progress of abnormal psychology has since shown to be entirely possible, became exposed to Hamlet's too often quoted rebuke to overweening philosophy. What is physically or, if you like, naturally impossible is what is logically incompatible with true laws of nature. So, if you mistake some proposition to express such a law when in fact it does not, then you are bound to be wrong also about the consequent practical impossibilities. But that a mode of argument must sometimes lead to false conclusions is no sufficient reason to reject it as unsound.

Nor is there any escape through contending either that there is something wrong with the concept of a miracle as a kind of naturally impossible event or that we can never in fact know what is and is not naturally impossible. For Christian apologetics absolutely presupposes that we all know a physical resurrection to be naturally impossible, that its occurrence would—as must have been thunderously maintained in a million Easter sermons—be the miracle of miracles. Were such events known to be merely marvellous and extremely unusual, then the physical resurrection of Jesus bar Joseph, even had it actually occurred, would amount to at best the weakest of reasons for holding to the Apostles' Creed.

(iii) To make clearer what is involved, consider an example derived from the work of the acknowledged father of critical history. This example has the advantage of being far removed from any ideologically sensitive area. Herodotus knew that, except where it is joined to Asia by an isthmus, Africa is surrounded by sea. But he did not know either that Earth is in fact—roughly—spherical and suspended in space, or all the consequences of these first facts. So, in chapter 42 of book 4 of his account of ancient Greece's Great Patriotic War, he writes: "Necos, the Egyptian king . . . desisting from the canal which he had begun between the Nile and the Arabian gulf, sent to sea a number of ships manned by Phoenicians with orders to make for the Straits of Gibraltar, and return to Egypt through them, and by the Mediterranean." This in due course they succeeded in doing. "On their return they declared—I for my part do not believe them, but perhaps others may—that in sailing round Africa they had the sun on their right hand."

The incredulity of Herodotus upon this particular point was, as we know, mistaken. Indeed the very feature of the whole tradition that provoked his suspicion constitutes for us the best reason for believing that a Phoenician expedition did indeed circumnavigate Africa. But that Herodotus here went wrong upon a point of fact does not show that his method was unsound. On the contrary: his verdict on this point is only discovered to have been mistaken when later historians, employing the same fundamental principles of assessment, reconsider it in the light of subsequent advances in astronomy and geography. It was entirely proper and reasonable for Herodotus to measure the likelihood of this Phoenician tale against the possibilities suggested by the best astronomical theory and geographical information available to him in the fifth century B.C., as well as against what he knew of the veracity of travellers in general, and of Phoenician sailors in particular. It was one thing to believe that they had set off and returned as reported. For he presumably had further confirming evidence for this in addition to the unsupported testimony of Phoenician sailors. And, if they had done these things, then they must have circumnavigated Africa, since it would have been impossible for them to overland their ships. It would have been quite another matter to believe a traveler's tale unsupported by other evidence, and not made probable by any promising theory.

Similar considerations and principles apply whether, as here, attention centers on an alleged impossibility, or whether, as more usually, it is a matter of what, granted always some presupposed framework of known possibilities and impossibilities, is only probable or improbable.

3. Possible counters to such methodological objections

Faced by this Humean argument, apologists are likely to respond in various ways. They might, for instance, recall that Hume himself was so imprudent as to dismiss stories of two wonders allegedly wrought by the Roman Emperor Vespasian, stories that we now have excellent reason to believe were true. The temptation then is to suggest that, with further advances in our knowledge, several of the miracle stories in the Bible might be similarly sustained.

(i) Indeed they might, and many, surely, have been. But this is not a bit of help to the apologist if the progressive verification is achieved— as in fact in that case it was, and always has to be—only at the price of showing that, although what was said to have happened did indeed happen, its happening was not after all miraculous. Suppose that all the miracle stories in the New Testament were true, but that none of the events occurring were genuinely miraculous. Then we are left with no evidencing reason for believing the fundamental, essential, defining Christian dogma, that Jesus bar Joseph was God incarnate.

Nor is there any apologetic profit to be got here from maintaining that the typically biblical notion is that of a sign, not necessarily involving any overriding of an established natural order. For, in so far as there now becomes nothing intrinsically remarkable and discernibly out of this world about the occurrences themselves, if any, these putatively revealing signs will have to be identified and interpreted as such by reference to precisely that system the claims of which require authentication.

Suppose, for the sake of argument, that we had been able to erect a solid and rich natural theology, a system that gave us good reason both for expecting that the God thus discovered has vouchsafed some supplementary revelation and for believing that this revelation is identifiable as the real McCoy by marks of such and such a sort. Then for these marks to suffice it would not have been necessary for their occurrence to constitute any kind of overriding of the ordinary order of nature.

But the fact remains that no suitably rich and strong system of natural theology is available. For, as was argued in earlier chapters, even if it were possible to prove the existence of a personal or quasi-personal Creator as the omnipotent and omniscient sustaining cause of the universe, still we could scarcely hope to find evidencing—repeat, evidencing[8]—natural reasons for believing either that the Creator (timelessly) abhors some kinds of human conduct and imperatively requires others, or that he (timelessly) proposes to reveal more of his nature and wishes and therefore provides reliable and effective natural means for identifying such revelations as authentic.

Again, someone is sure to want to remind us of Hume's own contention that we have and could have no experience of, and hence no conception or idea of, physical as opposed to logical necessities and impossibilities. Others will be eager to assert that modern science has had to jettison the notions both of causality and of laws of nature. There is, however, no call for us to try to refute such teachings here. For if Christian apologists are to produce good evidencing reasons for believing that they have a hold on an authentic revelation, then they have to presuppose the existence of a strong natural order, an order the maintenance of which is physically necessary and which it is humanly impossible to violate. If truly there is no such order, then there can be no question of any overridings of it and hence no question of referring to any alleged overridings in order to validate anything.

(ii) Hume was surely correct in the main contention of section 10 of his first *Enquiry*: "A miracle can never be proved so as to be the foundation of a system of religion." But it is essential to realize that this conclusion depends upon two things: first, an understanding of the methodological presuppositions of critical history, and second, a recognition of the impossibility of supplementing these by appealing to natural theology. Neither alone could be decisive. The two in combination are. To ignore either, or not to appreciate how they complement one another, is to fail to take the measure of the force and the generalship of the Humean offensive. We have, therefore, to appreciate that sections 10 and 11 of this *Enquiry* are complementary: the former recognizing the presuppositions of critical history, and drawing out relevant implications, and the latter confronting the project of a natural theology at its apparent strongest, and laboring to show it to be fundamentally misconceived.[9]

With respect to the thesis of section 10, Hume's most worthy opponent was perhaps Cardinal Newman. Yet even he appears to have failed to appreciate the complementarity between it and the subsequent section 11. For, while he is prepared to allow the general soundness of Hume's principles for the assessment of testimonial evidence, he nevertheless challenges their application to "these particular miracles, ascribed to the particular Peter, James, and John." What we have to ask, according to Newman, is whether such miraculous events really are "unlikely supposing there is a Power, external to the world, who can bring them about; supposing they are the only means by which He can reveal himself to those who need a revelation; supposing that He is likely to reveal himself; that He has a great end in doing so."[10]

If these suppositions could indeed be granted, then perhaps it would be reasonable to draw the conclusions desired. But Hume had in that subsequent section 11 developed a most powerful argument for saying not only that we do not have any natural knowledge of the existence of such a Power, but also, and here perhaps even more relevantly, that we could have no warrant for conjectures as to what upon that supposition might reasonably be expected. For what Hume loved to call "the religious hypothesis" is that of "a single being . . . not comprehended under any species or genus, from whose experienced attributes or qualities, we can, by analogy, infer any attribute or quality in him." The response to Newman's rhetorical questions should therefore be that any such conclusions about either likelihoods or unlikelihoods upon that hypothesis must necessarily be altogether groundless and arbitrary. As Hume himself argued, "It must evidently appear contrary to all rule of analogy to reason from the projects and intentions of men to those of a Being so different and so much superior."

4. Impossibility and unrepeatability

(i) Suppose now that we try to apply similar methodological principles to the phenomena or alleged phenomena of parapsychology. The psi phenomena, the putative subject matter of parapsychology, are, or would be, phenomena whose occurrence all of us—including most of the time the believing and practicing parapsychologists themselves—would with complete confidence rule out as physically (or practically or contingently) impossible. This point has in a way been recognized by all those who have insisted that psi phenomena are (or would be) inconsistent with (what are currently believed to be) the laws of physics. (This is, surely, most of what J. B. Rhine and others have had in mind when they have claimed that psi phenomena are, or would be, *non*physical.)

But the truth, as C. D. Broad argued long ago in a landmark paper,[11] is that the basic limiting principles (BLPs) that rule out such goings-on as, in this sense, impossible are both prior to and less sophisticated than the development of physical science. They also have been, and remain, largely independent of its development. Broad himself originally stated these BLPs in a manner not only highly abstract but also unwarrantedly Cartesian. Both their nature and their importance will come out more clearly in the un-Cartesian concrete.

Suppose, for instance, that there has been yet another security leak in Washington, or Bonn, or London. Then everyone, or almost everyone, assumes that some hostile agent has had some form of direct or indirect sensory access to the top-secret material that is now secret no longer. It never seriously enters most people's heads that that material might have been telepathically or clairvoyantly read by an agent who at no time came within normal sensory range. Extrasensory perception is thus in practice ruled out as impossible. That information can be acquired without employment of the normal senses is thus precluded by a BLP.

Suppose, again, that there had actually been an explosion in the nuclear power station at Three Mile Island. No one, or almost no one, would have suggested that this might have been a case of sabotage by psychokinesis. That too is by another BLP precluded as physically impossible.

A second thing to notice about these BLPs, in addition to the fact that they are both familiar and more fundamental than any of the named laws of physics, is that to appeal to them as reasons for dismissing some alleged occurrence as physically (or practically or contingently) impossible is not—any more than to appeal in a similar context to some named law of established physics—to dismiss such allegations dogmatically and a priori.

Many of those who with good reason pride themselves upon their skeptical and inquiring approach are quite unnecessarily embarrassed by, while making dreadfully heavy weather of, such charges of a priori dogmatism. Certainly, since none of us is infallible, we ought to be always ready to consider any strong evidence suggesting that some proposition we had believed expressed a true BLP or a true law of nature is, after all, false. Yet it is simply grotesque to complain, in the absence of any such decisive falsifying evidence, that these appeals to the BLPs and the named laws of established physics are exercises in a priori dogmatism. For what "a priori" means is prior to and independent of experience. But in both of these kinds of cases we have an enormous mass of experience supporting our present beliefs and our present incredulities.

(ii) So what sort of evidence should we demand as sufficient to show that we had, after all, been mistaken in dismissing all alleged psi phenomena as physically impossible? When, back in 1955, G. R. Price made the first attempt to deploy Hume's argument "Of Miracles" as a challenge to parapsychology,[12] Price called not for a demonstration type but a demonstration *token*. He demanded, that is to say, not an algorithm for setting up an exhibition of the reality of psi phenomena wherever and whenever that should be required, but instead a single, once-and-for-all decisive, knock-down falsification of one or all of the precluding BLPs. In this Price revealed that he had never fully appreciated either the strengths and the weaknesses of Hume's original argument or the possibility of remedying these weaknesses by strengthening amendment.

Certainly inferences from actuality to possibility are, always and necessarily, valid. So, if we could indeed truly know even that one single, solitary case of extrasensory perception or psychokinesis had once upon a time actually occurred, then we should be in a position to infer that any BLP or BLPs precluding such occurrences must be false. It might therefore appear reasonable to attempt to discover or to stage some not-in-practice-repeatable yet nevertheless once-and-for-all-decisive demonstration of the reality of psi phenomena.

To nourish such a hope, however, is to fail to take the measure of the Humean argument developed in section 2 above. That argument, it will be remembered, was epistemological rather than ontological. If sound, what it shows is not that no events precluded by BLPs have ever occurred, but that, until and unless those precluding BLPs are first known to be false, such events, even though they may well have occurred, nevertheless cannot be known to have occurred. So what is needed in order decisively to falsify a BLP precluding the occurrence of phenomena of a particular kind is "an algorithm for setting up an exhibition of the reality of" such "phenomena wherever and whenever that should be required."

To develop such an algorithm for the psi phenomena would be to provide for a repeatable demonstration of their reality. By providing this you would succeed in establishing truth of a nomological proposition, that is to say, a proposition of the same form as those of BLPs, and carrying similar implications. For you would have shown that the conditions (or it might be only some of the conditions) that guarantee the manifestation of psi phenomena are conditions that make the occurrence of those phenomena physically necessary and their nonoccurrence physically impossible. This truth established, we become licensed to infer not only that BLPs precluding the occurrence of psi phenomena are false, but also that many conditional propositions, both about the future and about the past, must be true. It thus becomes possible to know both that, if the appropriate conditions are satisfied, then psi phenomena will occur, and that if they had in the past been satisfied—even though in fact they were not—then psi phenomena would have occurred.

5. Disturbing peculiarities of parapsychology

(i) There are several further, reinforcing reasons for demanding full repeatability and for refusing to accept any substitute. In the first place parapsychology is by now a fairly old subject. The (original, British) Society for Psychical Research was founded in 1882. Serious work has been going on for more than a century, while the amount done each year appears still to be increasing. Nevertheless, the long-sought repeatable demonstration of any psi phenomenon seems to be as far away as ever. It is still stubbornly the case that those best-informed about the field automatically assume that people claiming to demonstrate psi capacities with night-after-night regularity must be some sort of frauds, achieving their effects by mere conjuring tricks. So long as this situation continues, there will every year be better and better reason to close the books, concluding that the whole business was a wild goose chase up a blind alley.

Another depressing and damaging feature of the history of the subject is the ever-lengthening succession of shameful, shabby cases, cases that at one time and to many people had seemed to constitute decisive demonstrations of the reality of these putative phenomena but have since been definitively discredited as fraudulent. For instance, this applies to every one of the cases commended by the various contributors to J. Ludwig, ed., *Philosophy and Parapsychology* (Buffalo, N.Y.: Prometheus Books, 1978). In particular, it is true of the once famous and now notorious work of S. G. Soal on Gloria Stewart and Basil Shackleton.[13]

Yet another reason for viewing the whole business with the deepest suspicion, and one reinforcing the demand for repeatability or nothing, is the fact that no one has been able to think up any halfway plausible theory accounting for the occurrence of any psi phenomenon. This is important, because a plausible theory relating these putative phenomena to something that undoubtedly does occur promises not only to explain but also to make probable their actual occurrence.[14]

(ii) A final disturbing peculiarity deserves more extended attention. It is that all the psi concepts are negatively defined. Because such expressions as "by telepathy" and "by psychokinesis" sound like the expressions "by telephony" and "by psychoanalysis," this important truth is often overlooked. But the fact, of course, is that all the psi terms refer rather to the absence of any means or mechanism, or at any rate to the absence of any normal and understood means or mechanism.

One consequence is that no sense has been given to a distinction between single hits achieved by ESP and single hits due to chance alone. Only when, after a series of guesses (or whatever) has been made and has been scored up against the targets, it turns out that there have been significantly more hits than we could have expected by chance alone are we entitled to begin to talk of psi, or of a psi factor. The phenomenon, therefore, is, so far at least, defined as essentially statistical. Furthermore, and despite some protests to the contrary, the same applies not only to the experimental work but also to the supposed spontaneous or sporadic phenomena. If, for instance, someone has a dream of a maritime disaster "on the night when that great ship went down," then there is no way of identifying this dream as a psi phenomenon save by summing single items of correspondence between dream and reality and arguing that there are too many correspondences, and too few noncorrespondences, to be put down to chance alone.

Psychokinesis (PK), on the other hand, should not be similarly statistical, nor would it have been, had the evidence actually offered on PK been what we ought to have expected. For, if people really were able at will to exert some force at a distance on other objects, then we should have expected this to be demonstrated by the use of some extremely delicate and very carefully shielded apparatus. If the subject's willings were always followed by the occurrences of the willed movement, and that movement was one that we had taken every care to ensure would not otherwise occur, then we would be home and dry, and, presumably, we should in this have a repeatable demonstration.

But the actual "dice work" has been different. In fact, it is once again essentially statistical. Several dice are tossed mechanically, and the subject is told to will them all to come up on one particular side. The procedure is repeated ad nauseam, and well beyond. The experimenter's hope is that he will find significantly more willed sides turning up than chance alone would lead us to expect. If that hope is fulfilled, the experimenter reports a PK effect. So, once again, no operational sense is in fact given to the notion of a single PK hit, as opposed to a run of falls suggesting the operation of a PK factor.[15]

The second and further consequence of all this is that there is no way of decisively identifying even a single run in which a psi factor has operated. Since no identifiable means or mechanism is being employed, it must remain always possible to say that any single run was no more than a statistical freak—however improbable, not impossible. There is therefore once again no substitute for what there is ever less reason for expecting we shall in fact get, namely, a repeatable demonstration showing psi phenomena being produced and inhibited at the will of the experimenters and/or their subjects. Only this would really demonstrate that the targets actually are causing the subjects to come up with correct guesses and/or that subjects actually are influencing the fall of the dice.

Notes

1. It is, I suggest, significant that there appears to be no such generally accepted program today. Certainly, when in the early sixties I was working on the book since republished as *God: A Critical Enquiry* (La Salle, Ill.: Open Court, 1984), "I did ask several Christian friends to name the work or works which they believed provided the most formidable advocacy." But "they found great difficulty in thinking of anything which seemed to them to be even halfway adequate, and there was almost no overlap between the different lists eventually provided" (p. x).

2. See H. Denzinger, ed., *Enchiridion Symbolorum* (Freiburg im Breisgau: Herder, 29th revised edition, 1953), § 1806. Instead of "be known for certain" (*certo cognosci*) an earlier draft read "be demonstrated" (*demonstrari*).

3. Ibid., § 1813.

4. I Corinthians, 15, 14. In England today, and no doubt elsewhere also, it is impossible to underline St. Paul's point too heavily, for we have numerous clerics who, while ever eager to present their conventionally left-wing politics as part if not the whole of the teachings of Christianity, are in fact themselves not, in any traditional understanding, Christians at all. For instance, a few years ago a man was appointed to a senior see in the United Kingdom who had referred to the very idea of a physical resurrection in studiously and gratuitously offensive terms such that I, as a vice president of the Rationalist Press Association, would never have dreamed of employing.

5. For discussion of Hume's original argument compare either my *Hume's Philosophy of Belief* (London, and New York: Routledge and Kegan Paul, and Humanities, 1961), chapter 8, or my *David Hume: Philosopher of Moral Science* (Oxford: Blackwell, 1986), chapter 5.

6. David Hume, *The History of England from the Invasion of Julius Caesar to the Revolution in 1688* (Indianapolis, Ind.: Liberty, 1983).

7. The sneer quotes around the word "proved" were not, of course, supplied by Hume.

8. The contrast is between evidencing and motivating reasons. See, for instance, my discussion of the Wager Argument of Pascal in *An Introduction to Western Philosophy* (London: Thames and Hudson, revised edition, 1989).

9. For a discussion of this radical critique compare, for instance, Flew, 1961, chapter 9.

10. "Essay on the Miracles Recorded in Ecclesiastical History," in *The Ecclesiastical History of M. L'Abbé Fleury* (Oxford: J. H. Parker, 1842), 2(8) 2.

11. "The Relevance of Psychical Research to Philosophy" was originally published in *Philosophy* 24 (1949): 291–309. But all the presently relevant material is perhaps more easily to be found, along with a great deal of further discussion, in Antony Flew, ed., *Readings in the Philosophic Problems of Parapsychology* (Buffalo, N.Y.: Prometheus Books, 1987).

12. "Science and the Supernatural" was originally published in *Science* 131 (no. 3265): 359–67. But again the presently most relevant parts are perhaps more easily found in Flew, ed., *Readings,* pp. 214–26.

13. Compare, for instance, ibid., passim.

14. Compare, for instance, ibid., part 2.

15. The first thorough critical survey of this "dice work" was "A Review of Psychokinesis (PK)" by Edward Girden, published in the *Psychological Bulletin* 59, no. 5 (September 1962): 353–88. Girden rightly placed heavy emphasis upon the significance of the failure to perform, or at any rate to report the (presumably negative) findings of nonstatistical investigations of this alleged phenomenon.

4

Can We Survive Our Own Deaths?

Whether we are to live in a future state, as it is the most important question which can possibly be asked, so it is the most intelligible one which can be expressed in language. Yet strange perplexities have been raised about the meaning of that identity or sameness of person, which is implied in the notion of our living now and hereafter, or in any two successive moments.

Joseph Butler (1692–1752)[1]

It is because the idea of a life after mortal death, and above all the threat of an eternal life in torment, appears so immediately intelligible, and so overwhelmingly formidable, that Butler and so many others have not been and are not greatly distressed by the indefeasibility in this life of "the religious hypothesis." For they could be confident that in that infinite future all would be made plain. The solution to the Problem of Evil would be revealed, wrongs would all be righted, and the divine justice vindicated.

The promise of such eschatological verification is, of course, paradoxical. Unbelievers are eventually to learn the grim truth, but only when it will be too late for prudent, saving action. To our protests that we never knew, and could not have known, the response will be that made to a parallel protest by an old-time Scots Judge: "Well, ye ken noo!" If however it is the believers who are mistaken, then they will never be embarrassed by a posthumous awareness of their error, any more than we can expect to enjoy the satisfaction of saying to them, "We told you so!" For, as the Epicureans used to urge, it will be for us mortals after death as it was before we were born:

> If it is going to be wretched and miserable for anyone in the future, then he to whom the bad things may happen has also got to exist at that time. Since death prevents that possibility . . . we can know that there is nothing to be feared after death, that he who does not exist cannot be miserable. It makes not a jot of difference . . . when immortal death has taken away his mortal life.[2]

1. Setting the problem: The great obstacle

Surely Butler was right. "Whether we are to live in a future state, as it is the most important question which can possibly be asked, so it is the most intelligible one which can be expressed in language." Surely we can understand the fears of those warned of the fate of the damned and the hopes of warriors of Allah expecting if they die in Holy Wars to go straight to the arms of the black-eyed houris in Paradise. Of course we can: they both expect—and what could be more intelligible than this?—that, if they do certain things, then they will in consequence enjoy or suffer certain rewards or punishments. And, if this future life is supposed to last forever, then clearly the question of whether or not we shall have it (and, if so, the consequent problem of ensuring that we shall pass it agreeably) is of quite overwhelming existential importance. For what are three-score years and ten compared with all eternity?

Now wait a minute, the skeptic protests. Surely something crucial is being overlooked. For this future life is supposed to continue even *after* physical dissolution, even *after* the slow corruption in the cemetery or the swift consumption in the crematorium. Of course we can understand the myth of Er[3] or stories of Valhalla. But to expect that after my death and dissolution such things might happen to me is to overlook that I shall not then exist. To expect such things, through overlooking this, is surely like accepting a fairy tale as history, through ignoring the prefatory rubric: "Once upon a time, in a world that never was . . ."

That first exchange gets us to the heart of the matter, by establishing two fundamentals. One of these is that the essence of any doctrine of *personal* survival (or *personal* immortality) must be that it should assert that *we ourselves* shall in some fashion do things and suffer things after *our own* deaths (forever). It is this, and this alone, that warrants, or rather constitutes, what John Wisdom so correctly characterized as "the logically unique expectation."[4] It is important to emphasize that this is indeed of the essence: both because some doctrines employing the word immortality have from the beginning not been of this kind—Aristotle on the alleged immortality of the intellect, for instance—and because others, which started as genuine doctrines of personal immortality, have been so interpreted and reinterpreted that they have surreptitiously ceased to be anything of the such. (These latter have thus suffered "the death by a thousand qualifications."[5]) It is also, it seems, sometimes necessary to point out that personal survival is presupposed by, and is no sort of alternative to, personal immortality.[6] For, as was famously said with regard to another remarkable claim to survival: "It is the first step which counts."

The second fundamental is this. Any doctrine of personal survival or personal immortality has got to find some way around or over an enormous initial obstacle. In the ordinary, everyday understandings of the words involved, to say that someone survived death is to contradict yourself, while to assert that we all of us live forever is to assert a manifest falsehood, the flat contrary of a universally known universal truth: namely, the truth, hallowed in the traditional formal logic, that "All men are mortal."

2. Possible routes around or over that obstacle

We may distinguish three sorts of ways in which we might attempt to circumvent or to overcome this formidable barrier, although the route-finding image becomes awkward when we notice that most living faiths have incorporated elements of more than one. Let us label these three ways "Reconstitutionist," "Astral Body," and "Platonic-Cartesian."

*   *   *

(i) The first of these cannot be better explained than by unrolling a pair of quotations. One is an epitaph composed for himself by Benjamin Franklin. I copied it from a plaque erected not on but beside his grave in Christ Church cemetery, Philadelphia: "The body of B. Franklin, Printer, Like the Cover of an old Book, Its Contents torn out, And stript of its Lettering and Gilding, Lies Here, Food for Worms. But the work shall not be lost; for it will, as he believ'd, appear once more in a new and more elegant Edition Corrected and improved By the Author."

The other comes from chapter 12 "The Night Journey" in the Koran. As usual, it is Allah speaking: "Thus shall they be rewarded: because they disbelieved our revelations and said, 'When we are turned to bones and dust shall we be raised to life?' Do they not see that Allah, who has created the heavens and the earth, has power to create their like? Their fate is preordained beyond all doubt. Yet the wrongdoers persist in unbelief."[7]

This direct Reconstitutionist Way is blocked by the Replica Objection. This is that the "new and more elegant edition" would not be the original Founding Father, Signer of the American Declaration of Independence, but only a replica, and that Allah spoke more truly than his Prophet realized when he claimed, not the ability to reconstitute the same persons, but only the "power to create their like." The force of the Replica Objection is all the greater, and all the more decisive, in as much as the "new . . . edition" and "their like" are both to be the creations of a quasipersonal, rewarding and punishing Creator, not just things that occur unintended.[8]

It is clear that Aquinas, unlike some of our contemporaries who think to follow him, appreciated all this. But his Reconstitutionism incorporated an element of our third kind. For he believed that a soul, which is a substance, in the sense of something that can significantly be said to exist separately yet is most emphatically not in such separate existence a whole person, survives what would normally be called death and dissolution. This soul will eventually be—shall we say?—incorporated into what, had provision not been made for this element of partly personal continuity, might otherwise have had to be dismissed as merely a replica of the original person.[9]

About this Thomist response the only thing we need to say at this stage is that this sort of semisoul, which is not by itself a whole person, must be exposed to all the objections that can be brought against a full Platonic soul, which is, or could be. Also, to the extent that the Thomist soul is not a whole person, its claim to constitute the essential but sufficient link maintaining personal identity is bound to weaken.

(ii) To explain the Astral Body approach it is best to think of cinematic representations—for example, in the movie version of Noel Coward's *Blithe Spirit*—in which a shadow person, visible only sometimes and only to some of the characters, detaches itself from a person shown as dead, and thereafter continues to participate in the developing action, at one time discernibly and at another time not. This elusive entity is taken to be itself the real, the essential, person.

It is not, however, essential for our present purposes that an astral body be of human shape, much less that, even after the traumatic detachment of death, it should remain—as in those decent old days it did—neatly and conventionally clad. The crux is that it should possess the corporeal characteristics of size, shape, and position, and that—although eluding crude, untutored, observation—it should nevertheless be in principle detectable. If it were not both in this minimum sense corporeal and in principle detectable, it would not be relevantly different from the Platonic-Cartesian soul. If it were not in practice excessively difficult to detect, no one could with any plausibility suggest that such a thing might slip away unnoticed from the deathbed.

The vulgar, materialist notion of souls—a notion Plato derides in the *Phaedo* (77D)—satisfies the present, studiously undemanding specification for astral bodies; that notion of souls surely was, as near as makes no matter, that of Epicurus and Lucretius. There seems reason to believe that many of the early Christian Fathers thought of souls as something less than totally and perfectly incorporeal.[10] So their souls also must for present purposes be classified as astral bodies.

The Way of the Astral Body runs between a rock and a hard place. For the more we make astral bodies like the ordinary flesh and blood persons from which they are supposedly detachable—in order to make sure that each person's astral body can be identified as the real and essential person—the more difficult it becomes to make out that it is not already known that no such astral bodies do in fact detach themselves at death. If, on the other hand, we take care so to specify the nature of our hypothesized astral bodies that the falsification of the hypothesis that such there be, while still possible in principle, is in practice indefinitely deferred, then we find that we have made it impossibly difficult to identify creatures of too, too solid flesh and blood with any such perennially elusive hypothetical entities. Under these and other pressures those who have started to attempt the Way of the Astral Body tend so to refine away the corporeal characteristics of these putative bodies that they become indiscernible from Platonic-Cartesian souls.

(iii) The third, Platonic-Cartesian Way is, of course, the most familiar. It is based upon, or consists in, two assumptions. The first is that what is ordinarily thought of as a person is in fact composed of two utterly disparate elements: the one, the body, earthy, corporeal and perishable; the other, the soul, incorporeal, invisible, intangible, and perhaps imperishable. The second assumption, and equally essential, is that the second of these elements is the real person, the agent, the rational being, the me or the you.

Traditionally these assumptions have been taken absolutely for granted; in discussions of survival and immortality, they still are. They are rarely even stated and distinguished. Still more rarely do we find anyone attempting justification. The founders of the British Society for Psychical Research hoped that its work might serve to verify what they feared that the advance of all the other sciences was falsifying: a Platonic-Cartesian view of the nature of man. In the middle decades of the present century J. B. Rhine cherished the same hope, and believed that the parapsychological work done in his laboratories at Durham, North Carolina, had indeed supplied the hoped-for verification. This is neither the place nor the occasion for yet another demonstration that these desired findings were in fact presupposed in prejudicial misdescriptions of that work, rather than supported by it.[11]

But it is perhaps just worth mentioning that when people construe out-of-body experiences as evidence for a Platonic-Cartesian view they make exactly the same mistake. If a patient claims to have "seen" something "when out of the body," something that she could not have seen with her eyes and from her bed, then the more economical as well as the more intelligible thing to say is that she "saw" that something clairvoyantly from her bed, rather than that it was "seen," equally clairvoyantly, by her temporarily detached soul.

3. What Butler saw as "strange perplexities"

Whether or not the two assumptions that together define the Platonic-Cartesian Way can in the end be justified, it most certainly will not do, notwithstanding that this is what usually is done, to take them as from the beginning given, as if they either required no proof or had been proved already. The truth is that it is very far from obvious that disembodied personal survival is conceivable, that is, that talk of persons as substantial incorporeal souls is coherent. For in their ordinary, everyday understanding of person words—the personal pronouns, personal names, words for persons playing particular roles (such as "spokesperson," "official," "Premier," "aviator," etc.), and so on—all these are words employed to name or otherwise refer to members of a very special class of creatures of flesh and blood.

In this ordinary, everyday understanding—what other do we have?—incorporeal persons are no more a sort of persons than are imaginary, fictitious, or otherwise nonexistent persons. "Incorporeal" is here, like those others, an alienans adjective.[12] To put the point less technically but more harshly: to assert, in that ordinary, everyday understanding, that somebody survived death, but disembodied, is to contradict yourself. Hence the incorrigible Thomas Hobbes was so rude as to say that, "If a man talks to me of 'a round quadrangle'; or 'accidents of bread in cheese'; or 'immaterial substances'; . . . I should not say that he was in error, but that his words were without meaning: that is to say, absurd."[13]

(i) This absurdity is very rarely recognized and admitted as such. Even Richard Swinburne, whose theological trilogy constitutes the most formidable of all contemporary defenses of theism, is sometimes inclined to take these two Platonic-Cartesian assumptions as given. Thus the second sentence of *The Coherence of Theism* reads: "By a 'God' he [the theist] understands something like a person without a body (i.e., a spirit) . . ." Later we are told that "Human persons have bodies: he [God] does not."[14] Again, in the course of a discussion of "What it is for a body to be mine," Swinburne, having first listed various peculiarly personal characteristics, tells us that "we learn to apply the term 'person' to various individuals around us in virtue of their possession of the characteristics which I have outlined."

This, surely, is all wrong. If persons really were creatures *possessing* bodies, rather than, as in fact we are, creatures that just essentially *are* members of one special sort of creatures of flesh and blood, then it would make sense to speak of a whole body amputation. Who is it, too, who is presupposed to be able sensibly to ask which of various bodies is his, or hers? How is such a puzzled person to be identified, or to self-identify, save by reference to the living organism he or she actually is?

As for Swinburne's suggestion that we could, and even do, learn to apply the word "person" to "various individuals around us" by first learning how to pick out certain peculiarly personal characteristics, and then identifying persons as creatures of the kind that possess these characteristics, this constitutes a perfect paradigm of the literally preposterous. For the manifest truth is that our only experience of any peculiarly personal characteristics is, and indeed has to be, of these as characteristics peculiar to that particular kind of creatures we have first learnt to identify as mature and normal human beings. The identification of such peculiarly personal characteristics therefore is and must be posterior rather than prior to the identification of members of the particular kind of creatures to which alone these characteristics can be and are attributed.

Swinburne thought to deflect the ferocity of such critical onslaughts by making the emollient point that no one has any business to argue, just because all the so-and-sos with which they happen themselves to have been acquainted with were such-and-such, that therefore such-and-suchness must be an essential characteristic of anything that is to be properly rated a so-and-so.[15] This is, of course, correct. Certainly it would be preposterous, and worse, to argue that because all the human beings with whom you had so far become acquainted had had black skins that therefore anyone with any other skin pigmentation must be disqualified as a human being.

Incorporeality, however, is a very different kettle of fish, or, more like, no kettle and no fish. For to characterize something as incorporeal is to make an assertion that is at one and the same time both extremely comprehensive and wholly negative. Those proposing to do this surely owe it both to themselves and to others not only to indicate what positive characteristics might significantly be attributed to their putative incorporeal entities but also to specify how such entities could, if only in principle, be identified and reidentified. It is not exclusively, or even primarily, a question of what predicates these putative spiritual subjects might take, but of how they themselves might be identified in the first place, and only after that reidentified as numerically the same through an effluxion of time.

(ii) The main reason the need to attempt answers to these questions is so rarely recognized must be, surely, the easy and widespread assumption that common knowledge of the untechnical vernacular equips us with a concept of incorporeal persons, and hence that what ought to be meant by talk of the identity of such entities is already determined. It is this assumption that supports and is in turn supported by those reckless claims to be able to image (to form a private mental image of) personal survival in a disembodied state. The assumption itself is sustained by the familiarity both of talk about minds or souls and of talk about survival or immortality. Since both sorts of talk are without doubt intelligible, does it not follow that we do have concepts of soul and of mind, as well as of disembodied personal existence? No, or rather, yes and no.

Just because we can indeed understand hopes or fears of survival or immortality it does not follow that we can conceive, much less image, existence as persons, but disembodied. No one has ever emphasized and commended incorporeality more strongly than Plato. Yet when in the myth of Er he labors to describe the future life awaiting his supposedly disembodied souls, everything even that master craftsman of the pen has to say about them presupposes that they will still be just such creatures of flesh and blood as we are now and he was then.

On the other hand, the familiarity and intelligibility of talk about minds and about souls does entitle us to infer that we possess both a concept of mind and a concept of soul. But these particular semantic possessions are precisely not what is needed if doctrines of the survival and perhaps the immortality of souls or of minds are to be viable. The crux is that, in their everyday understandings, the words "minds" and "souls" are not words for sorts of substances, not words, that is, for what could significantly be said to survive the deaths and dissolutions of those flesh and blood persons whose minds or souls they are. To construe the question whether she has a mind of her own, or the assertion that he is a mean-souled man, as a question, or an assertion, about some hypothesized incorporeal substances is like taking the loss of the Red Queen's dog's temper as if this was on all fours with his loss of his bone, or like looking for the grin remaining after the Cheshire Cat has vanished.[16]

This distinction is crucial to my argument. Certainly the fact that we can say so many sensible and intelligible things about minds or souls does show that we have concepts of minds or souls, just as the facts that we can talk sensibly about grins or tempers shows that we have concepts both of a grin and of a temper. But none of this shows, what is not the case, that we can sensibly talk of grins and tempers existing separately from the faces of which they are configurations or of the people who sometimes lose them or—and this is vital—that we can talk sensibly about the mind or soul surviving the dissolution of the flesh and blood person whose mind or soul it was.

(iii) Earlier I mentioned, and described as reckless, claims that we can not merely conceive but also image—form mental pictures of—disembodied survival. In the twentieth-century literature this claim was, I believe, first made by Moritz Schlick:

> In fact I can easily imagine, e.g. witnessing the funeral of my own body and continuing to exist without a body, for nothing is easier

than to describe a world which differs from our ordinary world only in the complete absence of all data which I would call parts of my own body. We must conclude that immortality, in the sense defined, should . . . be regarded . . . as an empirical hypothesis, because it possesses logical verifiability. It could be verified by following the prescription "Wait until you die!"[17]

A more puckishly picturesque version was later provided by John Wisdom: "I know indeed what it would be like to witness my own funeral—the men in tall silk hats, the flowers, and the face beneath the glass-topped coffin."[18]

This is a thesis that was, so far as I know, first challenged by me, in a paper first published twenty years after that of Schlick.[19] In the subsequent thirty-seven years there has, again so far as I know, been no counter-challenge, although my paper has been reprinted at least five times. My point, which I now repeat, was that Schlick's thesis can and should be challenged, and the challenge can be pressed home without presuming to draw limits to Wisdom's no doubt extremely extensive powers of private mental picturing. The crux is that there is a world of difference between, on the one hand, imagining what it would be like to witness my own funeral, and, on the other hand, imagining what it would be like for *me* to witness my own funeral. What Schlick and Wisdom and everyone else can certainly do is the former. What would be needed to warrant Schlick's conclusions is the latter. The question at issue is a question about possible pictures and possible captions. Everyone knows what picture fits the first caption. What picture fits, and justifies, the second?

If it is really I who witness, then it is not my funeral but only "my funeral" (between disclaiming quotes). If it really is my funeral, then I cannot be a witness, since I shall be dead and in the coffin. Of course I can imagine (image) what might be described as my "watching my own funeral." For I can remember Harry Lime in the film *The Third Man* watching "his own funeral," and of course I can imagine being in the same situation as Harry Lime. But it was not really Lime's funeral. The crucial question remains: "Was the flesh and blood creature Flew really there, alive, or was there only his corpse in the coffin?"

What Schlick and Wisdom really were doing when they engaged in these misdescribed exercises of imagination was causing themselves to have the kind of nonperceptual visual experience that might conceivably be suffered by an incorporeal subject of consciousness, if indeed such an entity could conceivably be said to exist. Precisely because it would be by the hypothesis incorporeal such a hypothetical subject of consciousness could not be identified with Schlick or Wisdom or anyone else. So the kind of conscious experience under discussion would not be an experience had by a person, in any ordinary understanding of that crucial term, but one had by a hypothetical we know not what, for which no means of identification has yet been provided. In consequence this hypothetical we know not what has not been provided with any means of reidentification through time as one and the same individual we know not what.

That second and consequential point is surely much the more important of the two. For in most of our exercises of imaging we are not ourselves among the objects of that imaging. So we might easily be tempted to think that we were on these occasions imagining what it would be like for us to survive, but disembodied. But a long series of great and less great philosophers, working on the false assumption that persons, or at any rate, their "selves," are essentially incorporeal, have tried but failed to suggest any criterion for the identity of such postulated incorporeal entities.

4. The problem of personal identity

To say that Flew will survive what would ordinarily be accounted Flew's death is to say that someone or something then living will be the same person as I am now. So our present problem is, if not the same as, at least inseparably connected with, the philosophical problem of personal identity, the problem, that is to say, of what is meant by the expression "same person."

(i) Swinburne, who recognizes similarly serious and heavy problems about *The Coherence of Theism,* and who in that book labors long and hard to solve those problems, quickly concludes, about persons: "The identity of a person over time is something ultimate, not analysable in terms of bodily continuity or continuity of memory or character."[20] Given this conclusion, Swinburne allows—while still taking it for granted that people are essentially incorporeal—"We may use bodily continuity to reach conclusions about personal identity."[21]

This will not do. For what we actually use bodily criteria for is to establish bodily continuity. And this is not just a usually reliable criterion for, but a large part if not the whole of, what is meant by personal identity. (It would be, wouldn't it, if persons just are, as I maintain that we all know that we are, members of a very special sort of creatures of flesh and blood?)

Starting, like so many of the great and good, from the false assumption that people are, if not essentially incorporeal, at least not essentially corporeal, Swinburne proceeds to address the problem of personal identity, the problem, that is, of what it means to say that this at time two is the same person as that at time one. And, like everyone else who has started with a similar false assumption, Swinburne first tries somehow to give an answer in terms either of true memory or of honest but possibly mistaken memory claims.

Then, once again like so many others, Swinburne both overlooks the theoretical possibility and actual frequency of honest yet mistaken claims to be the same person as did this or suffered that *and* fails to appreciate the decisive force of Bishop Butler's refutation of any circular analysis of "being the same person as did that" in terms of "remembering being the same person as did that."[22] In consequence, whatever difficulties other people might confront in trying to reidentify some putative person as the same as the one who did that particular deed, or who enjoyed or suffered that particular experience, Swinburne is inclined to assume, first, that there must be a true answer to all possible questions about personal identity, and, second, that the putative person in question must always be in a position to know that true answer—if only he would tell us, and tell us true.

But now, first, if there is or even could be a true answer, then the question to which it is a true answer must already have sense. It must, to particularize, already make sense to speak of a disembodied person, and to go on to wonder whether "the identity of a person over time is [not] something ultimate, not analyzable in terms of bodily continuity or continuity of memory or character."

Arguing against Penelhum, Swinburne mistakes it that the objection to giving an account of the identity of disembodied persons in terms of memory claims is that such claims could not be checked, which he contends that they could be. But the decisive objection, put first and classically by Bishop Butler, is that true memory presupposes, and therefore cannot constitute, personal identity. (When I truly remember doing that, what I remember is that I am the same person as did it.)

Swinburne's second mistake here, and again it is an error in which he has a host of companions, is a matter of method. In a word, this seductive and popular mistake consists in the misuse of possible puzzle cases, cases which, if they actually occurred, and were thought likely to recur, would require us to make new decisions as to what in future correct verbal usage is to be. What is wrong is to assume that decisions, even the most rational decisions, about responses to purely hypothetical challenges, usually challenges we have no reason or less than no reason to expect to have to face in real life, must necessarily throw direct light upon the present meanings of the words concerned.

The truly disturbing conclusion to be derived from a proper employment of puzzle cases is one to which Swinburne seems to have blinded himself. It is that it is possible to conceive, and even to imagine (image), situations giving rise to questions about personal identity to which, in the present meanings of the key terms, there could be no unequivocally true or unequivocally false answer. So not even the person or persons themselves could know that answer. Consider, to reuse the example I first introduced over forty years ago, the questions that would arise if someone was told that she was going to split like an amoeba, and did. The two people resulting from this division, while indisputably different from each other, would both have equally indisputable claims to be the same person as the one who suffered the split.

(ii) The key to the philosophical problem of personal identity is, as so often, to start right. Against the whole Platonic-Cartesian tradition we have to insist that our paradigm persons are standard specimens of one particular visible, tangible, utterly familiar kind or species of essentially corporeal creatures. Given this, it then becomes inescapably obvious what the courts of justice mean when they ask whether the prisoner in the dock is the person who did the deed. It is essentially a question about physical continuity: Had witnesses to the crime pursued the criminal, never letting him out of their observation, would they be able to stand up in court and honestly testify, "That is the man!"? Certainly no real life, properly constituted court is ever likely to have such superlative evidence of guilt, although aficionados of good, old-fashioned Westerns will be able to recall such scenes from movies. Nevertheless it is the import of this ideal testimony that the prosecution is endeavoring to establish by the deployment of whatever inferior kinds of evidence happen to be available.

Of course the court expects that the prisoner, like other members of our species, will possess all those peculiar characteristics that Swinburne takes care to pick out. If it so happens that he does not, then the defense will certainly want to argue that he was incapable of forming a *mens rea* [guilty mind]. Again, if there has been some drastic personality change in the defendant since the commission of the crime, similarly wide-awake defense lawyers will want to argue that, in a secondary sense, the defendant is now "quite a different person" from the man who did the deed and hence should suffer some lesser or no penalty. (This secondary presupposes the primary sense: no one would say their son was quite a different person since he passed through Marine Corps boot camp if they were not sure that he was, in the primary sense, the same.)

Of course, too, we might someday discover that some other species, perhaps in some other inhabited world, also possessed some or all of our peculiarly personal characteristics. But, before any "survival hypothesis" can get off the ground, proponents have got to explain how both an incorporeal or spiritual substance could be identified as a bearer of these peculiarly personal characteristics, and how, even if it could be identified in the first place, it could then be reidentified as numerically the same as some former, flesh and blood human being. Until and unless it appears that this can be done I propose to conclude with a one-verse Chinese burial song, a song sung, the translator tells us, only at the burial of kings and princes:

> *How swiftly it dries,*
> *The dew on the garlic-leaf,*
> *The dew that dries so fast*
> *Tomorrow will fall again.*
> *But he whom we carry to the grave*
> *Will never more return.*[23]

Notes

1. Joseph Butler, "A Dissertation of Personal Identity," in *Butler's Works,* edited by W. E. Gladstone (Oxford: Clarendon, 1896), vol. 1, p. 387.

2. Lucretius, *de Rerum Natura* [On the Nature of Things], translated by W. H. D. Rouse (London, and Cambridge, Mass.: Heinemann, and Harvard University Press), 3.862–69.

3. Plato, *The Republic,* 10.614B–621D.

4. *Philosophy and Psychoanalysis* (Oxford: Blackwell, 1953), p. 150.

5. "Theology and Falsification," in Antony Flew and Alasdair MacIntyre, eds., *New Essays in Philosophical Theology* (London: SCM Press, 1955), p. 97; also, in various languages, in at least thirty other places later.

6. Contrast Roy Holland, reviewing C. B. Martin, *Religious Belief* (Ithaca, N.Y.: Cornell University Press, 1959), in *Mind* (1961): 572.

7. The Koran, translated by W. J. Dawood (Harmondsworth: Penguin), p. 234.

8. Does anyone really believe that posthumous justice could be done to Hitler or Stalin or any of the other multimillion murderers of our tormented century if only we had the technology to create such replicas?

9. See the Reply to Object 4 in Article 2 under Question 79 of Book III of the *Summa Theologica.* We have here another example of the great synthesizer trying to have it both ways.

10. See, for instance, Tertullian's *de Anima* [Concerning the Soul]. In chapter 7 he finds "in the Gospel itself . . . the clearest evidence for the corporeal nature of the soul. . . . For an incorporeal thing suffers nothing, not having that which makes it capable of suffering; else, if it had such a capacity, it must be a bodily substance." (The reference is to Luke 16, 23–24, the story of Lazarus.) In chapter 9 Tertullian then tells a tale of "a sister whose lot it has been to be favoured with sundry gifts of revelation." She is said to

have testified, "A spirit has been in the habit of appearing to me; not, however, a void and empty illusion, but such as would offer itself to be even grasped by the hand, soft and transparent and of an etherial colour, and in form resembling a human being in every respect."

11. For extensive discussion of these and other related questions, compare Antony Flew, ed., *Readings in the Philosophical Problems of Parapsychology* (Buffalo, N.Y.: Prometheus Books, 1987).

12. "Alienans adjective" is a medieval, Scholastic technicality. Whereas, for example, the ordinary adjectival expression "red book" is used to imply that something is both red and a book, such alienans adjectives as imaginary, fictitious, or nonexistent are not similarly employed in order to pick out a subset for some more extensive set: imaginary books, unlike red books, are not species of the genus books!

13. *Leviathan,* chapter 5.

14. (Oxford: Clarendon, 1977), p. 51.

15. Ibid., p. 54.

16. In this crucial sense of "substance"—which is by no means the only sense in which that word has been employed—a substantial soul or life could significantly, even if not truly, be said not only to preexist but to survive whatever it had "animated" or "ensouled." Perhaps the most effective way of fixing this concept firmly in mind is by appealing to examples from Lewis Carroll's *Alice in Wonderland* and *Through the Looking Glass,* examples in which the absurdities are produced by treating words that everyone realizes are not words for sorts of substances as if they were. Remember, for instance, the subtraction sum the Red Queen set for Alice: "Take a bone from a dog, what would remain?" The answer that nothing would remain is rejected. For the dog losing its temper would depart, while the lost temper would remain. Or, again, what of the grinning Cheshire Cat, which progressively vanished, leaving only the grin behind?

17. See his "Meaning and Verification," in the *Philosophical Review* (1937), later reprinted in H. Feigl and W. Sellars, eds., *Readings in Philosophical Analysis* (New York: Appleton-Century-Crofts, 1949).

18. John Wisdom, *Other Minds* (Oxford: Blackwell, 1952), p. 36.

19. "Can a man witness his own funeral?" in the *Hibbert Journal* (1956) and later reprinted in J. Feinberg, ed., *Reason and Responsibility* (Belmont, Calif.: Dickenson, 1971); in W. J. Blackstone, ed., *Meaning and Existence* (New York: Holt, Reinhart and Winston, 1972); in F. A. Westphal, ed., *The Art of Philosophy* (Englewood Cliffs, N.J.: Prentice-Hall, 1972); and in P. A. French,

ed., *Exploring Philosophy* (Morristown, N.J.: General Learning Press, 1975). There is also a retitled and very much revised version in Antony Flew, *God, Freedom, and Immortality* (Buffalo, N.Y.: Prometheus Books, 1984).

20. Swinburne, *The Coherence of Theism,* p. 110.

21. Ibid., p. 109.

22. See his "A Dissertation of Personal Identity." Also compare my "Locke and the Problem of Personal Identity," in *Philosophy* (1951), later reprinted, with revisions, in both C. B. Martin and D. M. Armstrong, eds., *Locke and Berkeley* (New York: Doubleday, 1968) and B. Brody, ed., *Readings in the Philosophy of Religion* (Englewood Cliffs, N.J.: Prentice-Hall, 1976).

23. These lines first appeared in English translation in Arthur Waley *170 Chinese Poems* (London: Constable, 1918), p. 38. Having been captivated by that entire collection when I first read it as a schoolboy in the thirties, I bought permission to employ this particular verse as the epigraph for my Gifford Lectures on *The Logic of Mortality* (Oxford: Blackwell, 1987), a work to which anyone desiring a fuller development of the contentions of the present chapter is hereby referred.

Part Two

Defending Knowledge
and Responsibility

5

Must Naturalism Self-Destruct?

> When we hear of some new attempt to explain reasoning or language
> or choice naturalistically, we ought to react as if we were told someone
> had squared the circle or proved $\sqrt{2}$ to be rational: only the mildest
> curiosity is in order—how well has the fantasy been concealed?
>
> Peter Geach, The Virtues[1]

This chapter is a sermon preached on the above text. Section 1 distinguishes evidencing from motivating reasons for believing, arguing that
the presence of the latter does not foreclose on the possibility of someone
having and knowing that they have the former also. The psychologizing
and sociologizing of believers is, therefore, no substitute for the rational
examination of beliefs. Section 2 ridicules and refutes reckless and arrogant claims made on behalf of both psychoanalysis and the sociology
of belief, claims which imply that there is no such thing as knowledge
properly so credited. Section 3 contends that it must be similarly suicidal
to pretend to have discovered that we humans are all subject to an
all-inclusive necessitation precluding any possibility of actual choice. The
crux here is that knowing presupposes a capacity to maintain or to
abandon beliefs in the light of truth-directed criticism, which is a matter
of choosing. Section 4 draws out corollaries concerning the crucial
importance of such criticism in both theoretical and practical enquiries.

Section 5 shows that, whatever may be true of imprudent individual scientists, the natural and social sciences are not as such committed to the intellectual suicide of denying that human beings possess those peculiar potentialities that alone make knowledge possible. This demonstration consists in developing a suggestion made earlier, in section 6 of chapter 2, that only agents—creatures able both to do and to do other than they do do—could even understand the concepts either of choice or of natural necessitation and the contrary-to-fact. Finally, section 6 constitutes an epilogue.

1. Explanations as answers to questions

In explaining and justifying our chosen motto the first points to seize are that every explanation is an answer to a question and hence that, whenever more than one question can be asked, there must be room for more than one answering explanation. Such alternative explanations, therefore, will not necessarily be rivals for the same logical space.

(i) The primary contention that explanations are answers to questions can be somewhat frivolously enforced, yet enforced none the less effectively, by reference to a recent Andy Capp comic strip. The tried and suffering Flo is shown protesting, "There was twelve light ales in the pantry this mornin'—now there's only ONE! 'ow d'yer explain THAT?" To which her incorrigible husband responds, with deadly predictability, "It was that dark in there, I didn't see it." The cartoonist Smythe felt no call to spell out the ways in which the intended question—about the eleven—differed from the question answered—about the one. Any such superfluous and heavy-footed spelling out should have taken notice also of the fractionally less obvious truth that the original challenge was, as so often, rather to justify the questionable than to explain the perplexing. The corollary of this primary contention—which is that explanations or, for that matter, justifications directed at different questions do not of necessity have to be competitors—had better be illustrated in a less light-hearted and more abstract way. So consider next the speech act of asserting the familiar, colorless, universally representative proposition p.

There are certainly two, and indeed more than two, categorically different questions that can be asked about this pedestrian performance. One, in requesting an explanation why the performer believes that *p*, asks for a statement of that performer's warrant for so believing. It asks, that is to say, for his or her evidencing reasons for harboring the belief that *p*, for his or her evidencing justification for so doing. The other, in requesting an explanation why the same performer chose this particular occasion to express the belief that *p*, asks the point and purpose of this particular speech act. It asks, that is to say, for his or her motivating reasons for so acting. The answer given is always in the first instance an explanation, though sometimes it may also constitute an attempt at justification.

(ii) The crucial distinction between these two kinds of reason—the two senses, that is, both of the word "reason" and of several associated terms and expressions—can be fixed firmly in mind by reflecting on Pascal's Wager.[2] In presenting that argument Pascal begins by assuming that we have no sufficient evidencing reasons for holding that the propositions of the Roman Catholic religion are true. He then offers motivating reasons why we should nevertheless labor to become persuaded of their truth. Once the key distinction has been mastered we are well on the way to losing all temptation to assume that evidencing reasons exclude motivating ones, or the other way about. It becomes easy to recognize that one and the same person can at one and the same time have both the strongest of motivating reasons for wanting to believe that *p*, and completely sufficient evidencing reasons to justify their in fact holding that boring old belief in that *p*.

A further source of temptation lies in the fact that most people make inquiries or press charges about possible motivating reasons for believing or not believing only when they feel entitled to assume that the available evidencing reasons provide insufficient warrant. They are thus inclined to construe all suggested motivating reasons as shoddy and shiftless substitutes for what is assumed to be lacking, what may even have been shown to be lacking, namely, adequate evidencing reasons. They and others then proceed to mistake it to be, in order to discredit any disfavored belief, both necessary and sufficient simply to provide motivating reasons why their opponents might want to harbor and express that belief. (By preference, of course, these suggested motivating reasons will be thoroughly sordid and self-interested.)

The psychologizing and sociologizing of believers thus replaces the rational examination of beliefs. It is a development that cannot but be attractive to those who have contrived, notwithstanding their own inadequacies, to grasp the critical initiative. It is the more attractive when these people are both aware of and even embarrassed by their manifest inability to meet their opponents in fair and open intellectual combat, and in such combat straightforwardly to refute what the more formidable of those opponents do actually maintain.

2. "There is no such thing as knowledge: we know."

The first point made to elucidate and to defend the motto from Geach was that every explanation is an answer to a question, and hence that, wherever more than one question can be asked, there must be room for more than one answering explanation. In section 1 the concentration was upon cases in which on a particular occasion explanation in terms of motivating reasons is mistaken either to preclude or to be an adequate substitute for an explanation or justification in terms of evidencing reasons. Consider now the far more devastating cases in which it is either asserted or assumed that the same holds absolutely and in general.

(i) Take, as a terse and suitably textbook example, the reckless claim made by Dr. Charles Berg, who was in his day the leading British Freudian psychoanalyst:

> The analyst must above all be an analyst. That is to say he must know positively that all human emotional reactions, all human judgements, and even reason itself, are but the tools of the unconscious; and that such seemingly acute convictions which an intelligent person like this possesses are but the inevitable effect of causes which lie buried in the unconscious levels of his psyche.[3]

If this is truly knowledge, then what is here said to be known must be—for a start—true. Yet, if every time anyone asserts anything their speech acts are nothing but "the inevitable effect of causes which lie buried in the unconscious," then, surely, the implication is that there cannot be—or at any rate that we cannot have and realize that we do have—good evidencing reasons for believing any of these assertions. But, if this goes for everyone, then it must have gone for the whole Fellowship of the Ring,[4] not excluding even Dr. Freud himself.

In that case no one at all—not even the Founding Father—has ever known what we have just now been assured that at least every single working analyst must "know positively." The immediate consequence of Berg's Bombshell is thus simply that no one at all knows either that or indeed anything else whatever.

The psychoanalysts have got themselves into this preposterous predicament by the deft execution of a familiar yet misguided maneuver. It is a maneuver that has in the past been executed, and will in the future be executed again, both by recognized internal leaders of, and by self-appointed ideological commissars for, many other disciplines. Its nerve consists in turning a modest confession of professional limitation into a piece of aggressively deflationary metaphysics. What the spokesperson for psychoanalysis is perhaps both entitled and required to say, is that analysts must, *in their analytic hours,* limit their inquiries to the conscious and especially to the unconscious motives, purposes, intentions, and so forth of all the speech acts and other, as the behaviorists would say, behaviors of their patients. What such spokespersons are so often and so strongly tempted to do is to insist that their own professional kind of questions is the only kind which can ever legitimately be asked and answered by anyone. The claim then is that their own prized and precious discipline has discovered that reality has, and can have, no aspects other than those with which that discipline itself is exclusively concerned.

Other more or less significant tokens of the same type of maneuver are the claims, more or less seriously made, that (1) nutritional studies have shown that foods consist in nothing else but so much protein, so much carbohydrate, and so much what have you, and that any gustatory characteristics which we might uninstructedly attribute are only "in the mind"; (2) that an Aldiss Lamp being intelligently and competently employed in signalling can be fully described and fully understood without reference to the semantics of that signalling use; and (3) that physics has revealed that things and happenings in the universe around us possess in reality only those primary qualities that physicists have found it possible to measure and profitable to incorporate into their most fundamental theories.

(ii) Turning next to what is still stubbornly miscalled the sociology of knowledge, we find similarly rash and intellectually suicidal claims being made, with perhaps even less awareness of the dangers of turning confessions of professional limitation into aggressively deflationary metaphysics.

When he published *Scientific Knowledge and Sociological Theory* (London: Routledge and Kegan Paul, 1974) Barry Barnes was a member of the Science Studies Unit of the University of Edinburgh. So we might have hoped for better things. And at first that hope is not disappointed. For Barnes is prepared to assert outright the existence of a real, mind-independent, material world, a world that is not any sort of ideal social construction. He also recognizes that the subject matter of some beliefs does exercise some constraint upon what is in fact believed. Thus his preface notices that the available literature "does, however, tend to skirt around the question of what the world has to do with what is believed" (p. vii). Later (p. 19) he says:

> Perhaps it should be explicitly emphasized that nothing here argued suggests that the individual may choose what he sees or experiences in a given situation, or that reality does not constrain the possibilities of human thought or belief. However, it will be valuable to reveal the social element in the definition of what are accepted facts.

Later still Barnes explicitly rejects idealism, although it is, surely, significant that he rejects it on grounds other than that it denies the existence of a mind-independent material world. "Idealism," Barnes maintains, "is to be rejected because of its hostility to causality and determinism. The opposition . . . between causes and reasons as explanations of actions, is of central importance in idealist thought" (p. 70).

When, however, we come to the first words of a chapter on "The Sociologist and the Concept of Rationality" we find that none of this prevents Barnes from writing:

> If due weight is given to the preceding arguments, no particular set of natural beliefs can be identified as reasonable, or as uniquely "the truth" . . . What is implied is . . . that the sociologist cannot single out beliefs for special consideration because they are *the* truth. (p. 22, italics original)

Had this passage stood alone it should perhaps have been construed in some alternative, more charitable way. But before the chapter ends Barnes goes on to make both himself and his aspiring discipline ridiculous by repudiating a rival sociologist's claim to know even what in my boyhood our elders used to pick out as "the facts of life." Poor Steven Lukes, who might as a radical activist have hoped for rather more sympathetic treatment, is put down first for his "rampant inductivism." Worse still: "Lukes refers to the ignorance of physiological paternity among some people and their 'magical' notions of conception; he regards these notions as in violation of objective rationality criteria without making any attempt to show why" (p. 36). May we for our part not make so bold as to conjecture that Lukes, like most if not quite all contemporary adults, knows—repeat, *knows*—that those ignorant or magical beliefs are not merely thought to be, but nothing more nor less than are, false? For Lukes himself does not appear to be inhibited by any philosophical muddles or misconceptions requiring him to pretend to a heroically total nescience.

Of course Barnes himself cannot with complete consistency sustain this level of pretended nescience; he refers, for instance, to Kuhn's "observation that paradigms necessarily include concrete achievements." But then he goes on to warn readers that these cannot be allowed to comprise discoveries of anything that is in fact the case, or to permit any claims to know rather than to "know" that some statement is— spare the mark—not "true" but true. Then again, at the beginning of the following chapter 4, he tells us that we have just been shown "how

the culture of natural science may be made intelligible without recourse
to externally based, 'objective' assessments of the 'truth' of its beliefs
or the rationality of its activities" (p. 69).[5]

With Barnes as with Berg we must not in the end refrain from
pressing the sixty-four-thousand-dollar question: "What status do you
claim for your own work?" If, as Barnes says, "The sociologist cannot
single out beliefs for special consideration because they are the truth,"
then what does Barnes think he is doing in thus presenting to a wider
public his particular collection concerning *Scientific Knowledge and
Sociological Theory*? Are these thus recommended beliefs, too, no more
than "the informal understandings negotiated among members of an
organized intellectual community"[6]—one particular Edinburgh sept of
the sociological clan?

(iii) A second sociological example is provided by a formidably influential
Open University set-book, *Knowledge and Control*.[7] For twenty or more
years its profoundly obscurantist and educationally subversive doctrines[8]
have been preached to a large proportion of Britain's intending or actual
schoolteachers, preached as revealed truth, it would seem, both from
the electronic pulpits of the Open University and in the more conventional
lecture halls of the University of London Institute of Education.

The key contention, the misguiding thread, is never formulated in
a properly terse, explicit, or completely categorical form. It is, nevertheless,
perfectly clear what it is. It is that the mere possibility of developing
some sociological account of the desires and interests supporting the
making of some kind of discrimination constitutes a sufficient demonstration that there is no objective basis for anything of the sort, that
there are, that is to say, no corresponding differences "without the mind."
The reason for describing this doctrine as educationally subversive is,
therefore, quite simply, that it is. It forecloses on the possibility that
any distinctions made by examiners may correspond to actual differences
in the quality of the work and of the candidates examined. So what,
please, are teachers supposed to be doing if it is not helping to bring
about real improvements in the capacities and performances of their
pupils?

The editor of this dreadful book, in a note to his own contribution, faults the authors of "an otherwise excellent paper" for "drawing a *metaphysical* 'out there' in terms of which they claim, we must check our theories." (p. 43n, italics original). Again, Nell Keddie, one of his favorite contributors, after noting that "teachers differentiate . . . between pupils perceived as of high and low ability," forthwith dismisses the very idea that such perceived differences might actually subsist between those teachers' pupils: "The origins of these categories are likely to lie outside the school and within the structure of the society itself in its wider distribution of power" (p. 156).[9]

You may think this bad enough. Nevertheless, compared with her fellow contributor Alan Blum, Nell Keddie could almost pass as an unprejudiced research worker. Blum's bizarre essay is written from New York University. I will not resist quoting its climactic claim to a collective divinity of sociologists: "It is not," he says, "an objectively discernible, purely existing external world which accounts for sociology, it is the methods and procedures of sociology which create and sustain that world. . . . Sociologists have managed to negotiate a set of practices for creating and acting upon external worlds" (p. 131).

The Blessed and Undivided Trinity, therefore, has now to yield place to the American Sociological Association! Our immediate concern here, however, is with Blum's less megalomaniac yet equally wrongheaded denial of any genuine knowledge:

> Scholars who have traditionally sought to discover "objective" knowledge have had to contend with the fact that the search for and discovery of such knowledge is socially organized. . . . The implication is this: if objective knowledge is taken to mean knowledge of a reality independent of language, or presuppositionless knowledge, or knowledge of the world which is independent of the observer's procedures for finding and producing the knowledge, then there is no such thing as objective knowledge (p. 128).

It is thus clear that Blum too believes that the sociology of belief reveals the impossibility of knowledge. Indeed one of the two sentences omitted from the passage quoted indicates that he has in his own fashion recognized this as a slightly awkward consequence of his position, although not one for him to worry about: "Philosophically, this has often constituted a dilemma."

About Blum's too modestly minimized "dilemma" there is nothing more for us to say now. But even at this stage it is worth insisting that if Blum is not being merely slovenly in his word ordering, and if he does really mean to deny "knowledge of a reality independent of language," then his denial is grotesque. For it is indeed just plumb grotesque to maintain that—say—the stars in their courses are in any way dependent on what we say or do not say; and it is not for any sociologist to deny the claims of the natural scientists to know that this earth existed long before it bore any language-using creatures. If, on the other hand, Blum really intends to deny only propositional knowledge independent of language, then this is unexceptionable; or, rather, it is unexceptionable so long as it is not mistaken to imply that the truths we have to express in a particular form of words would not be true at all until and unless someone had formulated those truths in these or equivalent words. The crucial distinctions are: first, between knowing and the truths that are known, and, second, between knowledge of a reality that is independent of language and knowledge that is itself independent of language.

It is one thing, and scarcely disputatious or exciting, to say that the extent of our knowledge must be limited by, among other things, the quality and the quantity of the conceptual equipment that happens to be available to us. It is quite another, and as we have been reminding ourselves, utterly paradoxical and preposterous, to hold that every reality of which we can have knowledge must be dependent upon our presence, our activities, our "observer's procedures," and on our having the concepts required to possess and to express that knowledge. Embarrassing though the observation is, it does appear to be true that the shamefully simple confusions removed in this and the previous paragraph have been and remain perennial chief sources of the demoralizing dogma that any knowledge that we do possess must be, in some depreciatory and emasculating sense, essentially and only relative and subjective, the dogma— to put it in a brief, brutal and straightforward way—that there really neither is nor can be any such thing as, without prefix or suffix, knowledge.

3. Knowing presupposes choosing.

Geach warned against all attempts to explain reasoning or language or choice naturalistically. So far this chapter has concentrated its fire upon the assumption that, if it is possible to supply any kind of naturalistic causal or motivational explanation of people believing p, then there can remain no room for the believers to have, and to know that they have, sufficient evidencing reasons to justify their claims to know p. It is time now to move on. It is time to contend that, if there is no possibility of erroneously believing not-p, then there cannot be knowledge of that p. If that is so, then indeed there can be no question of discovering inexorably necessitating sufficient causes for all the speech acts and other ongoings which are in fact involved when people are truly said to have come to recognize the excellent evidencing reasons they have for believing p—and hence, on occasion, for nothing more no less than actually knowing that p.

(i) Consider now one throwaway statement from a generally excellent book described by *Fortune* magazine as "a powerful indictment of the American criminal justice system":

> Stated another way, if causal theories explain why a criminal acts
> as he does, they also explain why he *must* act as he does and therefore
> they make any reliance on deterrence seem futile or irrelevant. (italics
> original)[10]

This, in what is here the appropriate sense of "cause," is false. It is as essential as it is uncommon to distinguish two fundamentally different senses of the word "cause." In one of these—the sense in which we speak both of the causes of astronomical phenomena and of ourselves as agents causing movements of inanimate objects—causes truly do, pace Hume and the whole Humean tradition, necessitate (not compel) their effects.[11] Given the total cause, then nothing except a miraculous exercise of supernatural power can prevent the occurrence of whatever is in fact the due effect. In this first, physical, or necessitating interpretation, complete causal theories do indeed explain why what does happen *must* happen.

Yet it is only in a second, quite different, personal or inclining sense that we can talk of the causes of human action, whether criminal or otherwise. If I give you good cause to celebrate—perhaps by sympathetically informing you of some massive misfortune afflicting your most detested enemy—then I provide you with a possible motivating reason for celebration. But I do not thereby necessitate the occurrence of appropriate celebrations. You yourself remain not merely an agent but, as far as this goes, an altogether free agent.

Hume made this fundamental distinction. But he had to make it in a somewhat less direct way: "By *moral* causes, I mean all circumstances, which are fitted to work on the mind as motives or reasons. . . . By *physical* causes I mean those qualities of the air and climate, which are supposed to work insensibly on the temper, by altering the tone and habit of the body."[12]

Certain criminologists, seeking the supposed concealed causes of crime, once asked a convicted multiple bankrobber: "Why did you rob banks?" He replied, with the shattering directness of an Andy Capp: "Because that was where the money was." Not yet corrupted by any supposedly rehabilitatory Open University courses in sociology, he did not pretend that his criminal actions had been anything but actions. As an agent he was not, and could not have been, inexorably necessitated. This has to be true since, from the mere fact that someone was in some respect an agent, it follows necessarily that they were in that respect able to do other than they did.

Once this basic distinction between the two causes is mastered it becomes obvious that we need a parallel distinction between two determinisms. Certainly, to say that some outcome is fully determined by physical causes does carry rigorous necessitarian implications. But, equally certainly, to say that someone's actions are completely determined by causes of the other sort—earlier called motivating reasons—is, if anything, to presuppose the contrary. The "psychic determinism" to which Freud appealed in the psychological area is thus not the local application of a universal determinism of the first, necessitating sort. Instead the two appear to be flatly incompatible.[13] It is, therefore, diametrically wrong to try to conscript what historians and other social scientists offer as explanations of human actions *qua* actions to serve as support for a necessitarian determinism.

(ii) The conclusions of the previous subsection provoke both a question and an objection. The question asks after the nature of the alleged link between choice and rationality. The objection is that, if agent choice implies that agents are not necessitatingly determined to act as they do act, but could have done other than they do, then there neither is nor could be any such thing.

A suggestion in answer to the former comes from the second volume of the *Postscript* to Sir Karl Popper's *The Logic of Scientific Discovery*, the volume entitled *The Open Universe*. But in order to overcome the latter it will be necessary, in section 5, to defy his warnings against plunging "into the morass of language philosophy."[14] Popper begins his treatment of the subject of the question by quoting an argument deployed by J. B. S. Haldane in *The Inequality of Man:*

> I am not myself a materialist because if materialism is true, it seems to me that we cannot know that it is true. If my opinions are the result of the chemical processes going on in my brain, they are determined by the laws of chemistry, not those of logic.[15]

As it stands this argument is vitiated by a false antithesis. Suppose we elaborate and refine upon the illustration offered and the distinctions made in section 1, above. Then we can now distinguish a third kind of question to be raised about all the ongoings involved in what would normally be described as the speech act of asserting the proposition *p*. This third kind of question asks about the physical necessitating causes of some or all these events. If we discount for the moment the necessitarian implications of such physical causation, then there would seem to be no inconsistency in asking at one and the same time both for the evidencing reasons the person had for believing *p*, and for the causes of all the various events that occurred in the course of that person's expressing the belief that *p*. On that first, temporary, discounting assumption no incompatibility subsists between—as Haldane at that stage put it—determination by the laws of chemistry and determination by the laws of logic.

But, after noticing that Haldane himself later repudiated both this argument and the conclusion that it was offered to support, Popper nevertheless urges that what Haldane really meant was something else:

> This is precisely Haldane's point. It is the assertion that, if "scientific" determinism is true, we cannot, in a rational manner, know that it is true; we believe it, or disbelieve it, but not because we freely judge the *arguments or reasons* in its favour to be sound, but because we happen to be so determined (so brainwashed) as to believe it, or even to believe that we judge it, and accept it rationally.[16]

Now the heart of the matter becomes not whether our beliefs were caused by evidencing reasons, rather than by chemical processes in our brains, but whether we could by any means have believed other than we did. Unless we could we cannot take credit for having, as rational beings, judged that these beliefs are true. Popper proceeds to add an important, correct comment:

> This somewhat strange argument does not, of course, refute the doctrine of "scientific" determinism. Even if it is accepted as valid, the world may still be as described by "scientific" determinism. But by pointing out that, if "scientific" determinism is true, we cannot know it or rationally discuss it, Haldane has given a refutation of the idea from which "scientific" determinism springs.

This seminal idea is, we must assume, part of what Geach would call naturalism; and naturalism is in this way refuted in as much as such a naturalist can be taken, as surely he must be, to be claiming nothing more nor less than to know that his scientifically grounded naturalism is nothing more nor less than true. If, however, this argument is to go through, it has to be allowed that no computer or other device, the ongoings in which are completely determined by necessitating causes, can correctly be said to know that any of its operations are valid or that any of its output is true. I myself gladly accept and affirm this essential limitation upon the potentialities of all such artifacts. Yet to

Popper that affirmation might seem uncomfortably like a worthwhile finding dredged up from "the morass of language philosophy."

4. Sincerity, rationality, and monitoring

Before taking a plunge in section 5 into that forbidden territory we must, in the present section 4, first notice that much if not all belief is in fact immediately necessitated. We can then go on to draw out important corollaries of the conclusion established in section 3. That at least some fundamental beliefs are immediately inescapable is best appreciated by recalling Hume's doctrine of what Kemp Smith christened "natural beliefs"—the belief, for instance, that in perception we are directly aware of some mind-independent reality.[17] The congenial corollary is that, the more beliefs we find that are in certain circumstances immediately inescapable, the more vital it becomes to try to withdraw from such possibly deceiving situations, and, in a cool hour and a quiet place, to expose ourselves and both these and other beliefs to the full force of all rational and truth-directed objections—that is, to criticism.

(i) Such openminded willingness to expose both our theoretical ideas and our practical policies to serious and honest criticism certainly is always, if not always quite immediately, within our power. It also provides both the criterion of the sincerity of our personal commitment to the search for theoretical truth and the touchstone of the genuineness of our professed dedication to the stated objectives of whatever practical policies we may choose to favor. In this understanding openmindedness is a matter both of rationality and of good faith.

Suppose, for instance, that someone is so old fashioned as to proclaim a quest for the Holy Grail. And suppose then that, almost before the fanfares have died, that person settles for the first antique-seeming mug offered by the first fluent rogue in the local bazaar. We surely have to say that this neglect of any systematic inquiry, this total lack of interest in either the true history of the purchase put in the place of honor on the mantelpiece or the evidence that perhaps the real thing does survive somewhere, all conspire together to show that, whatever else they may have been after, it certainly was not to unearth and acquire the vessel actually employed in the original Last Supper, if such there was. Sincerity absolutely presupposes a strong concern to know whether the purpose professedly entertained has been or is actually being achieved.

Again, since many find it hard to accept that a point so down to earth can be enforced by an illustration so farfetched, consider two more pedestrian alternatives. Suppose someone professes to be in business in order, no doubt among other things, to turn a profit; or suppose that the captain of a cricket team says that he is playing, no doubt again among other things, in order to win. Then what credence could we give to these professions if there is no care to keep, in the one case, accounts and, in the other, the score? Descartes used to say that he preferred to judge what people sincerely believe by what they do rather than by what they say. The same shrewd principle applies equally well to the determination of true intentions and present purposes.

That there is this universal and necessary connection between sincerity of purpose and the monitoring of progress is, once it has been pointed out, too obvious a logical truth to require illustration or proof.[18] Yet it is one of those obvious logical truths from which, as we shall be seeing, it is possible to derive exciting and therefore contested conclusions.

(ii) The next step is to relate these logically necessary connections to Popperian methodology.[19] They refer to both theoretical science and practical policy. In each case the methodological recommendations can be seen as the direct and necessary outcomes of the appropriate purposes. It is the more worthwhile to represent these recommendations in this way in as much as Popper seems never to have done so himself. His apparent reluctance, and the consequent failure to deploy what are perhaps the most powerful supporting arguments, are probably to be explained by reference to a generous yet unrealistic unwillingness to recognize discreditable distractions or even sheer bad faith in any opponents.

The aim of all theoretical science is truth. If that is what we are sincerely seeking, then we have to adopt what Popper calls the critical approach. For people who truly want to discover the truth, like knights who with pure hearts and single minds seek the Holy Grail, cannot and will not embrace unexamined candidates. They must and will be ever ready to test, and test, and test again. And in the present context criticism is just this sort of testing.

It is testing by raising and pressing relevant questions. Are there, for a start, any inconsistencies within or between the propositions propounded? And are these propositions all compatible with whatever else we know or believe that we know? It is of course precisely in as much as critics are sincerely seeking the truth that they refuse to tolerate contradictions. For though two contradictory propositions may both be false they cannot, being mutually contradictory, both be true. So the sincere truth-seeker urgently requires to discover which, if either, actually is true.[20]

Suppose now that the claims made are both internally consistent and consistent with everything that is already known. Then we have to ask: "What else follows from the theory or hypothesis proposed, and how are we to set about discovering whether these further consequences do in fact obtain?" Paradoxically Popper maintains that, having started by making bold conjectures—conjectures apparently fitting all available facts while also carrying extensive implications of what else must be the case if these bold conjectures are correct—scientists should then seek strenuously to falsify those conjectures, that is, to show that they are, after all, false. In consequence the proper method of science, whether natural or social, becomes that of *Conjectures and Refutations* (London: Routledge and Kegan Paul, 1963).

Honest inquirers, therefore, though they will naturally want their own theories and their own hypotheses to turn out to have been correct, must to the extent that they are indeed sincere truth-seekers necessarily labor to show that all theories and hypotheses proposed—most especially their own—are after all false. Suppose that one nevertheless survives the most rigorous and comprehensive criticism. Then, however temporarily, the hopes of its sponsors are fulfilled. On the other hand, when a promising theory or hypothesis is falsified, its sponsors can console themselves with the thought that the strenuous testing culminating in this conclusion must surely have advanced research. So the successor theory or hypothesis should be, if not the final truth, at least significantly nearer to it.

The reason for seeking not confirming instances but falsifications is, in the oft-quoted words of Francis Bacon,[21] that "the force of the negative instance is greater." For conclusively to falsify any unrestricted universal generalization—any proposition, that is, of the form "All so-and-sos, without restriction of time or place, are such-and-such"—it is sufficient to produce a single counter-example, a single case, that is, of a so-and-so that is not a such-and-such. It is, however, impossible equally conclusively to verify a proposition of this form. For, provided that these "All so-and-sos" are not restricted to only "All so-and-sos in such-and such a place or during such-and-such a period," there remains always, no matter how many so-and-sos are found to be such and such, at least the theoretical if not the live practical possibility of eventually discovering a counter-example.[22]

(iii) Whereas the single aim of theoretical science is truth, the purposes of practical policies, and of the institutions established for the implementation of those policies, and the fulfillment of those purposes, are as multifarious as human desires. Yet parallel considerations apply here too. If, therefore, you want to claim that it was in order to secure some particular goods that a policy was originally introduced, and/or that those are still the objectives for which it continues to be sustained, then you have to show that both the people who first introduced the policy, and the people who now support and sustain that policy and its related institutions, were, and are, keen to monitor success or failure by that same stated standard. How, for instance, can anyone in good faith and with any pretensions to rationality pretend that it is with the aim of raising levels of learning achievement that they are restructuring a public school system when they are at the same time by every means available discouraging the discovery, and still more the publication, of all relevant performance data?[23]

These insights can help us to appreciate Popper's advocacy of what he distinguishes as piecemeal, reformist, social engineering, as opposed to the wholesale, Utopian, revolutionary alternative. That advocacy here is consequence and expression of his sincere and rational concern for the welfare of the subjects of such social engineering, the, so to speak, socially engineered. For Popper's crucial objection to the wholesale Utopian variety precisely is that this must make impossible the effective monitoring of success or failure in achieving the goods supposedly intended by the social engineers. It therefore makes it equally impossible for them to recognize and to learn from their mistakes, and then to apply the lessons learnt to the amendment of their policies. So there is an obvious Popperian answer to a frequently pressed question: "Just how wide-ranging and upsetting does a program have to be before its implementation ceases to count as piecemeal, and begins to rate as wholesale social engineering?"

The answer is: "Just so soon as it becomes impossible effectively to monitor success or failure, and to make cybernetic corrections of perceived mistakes." Popper himself says, "The reconstruction of society is a big undertaking which must cause considerable inconvenience to many and for a considerable span of time. Accordingly, the Utopian engineer will have to be deaf to many complaints: in fact it will be part of his business to suppress unreasonable objections. He will say, like Lenin, 'You can't make an omelette without breaking eggs.' But with it, he must invariably suppress reasonable criticism also."[24]

In this perspective it is easy to see how inept it was to describe the enormous exercises of social engineering made possible by the Bolshevik October coup as features of "that great social experiment in Russia"—notwithstanding that these were in the twenties and the thirties frequently so described. With reference to the compulsory and almost unbelievably mass-murderous collectivization of agriculture, for instance,[25] there was absolutely no willingness to change course when and as it became clear that, whatever its other attractions to the ruling class and party, collectivization had been and remained an economic disaster.

Since, both in the USSR and in numerous other countries subjected to similar regimes, such exercises have been executed in the name of what calls itself Scientific Socialism, it becomes very much to the point to quote Popper's counter-claim—that the critical approach would "lead to the happy situation where politicians begin to look out for their own mistakes instead of trying . . . to prove that they have always been right. This—and not Utopian planning or historical prophecy—would mean the introduction of scientific method into politics, *since the whole secret of scientific method is a readiness to learn from mistakes.*"[26]

5. Only choosers know either choice or necessity.

At the beginning of *The Open Universe* Popper announces his intention to present "my reasons for being an indeterminist." At once he adds: "I shall not include among these reasons the intuitive idea of free will: as a rational argument in favour of indeterminism it is useless" (p. 1). His warrant for saying that any such direct appeal to experience is useless, a reason he formulates in a fashion too misleading to quote here, is that he may be mistaken even about the nature of what the behaviorist would call one of his own behaviors. In so far as this is a token of an argument of a Cartesian type—one contending that, in any area where we may conceivably be mistaken, we can never truly know—its validity, if it were valid, would have to be recognized as putting an insuperable obstacle in the way of the achieving by any fallible being of any knowledge whatsoever.[27] Happily the truth is that to know it is sufficient to believe what is in fact true, and to be rationally justified in that belief.

Even Popper's original disclaimer, referring as it does to "the intuitive idea of free will," is importantly misleading. For, as was argued in section 6 of chapter 2, the crucial question is not whether we ever act of our own free will, but whether we ever act at all. When we say of someone that they acted not of their own free will but under compulsion, still they did act. The case of the businessman, who received from the Godfather an offer he could not refuse, is thus vitally different from that of the errant mafioso, who was without warning gunned down from behind.

We may both truly and colloquially say of the former, offered the urgent choice of having either his signature or his brains on a document within thirty seconds, that he had no choice, and hence that he could not have done other than he did. (He signed away the whole family business to—if that is the correct expression—the Organization.) But of course these everyday idioms must not be misconstrued, as so often they are, at the foot of the letter. For in more fundamental senses the businessman who acted under compulsion did have a choice, and could have acted other than he did, however understandably intolerable the only alternative remaining open to him. In these same more fundamental senses, to have a choice, to be able to do otherwise, is essential to what it is to be an agent. In these same more fundamental senses, again, the errant mafioso actually did have no choice; and, because he did not do anything, he could not have done otherwise. For, in that moment of unexpected and sudden death, he ceased both to do and to be.

In the brief treatment of this topic in subsection 6(iii) of chapter 2, the prime concern was simply to show that the "Free will Defense" is impotent to spare the Mosaic God ultimate and total responsibility for all the sins for which—as a manifestation, look you, of transcendent Justice—that God threatens to punish with extremes of torment creatures originated and eternally maintained for that purpose. The aim now in a more extensive treatment is to reveal where, absent any such Creator, responsibility must rest.

(i) As was suggested earlier the best place from which to start is the chapter "Of Power" in Locke's *Essay concerning Human Understanding.* It is as certain as this sort of thing can be, without direct testimonial evidence, that Hume had this chapter most in mind, perhaps even open before him, when in both the *Treatise* and the first *Enquiry* he composed his enormously yet not always happily influential sections "Of the Idea of Necessary Connexion" and "Of Liberty and Necessity." Yet Hume, "one of the very greatest philosophers of all time,"[28] missed its message. He missed it, as did Kant later, because he could not entertain any idea of necessity other than the logical, and because he had above all to defend his insight that causal propositions cannot even if true be necessarily true.

In this chapter Locke was concerned with power in the sense in which power can be predicated only of people, or of such other putative quasipersonal beings as the theist's God, the Olympian gods, angels, devils, and assorted originally bodiless or disembodied spirits. Let us, therefore, attach to this prime kind of power the label "power (personal)." In another sense, which is the only sense in which the word can be applied to inanimate objects and to most of animate nature, a power simply is a disposition to behave in such and such a way, given that such and such preconditions are satisfied. Thus we might say that the "nuclear device" dropped at Nagasaki possessed an explosive power equivalent to that of so many tons of TNT, or that full-weight nylon climbing rope has a breaking strain of (a power to hold up to) 4,500 pounds. Let us label this secondary sort of power "power (physical)."

What a study of this chapter can bring out is that we all have the most direct and the most inexpugnably certain experience: not only of both physical (as opposed to logical) necessity and physical (as opposed to logical) impossibility, but also of both being able—possessing the power (personal)—to do other than we do do and of being unable—lacking the power (personal)—to behave in any other way than that in which we are behaving. Once seized of these truths we should be ready to recognize that there is no way in which creatures neither enjoying nor suffering experiences of both these two contrasting kinds could either acquire for themselves, or explicate to others, any of the corresponding notions. Locke starts with a statement of what he proposes to prove:

> Every one, I think, finds in himself a Power to begin or forbear, continue or put an end to several Actions in himself. From the considerations of the extent of this power of the mind over the actions of the Man, which everyone finds in himself, arise the *Ideas* of *Liberty* and *Necessity*.[29]

Locke's technique for enforcing this point about our familiarity with our agent powers—our experience of them—is to contrast what we do know or may know about what we can do with what we do know or may know about what we cannot do. Unfortunately, Locke, like Popper, wrongly assumes that the sixty-four-thousand-dollar question is not whether we are, and can know that we are, agents choosing this alternative when we could have chosen that, but whether we are, and can know that we are, free agents choosing between alternatives at least one of which we find passing tolerable. This fault we have simply to discount, making the necessary mental transposition as we go along:

We have instances enough, and often more than enough in our own bodies. A Man's Heart beats, and the Blood circulates, which 'tis not in his Power . . . to stop; and therefore in respect of these Motions, where rest depends not on his choice . . . he is not a *free agent.* Convulsive Motions agitate his legs, so that though he wills it never so much, he cannot . . . stop their motion (as in that odd disease called *Chorea Sancti Viti*), but he is perpetually dancing: He is . . . under as much Necessity of moving, as a Stone that falls or a Tennis-ball struck with a Racket. On the other side, a palsy or the stocks hinder his legs from obeying the determination of his mind, if it would thereby transfer his body to another place. In all these there is a want of freedom.[30]

What truly there is want of, we must repeat, is not *freedom* but *agency,* not the lack of any tolerable and uncoerced alternatives, but the lack of any alternatives at all. Against this straightforward appeal to experience Popper would argue that it is always conceivable that we are mistaken about what is or is not in fact subject to our wills: that some of us in the past have been afflicted by sudden paralyses, or that we any of us may now have suddenly acquired powers of psychokinesis. Certainly this is conceivable: we are none of us either infallible or all-knowing. But here the fundamental and characteristically Cartesian mistake is to assume that knowledge presupposes infallibility, and that, where we may conceivably be mistaken, there we can never really know.

Locke goes on to suggest, albeit in a less satisfactory terminology, that where action is not, there necessity reigns, that the human behaviors that are not actions must be necessary. Thus he writes, "Wherever Thought is wholly wanting, or the power to act or forbear according to the direction of Thought, there *Necessity* takes place."[31] And, a page or two earlier, we read:

A Tennis-ball, whether in motion by a stroke of a Racket, or lying still at rest, is not by anyone taken to be a *free Agent* . . . because we conceive not a Tennis-ball to think, and consequently not to have any Volition, or preference of Motion to rest, or *vice versa;* and therefore . . . is not a free Agent; but all its both Motion and Rest come under our idea of necessary, and are so call'd. . . . So a Man striking himself, or his Friend, by a Convulsive motion of his Arm, which is not in his Power . . . to stop, or forbear; . . . every one pities him as acting by Necessity and Constraint.[32]

Once again, of course, the reason we should pity such persons is not that they would be acting under constraint, but that their behaviors would be completely necessitated, and therefore not actions at all. Especially to those familiar with Hume's criticisms of this chapter what is most curious is Locke's actual failure to go on to emphasize that, notwithstanding that those behaviors that are actions cannot have been necessitated, since the agents must as such have been able to do other than they did, still the behaviors aforesaid may themselves necessitate. For actions may bring about effects, making one alternative physically (as opposed to logically) necessary and another physically (as opposed to logically) impossible.[33]

(ii) It is from experience of the kinds indicated by Locke, experience of making things happen and of trying but failing to make things happen, that we can and must derive the fundamental concepts of agency and necessity, as well as such other necessarily connected concepts as those of power (personal), of being able to do other than we do do, and hence of being able to choose and having to choose between alternative possible courses of action. Since all these indispensable concepts are and can only be derived from, and ostensively defined by reference to, universal human experience, it is utterly out of the question to maintain that they have and can have no correct application in this universe, that it is and must be a presupposition of any science of human psychology that, really, no one could do other than they do do.[34]

It can be instructive here to seek the sources of Hume's failure to find the "impression" (experience) from which the "idea" (concept) of physical necessity and physical impossibility might be derived. Hume, like so many successors of Descartes, was handicapped by the conviction that all philosophical investigations had to start from the position reached in the second paragraph of part IV of the *Discourse on the Method*.[35]

When he was, so to speak, on his philosophical best behavior, Hume thus had to think of himself as an incorporeal pure observer rather than as the flesh and blood observer-cum-agent that he actually was, and as all of us are.[36] This incorporeal pure observer was committed to a narrow, exclusively private, Cartesian conception of experience. Berkeley had opened *The Principles of Human Knowledge* by claiming that the objects of such knowledge are always and only ideas "in the mind" of the knower. This unbelievably pessimistic assertion is in substance repeated in the first sentence of *A Treatise of Human Nature,* albeit with the addition of a new distinction of Berkeley's ideas into two kinds: "All the perceptions of the human mind resolve themselves into two kinds, which I shall call *impressions* and *ideas.*"

We have here to remind ourselves that, whereas the plain person confines his talk of perceptions to cases in which some creature of flesh and blood is immediately aware of a mind-independent reality, Hume's "perceptions of the mind" carry no such external implications, while their subjects are supposed to be—just as in Descartes and in Berkeley—incorporeal. His empiricism is thus one that construes experience as consisting in the passive reception of impressions—a sort of formless gawping at, and inert acceptance of, what an earlier philosophical generation used to call "the given." This is holus bolus different from the down-to-earth, active empiricism that has so strong an appeal to realistic common sense. For that everyday, out-of-the-study empiricism sensibly insists, for instance, that anyone claiming to have had experience of cows is claiming to have perceived and in one way or another manipulated a fair number of real, flesh and blood cows. Their claim is to have herded and milked, felt and smelt, Gertrude and Mary and Elsie and Jemima and a whole lot of others. There would, and rightly, be short shrift down on the farm for job applicants admitting only to their past enjoyment of cowish sense-data, while daring to deny the very possibility of actual knowledge of either real flesh and blood cows or any other three-dimensional denizens of the External World![37]

However much common sense might keep breaking through Hume remained officially committed to the contention that the philosophically initiated cannot but embrace a narrow, artificial, exotic, veil-of-appearance conception of experience. Thus in the first subsection of section 12 of *An Enquiry concerning Human Understanding* he assures us that "the slightest philosophy" dictates that "the existences which we consider, when we say *this house* or *that tree,* are nothing but perceptions in the mind." Hume thus presents "a paralytic's eye view of causation."[38]

All that such inert and passive observers could discriminate in "the given" would be the constant conjunction and regular succession of (sorts of) ideas and (sorts of) impressions. By mere observation they most certainly could never, in the everyday understanding, have experience of physical (as opposed to logical) necessity—of bringing something about by making it physically necessary to happen and physically impossible not to happen. They must therefore be disqualified from even understanding any nomological propositions, any propositions, that is, that state that given such and such conditions some kinds of happenings would be physically necessary while other kinds would be physically impossible. Because such propositions state physical necessities and physical impossibilities, they license counterfactual inferences: if such and such conditions were to obtain, which in fact they will not, then, as a matter of physical necessity this and that would happen.

Like some other things in Hume this bold attempt—made "by one of the very greatest philosophers of all time"—has its highest value as an unintended demonstration of what surely cannot be done. For however could any pure observer, the incorporeal subject of essentially private experience, acquire any of these fundamental and indispensable notions? However could they be acquired, if not as they surely are in fact acquired, in and through our everyday experience as agents, experience, that is, as corporeal things causing effects upon other corporeal things, experience too as agents who, in their understanding of the possibility of doing otherwise, grasp the crucial concept of the contrary-to-fact? If someone believes that it either is or could be done in some alternative way, then we will have to respond, with the archetypically incredulous man from Missouri: "Show me!"

6. Epilogue: A sober and compatible naturalism

The present chapter has consisted in an attempt to explain and defend the motto from which it began. It must not conclude without a reiteration that it has at best provided and accepted a refutation only of those recklessly aggressive forms of naturalism that promise to banish "reasonings or language or choice." But such claims in truth are not, though they are often believed to be, essential to naturalism. Consider, for instance, and not for the first time, the consistently Aristotelian naturalism of Strato of Lampsacus, who was next but one to The Philosopher himself as director of the Lyceum. Neither Aristotle nor his followers seem to have suggested anything of the sort. They had, poor things, never heard of the sociology of belief, nor did they feel bound to labor to explain human action in the same necessitarian terms as were found convenient in astronomy or meteorology. If we are to accept Geach's motto, then we must interpret the words "explain . . . naturalistically" as entailing discredit, denial, and explaining away. In that understanding, but in that understanding alone,

> when we hear of some new attempt to explain reasoning or language or choice naturalistically, we ought to react as if we were told someone had squared the circle or proved $\sqrt{2}$ to be rational: only the mildest curiosity is in order—how well has the fallacy been concealed?

But what, finally, is to be said about choice and about the responsibility of agents for the choices that as agents they do in fact make? Certainly human beings are organisms, creatures of flesh, blood, bones, and other sorts of stuff, and nothing else besides. So suppose that it appeared one day to be possible to explain all the movements of members of this very special kind of organism by reference to necessitating physical causes. Would that not show that, really, there is no such thing as choice, that really no one ever could have done, or could do, other than they did do, or will do, and—in terms of the distinction drawn in section 6 of chapter 2—that, really, all the movements of such organisms must have been, and be, motions rather than movings?

No, it would not. In the first place, as has been argued already at some length, explanations of the physical aspects of the behavior of these organisms in terms of physical causes are not necessarily irreconcilable rivals to explanations of other aspects of that behavior in irreducibly different terms. More immediately to the particular present point, the fact that all the crucial terms and expressions can be, and indeed have to be, defined ostensively, means that no future discoveries ever could show that those crucial terms and expressions never have had and never will have any correct application.

So is it possible to develop a new and perhaps higher form of Compatibilism? Since necessitated is conceptually opposed to chosen behavior, to agency, we cannot say that agents as such are necessitated to behave as they do, and could not have done otherwise. The most that we might perhaps have to allow is that we are somehow necessitated to be the people who, when they have to choose, choose as they actually do choose, even though, in any ordinary understanding, they could have done otherwise. Yet even this concession is, surely, excessive. For who can deny but that our present characters are, to a very large extent, products of our previous choices? And, furthermore, all such discussion ought to take note, much more often than it does, of the oddity of the position of contemporaries keen to insist that the most complicated creatures known are subject to a total necessitation, while at the same time they remain equally eager to maintain that the simplest particles discovered by microphysics are exempt from the rule of necessitating causality. Surely, if there is any indeterminism in our universe, it is more likely to be found among the most complex sort of objects rather than the least.

When Luther argued that God must be the ultimate necessitating cause of human sin, as well as of everything else, he proceeded to explain that "by 'necessarily' I do not mean 'compulsorily' . . . a man without the Spirit of God does not do evil against his will, under pressure, as though he were taken by the scruff of his neck and dragged into it, like a thief or a footpad being dragged off against his will to punishment; but he does it spontaneously and voluntarily."[39] This fact, as Luther so clearly saw, in no way diminishes God's ultimate responsibility for the sins for which sinful creatures are to be inordinately and eternally punished. But, absent any Creator, the implication is very different. It is that for each and every one of us, in the words of one of Missouri's greatest sons,[40] "The buck stops here!"

Notes

1. Peter Geach, *The Virtues* (Cambridge: Cambridge University Press, 1977), p. 52.

2. See, for instance, "Is Pascal's Wager the only Safe Bet?" in my *God, Freedom, and Immortality* (Buffalo, N.Y.: Prometheus Books, 1984), or my *An Introduction to Western Philosophy* (London: Thames and Hudson, revised edition, 1989), VI 7.

3. Charles Berg, *Deep Analysis* (London: George Allen and Unwin, 1946), p. 190.

4. Freud is said to have presented a gold ring to all the original members of his inner circle.

5. Here and elsewhere Barnes and his like lay themselves wide open to Paul Feyerabend's objection to Kuhn: "He has failed to discuss the *aim* of science." See I. Latakos and A. Musgrave, eds., *Criticism and the Growth of Knowledge* (Cambridge: Cambridge University Press, 1970), p. 201. That objection remains both fundamental and sound despite the deplored fact that its maker has long since abandoned that aim in favor of his own novel form of frivolous and irresponsible obscurantism. See his *Against Method* (London: New Left Books, 1975).

6. This sinister phrase actually comes from Alan Blum's "The Corpus of Knowledge as a Normative Order," in M. F. D. Young, ed., *Knowledge and Control* (London: Collier-Macmillan, 1971), p. 117.

7. See note 6.

8. I examined and labored to refute these doctrines in "Metaphysical Idealism and the Sociology of Knowledge," in my *Sociology, Equality and Education* (London, and New York: Macmillan, and Barnes and Noble, 1976). Later, in D. Anderson, ed., *The Pied Pipers of Education* (London: Social Affairs Unit, 1981), Graham Dawson argued for the complete excision of that part of the public education budget presently devoted to financing the initiation of intending or actual schoolteachers into any such educationally counter-productive sociology of education!

9. Keddie's contribution contains, by the way, a commendation of "countries like North Korea" (p. 40) as opposed to "capitalist societies" (p. 28). Remarkably, the former are praised for what in the latter is abused—the providing of education relevant to future employment.

10. James Q. Wilson, *Thinking about Crime* (New York: Random House, 1977), p. 58.

11. For supporting argument see, for instance, my *David Hume: Philosopher of Moral Science* (Oxford: Basil Blackwell, 1986).

12. David Hume, *Essays Moral Political and Literary,* ed. E. F. Miller (Indianapolis, Ind.: Liberty Press, 1985), p. 198.

13. See my *A Rational Animal: Philosophical Essays on the Nature of Man* (Oxford: Clarendon, 1978), chapter 8.

14. K. R. Popper, *The Open Universe: An Argument for Indeterminism* (London, and Totowa, N.J.: Hutchinson, and Rowman and Littlefield, 1982), p. xxi.

15. Ibid., p. 89.

16. Ibid., pp. 92–93, emphasis original.

17. See N. Kemp Smith, *The Philosophy of David Hume* (London: Macmillan, 1949), pp. 116ff. and passim, and note that the name phrase chosen by Kemp Smith is not one of the several employed by Hume. On belief generally see H. H. Price, *Belief* (London, and New York: Allen and Unwin, and Humanities Press, 1969).

18. This logical link is, in Humean terms, a matter of "the relations of ideas" rather than "a matter of fact and real existence."

19. K. R. Popper, *The Open Society and its Enemies,* 5th ed. (London: Routledge and Kegan Paul, 1963).

20. It was, therefore, an outrageous violation of the presuppositions of honest communication and truth-seeking inquiry when Herbert Marcuse borrowed a motto from his fellow Frankfurters, Adorno and Horkheimer— "The general concept which discursive logic has developed has its foundations in the reality of domination"—and went on to contend that we have to be emancipated, apparently willy-nilly, from the allegedly artificial and oppressive doctrine that "contradictions are a fault of incorrect thinking." No wonder that that Modern Master's sympathies were more with *Soviet Marxism* than with the "repressive tolerance" contradictorily attributed to liberal societies! See his *One Dimensional Man* (London: Routledge and Kegan Paul, 1964), chapter 5, and compare A. C. MacIntyre, *Marcuse* (London: Collins/Fontana, 1970), pp. 75–79.

21. American readers may be intrigued to learn that Bacon's fall from the most powerful office under the Crown was popularly attributed to the Affair of the Water Gate.

22. All this may seem too obvious to merit repetition. But it certainly has not been obvious to, for instance, judges and juries in recent U.S. tort trials. Compare P. W. Huber, *Galileo's Revenge: Junk Science in the Courtroom*

(New York: Basic, 1991).

23. American readers may obtain some rueful satisfaction from learning that, whereas in the United States a large proportion of high school graduates do take the independently assessed and criteria-related Scholastic Aptitude Tests, no similarly reliable tests are taken by any school leavers in the United Kingdom. By thus eschewing all valid indices of annual output, the maintained school monopoly—by any standard a major industry—effectively prevents reliable productivity calculations. *Cui bono*? See, for instance, D. G. Green, ed., *Empowering the Parents: How to Break the Schools Monopoly* (London: Institute of Economic Affairs, 1991), pp. 15–49.

24. Popper, *The Open Society,* vol 1, p. 160.

25. Compare, for instance, R. Conquest, *The Harvest of Sorrow: Soviet Collectivization and the Terror Famine* (New York, and London: Oxford University Press, 1986).

26. Popper, *The Open Society,* vol. 1, p. 163, emphasis added.

27. Contemplate the devastation wrought by firing off both skeptical barrels in the first paragraph of part IV of the *Discourse on the Method*: "On the grounds that our sense sometimes deceive us, I wanted to suppose that there was not anything corresponding to what they make us imagine. And because some men make mistakes in reasoning . . . and fall into fallacies . . . I rejected as unsound all the reasonings which I had hitherto taken for demonstrations."

28. K. R. Popper, *The Open Universe,* p. xix.

29. *An Essay Concerning Human Understanding,* ed. P. H. Nidditch (Oxford: Clarendon, 1975), 2 (21) 7, p. 237.

30. Ibid., 2 (21) 11, p. 239. The Latin translates "St. Vitus dance."

31. Ibid., 2 (21) 13, p. 240.

32. Ibid., 2 (21) 9, p. 238.

33. See Max Black, "Making Something Happen," in S. Hook, ed., *Determinism and Freedom* (New York: New York University Press, 1958); reprinted as chapter 8 of Black's *Models and Metaphors* (Ithaca, N.Y.: Cornell University Press, 1962).

34. For dicussion of B. F. Skinner's contention to this effect in his *Beyond Freedom and Dignity* (New York: Knopf, 1971) compare chapter 14 below.

35. For a development of this interpretation see my *David Hume: Philosopher of Moral Science* (Oxford: Basil Blackwell, 1986).

36. Ibid., chapter 6.

37. Today we find philosophers, especially radical philosophers, who announce the demise of empiricism without ever making the absolutely crucial

distinction developed in the text. Of course Marxist or Marxizing radicals cherish theories they must know to have been struck down by the supreme court of experience. So they may reasonably be suspected of hoping through such confusion about the extension of the word "experience" to discredit that properly decisive judgment.

38. See "Can an Effect Precede its Cause?" in *Proceedings of the Aristotelian Society,* supp., vol. 28 (1954): 49–50.

39. See the final subsection of chapter 3 above.

40. Harry S. Truman, president of the United States (1945–52).

6

Sociology of or against Knowledge?

None of us can be right against the Party. In the last instance the
Party is always right . . . One can be right only with the Party and
through the Party. . . .

Leon Trotsky[1]

We control matter because we control the mind. Reality is inside the
skull. You will learn by degrees, Winston. . . . The word you are trying
to think of is solipsism. But you are mistaken. This is not solipsism.
Collective solipsism if you like. But that is a different thing: in fact
the opposite thing.

O'Brien to Winston Smith[2]

David Bloor's *Knowledge and Social Imagery* (London: Routledge and
Kegan Paul, 1976) is an audacious, original essay in the sociology of
mathematics. It is, as Bloor himself introduces it, part of an attempt
to apply "the strong programme" of the sociology of knowledge to
mathematics and the hard sciences. There could scarcely be a better
occasion for considering the presuppositions and the implications of
exercises of this kind. The objective in this consideration is to show
that the findings of the sociology of knowledge or, more properly, belief,
do not and cannot threaten the possibility of knowing without quali-

141

fication that some arguments actually are valid and some propositions actually are true.

This "strong programme" is defined in terms of four tenets. First, it must be "causal, that is concerned with conditions which bring about belief or states of knowledge. Naturally there will be other types of causes apart from social ones." Second, it will be "impartial with respect to truth and falsity, rationality or irrationality, success or failure. Both sides of these dichotomies will require explanation." Third, it has to be "symmetrical in its style of explanation. The same types of cause would explain, say, true and false beliefs." Fourth, and finally, "In principle its patterns of explanation would have to be applicable to sociology itself" (pp. 4–5).

1. Facts as causes of beliefs about those facts themselves

There is no doubt that a lot of this is both correct and important. Certainly a sociology of "knowledge" should embrace belief of every kind—both true beliefs and false beliefs, both beliefs rationally and beliefs irrationally held, both well-evidenced and ill-evidenced beliefs, and even beliefs altogether baseless. (I shall later offer argument for insisting that to persist in calling a subject so defined the sociology of knowledge, or even of "knowledge," rather than the sociology of belief is much more and worse than to persist in a merely tiresome verbal bad habit.) Certainly too what is thus so stubbornly miscalled the sociology of knowledge must be concerned with the causes of beliefs rather than with whatever evidencing reasons there may be for harboring those beliefs. Again, and equally certainly, its explanations must be applicable to sociology itself, and applicable in such a way that their application thereto does not undermine their own cognitive status. Let us have no more self- and all-destructive accounts of how and why people as a matter of fact come to believe whatever it is they do in fact believe—accounts which by implication rule out the possibility of even those accounts themselves being known to be true.[3]

But now, the third tenet of Bloor's "strong programme" gives pause. Just how much is this saying? This discipline has to be "symmetrical in its style of explanation. The same types of cause would explain, say, true and false beliefs." Is Bloor demanding no more than that, where the layperson is content to explain well-evidenced rational beliefs by reference to that evidence, asking for the causes only of what is seen as silly or bigoted, his sociologist of knowledge must seek causes for every kind without discrimination? Then, so far, that's fine. What will not do is what, I suspect, sometimes is being covertly done: namely, to disqualify, as possible causes of the beliefs that do happen to be true, all the effects upon the believer of the facts about which he comes truly to believe, and this on the grounds that "the same types of cause" are obviously not operating, or not operating to the same effect, upon those whose beliefs in this matter happen to be largely or entirely false.

Professing sociologists of knowledge have been, and remain, apt to minimize or even to deny the importance of such effects upon belief of the facts to which those beliefs refer. For this the main, but not the only, reason is the traditional and continuing concentration of the practitioners upon just those kinds of belief that are related to the observable most indirectly and most tenuously, if indeed at all. It is significant that Bloor's own paradigm for the Humean "bold attempt" at a sociology of mathematics and the hard sciences is an investigation of what certainly he himself, and probably most of his colleagues also, would at least privately put down as superstition: "Durkheim's classic study 'The Elementary Forms of the Religious Life' shows," Bloor assures us, "how a sociologist can penetrate to the very depths of a form of *knowledge*" (p. 2, italics supplied).

Wait a moment! It is all very well to seek purely social causes for the Olympian belief system of the Greeks in the four hundreds of the pre-Christian era. After all, these gods were no more observable than any others; in some later centuries, although there had been no great change in the non-human environment, we find a very different system of religious beliefs. I will not resist the temptation to share here a true tale of my own first visit to that country. On a tourist bus between Athens and Delphi we were privileged to be served by a guide as proud and patriotic as she was charming and enthusiastic. She pointed out in turn where Phoebus Apollo had done this, where the Blessed Virgin had done that, and where the Athenian fleet had crushed the barbarians at Salamis; and every time—as that evening I was able most joyfully to report to my then supervisor Gilbert Ryle—"in exactly the same logical tone of voice."

If the "strong programme" is strong to insist only that it has to account for the harboring of all the beliefs that are in fact harboured, and not just either those presumed to be false or those known to be true, then at any rate that can safely be allowed to pass without question or protest. But if Bloor is going to insist that all beliefs are to be causally accounted for without any appeal to the facts to which those beliefs claim to refer, then at least that part of his programme must be held up as manifestly preposterous and, in its implications, catastrophically obscurantist.

Perhaps the most elegant way of justifying so vehement a dismissal is to point out that the causal efficacy of the object perceived is a logically necessary condition of the occurrence of perception. Whatever, therefore, may apply to all those other beliefs that are also items of knowledge, those perceptual beliefs that constitute perceptual knowledge cannot be causally explained without reference both to the presence and to the impact of the object actually perceived.

To bring out that the causal efficacy of the object perceived is indeed a logically necessary condition of the occurrence of perception, as opposed to mere "perception" (in disclaimer quotes), consider a case of a man with two ruined, sightless eyes. Let him be caused, by direct stimulation of the brain, to have the (private) "sensory" experience which he would have had if he had been able to see the giant panda eating bamboo shoots in the cage in front of him. It is surely, precisely, and only because the presence of that most engaging creature is no sort of causal condition of our blind man's having the (private) experiences that he is having, that we have to say that, notwithstanding perhaps that he also has all the appropriate true beliefs, still he has not seen and cannot see the giant panda. (The parenthetical insertions of the word "private" are required, since—in the everyday, nontechnical, public sense of the word "experience"—to claim to have had experience of giant pandas is to claim not only to have enjoyed giant panda sense-data but also to have had dealings with some real, flesh and blood, external world, giant pandas.)[4]

If we now accept "Durkheim's classic study 'The Elementary Forms of the Religous Life' " as some sort of paradigm, then we may well say: "So much for the Olympians, and so much perhaps for the appearance of the Blessed Virgin too." But the triumph of the Athenian fleet in the Battle of Salamis is another matter altogether. That actually happened, and was seen and otherwise perceived to happen both by participants afloat and by observers ashore.

No doubt our guide's belief that it happened is to be explained in much the same terms as her beliefs in the visitation of Phoebus Apollo and of the Virgin Mary. But the beliefs of the original observers of that battle, both participant and otherwise, cannot be causally explained without crucial reference to what it was they observed. When it is a question of accounting for what people have been taught by their elders, or picked up from their peers by social osmosis, then there is indeed plenty of room for social causes. But when we move to the opposite end of the cognitive scale, and it becomes a matter of accounting for the central content of beliefs about matters of everyday use and observation, or of beliefs about more esoteric matters that the individual has investigated for himself, then it is another story. The causes of our belief that the ferry canoe is where it is on the Zaire River do not lie wholly or even partly in the peculiar social structure of our tribe. They are to be found, instead, in certain intrusive nonsocial, physiological, and biological facts: that when we turn our eyes towards the right bit of the river the canoe causes appropriate sensory impressions, and that those heedlessly placing themselves in the water rather than in the canoe are incontinently eaten by crocodiles.

2. Social causes usurping reason's throne?

On that most crucial and fundamental issue—the part to be played in the sociology of belief by the subject matter of any beliefs thus sociologized—Bloor can be allowed to be, at best, ambivalent. There is a hint of one way the wind is blowing on the very first page of *Knowledge and Social Imagery:* "The sociology of knowledge might well have pressed more strongly," Bloor reflects, "in the area currently occupied by philosophers, who have been allowed to take upon themselves the task of defining the nature of knowledge." Bloor is surely not here giving vent to a mere jurisdictional, trades union aspiration. He is not, that is, suggesting only that a task traditionally performed by persons paid as philosophers should in future be performed by the persons paid as sociologists. The suggestion is, rather, that the whole conception of knowledge as some variation on the theme of justified or grounded true belief might with advantage be jettisoned in favor of some epistemologically denatured sociologist's alternative.

Yet on the following page Bloor appears to retreat from this first, reckless, forward position. Nevertheless he indicates its lines:

> The sociologist is concerned with knowledge, including scientific knowledge, purely as a natural phenomenon. His definition of knowledge will therefore be rather different from that of either the layman or the philosopher. Instead of defining it as true belief [Not *justified* true belief?—A. F.], knowledge for the sociologist is whatever men take to be knowledge. (p. 2)

On the more immediately relevant topic of the causal influences of the subject matter of beliefs upon the formation and preservation of these beliefs, there are similar indications of ambivalence. It is clear that this ambivalence arises because Bloor believes, or believes part of the time, that to admit any such influence would put his firm out of business: "When men behave rationally or logically it is tempting to say that their actions are governed by the requirements of reasonableness or logic. . . . If this is so it is not the sociologist or the psychologist but the logician who will provide the most important part of the explanation of belief" (p. 5). In that event the lay person is right: "Empirical or sociological explanations are confined to the irrational" (p. 7).

Here and elsewhere Bloor either altogether fails to make, or else collapses, distinctions between radically different questions that can be asked about belief. Here and everywhere, by speaking of knowledge, without prefix or suffix, where he himself maintains that he like all his colleagues means only belief, without prejudice to any and all disputes over the cognitive status of that belief, Bloor becomes committed in particular to devaluing genuinely cognitive assessments and in general to confusing both himself and others.

The failure to make, or the collapsing of, fundamental distinctions is seen *both* in his hint that a traditional and cognitive conception of knowledge might with profit be replaced by an alternative sociological conception of "knowledge," or "perceived" knowledge, *and* in his subsequent assumption that there can and should be one and only one "explanation of belief"—a single explanation to which any contributions from "the layman or the philosopher" or "the logician" must be inversely proportional to the contributions of "the sociologist or the psychologist." The depreciation of genuinely cognitive assessments is seen both in the same aspects of these two passages and in Bloor's inclination to urge not just that people paid as sociologists might do some of the work previously done by other specialists, but rather that such seemingly unfashionable activities could ideally be abandoned in favor of something strictly sociological.

We have to distinguish very different sorts of questions that can be asked about the phenomena of belief, and the very different, and hence by no means always and necessarily incompatible, explanations that may relevantly be offered in answer to such very different questions. There will be, or would be, a single explanation only for a phenomenon about which one single question is all that is or could be asked.[5] So consider now that most common kind of phenomenon describable in such words as: "She expressed her belief that *p*."

Confronted by this phenomenon, we may ask for and discuss her evidencing reasons. Then, if these appear to be insufficient, we may find other and better evidencing reasons that were not hers. Reasons of this first kind are such as may make it probable, or even prove, that *p* is true. Alternatively or additionally we may ask for her motivating reasons for expressing that belief on that occasion. Here any relevant answer to our question will be an explanation of the point of an action for the agent, and the kind of reasons offered will be such as have no necessary bearing on the question of the truth of *p*.

A third category of questions abstracts entirely from all the semantic aspects of the phenomenon. This interest now lies in the physiological and other preconditions of the emission of those sounds by and through which the subject both expressed her belief and performed her action. But the sounds themselves are considered as so much uninterpreted acoustic disturbance. Explanations of this third kind are bound to refer to many ongoings without which the subject could not in fact have reasons of the first two types. Presumably, for instance, it is not as a matter of fact possible for anyone either to have an evidencing reason for believing that p or to want to express their belief in that p unless their central nervous systems and other organs are present and working in some appropriate way. Nevertheless it would appear that none of the terms collected as characteristic of any of these three kinds of explanation is logically reducible to anything similarly characteristic of either of the other two. You cannot, that is to say, define "reason (evidence)" in terms of either "reason (motivating)" or "cause (physical)" or either of the other ways about.[6]

The upshot, therefore, of sections 1 and 2 together is that Bloor has no warrant either for his ambivalence about the part to be played in the sociology of belief by the subject matter or the beliefs sociologized, or for his suggestions that sociological might ultimately and properly replace epistemological accounts of all belief. The sociologist of belief is professionally committed to inquiries of our second and third kinds: "the strong programme" must be "causal, that is, concerned with conditions which bring about belief or states of knowledge." But, "naturally there will be other types of causes apart from social ones." Nor has any (evidencing) reason been given for thinking that these inquiries even permit—much less require—an assault on the layman's conception of knowledge.

3. The peculiar objects of mathematical belief

Bloor is, of course, investigating mathematical beliefs rather than beliefs about "matters of fact and real existence." So the intrusive nonsocial causes of which he should be taking account are of a different kind. They are, I presume, actually subsistent logical relations or, rather, the impact of the recognition of these upon the mathematicians.

Before proceeding further we need to remind ourselves, as Bloor does not remind either himself or us, of what about logical relations is and is not socially relative or socially determined. Different societies may have, for instance, different marriage institutions, involving different conceptions of a husband or a wife, while any vocable whatsoever can by convention be attached to any concept whatsoever. Yet, once given that the words "husband" and "wife" are being used in particular determinate ways and with particular determinate meanings, then all the logically necessary truths in the expression of which those terms can be employed are also and necessarily given. It is not within the power of either man or God to decide what necessary truths are to obtain, either here or elsewhere.

So it is quite wrong to suggest, as has occasionally been suggested even by some of those paid to know better, that we could, by prescribing some different use for one or more of the symbols that have been by previous convention employed to state, say, 7 + 5 = 12, miraculously transform that self-same proposition from a necessary truth into some sort of falsehood. What, and all, that could in reality be achieved by such an arbitrary prescription would be the pointless, and perhaps worse than pointless, disqualification of "7 + 5 = 12" as the proper expression of what could not but remain the same eternal, unchanging, and necessary truth, that same truth which, previous to this new ruling, was quite properly so expressed.

When, however, he does take account of the possible influence upon beliefs of their subject matter—and his attention to this strikes me as being reluctant, infrequent, and cursory—Bloor makes reference to science rather than to mathematics: "If sociologists make misperception a central feature of their analysis they may fail to come to terms with the reliability, repeatability, and dependability of science's empirical basis" (p. 20). Again, in a chapter on "Materialism and Sociological Explanation," he is prepared to insist: "No consistent sociology could ever present knowledge as a fantasy unconnected with man's experience of the material world around him. . . . All of these presuppose the reliability of perception and the ability to detect, retain, and act upon perceived regularities and discriminations" (p. 29).

As far as it goes, this is excellent. Unfortunately Bloor also has

something to say about the validity of arguments, although not in the
particular context of mathematics:

> Logic, it may seem, constitutes a set of connections between premises
> and conclusions and men's minds can trace out these connections.
> As long as they are being reasonable then the connections themselves
> would seem to provide the best explanation of the beliefs of the rea-
> soner. Like an engine on rails, the rails themselves dictate where it
> will go. . . . If this is so then it is not the sociologist or the psycholo-
> gist but the logician who will provide the most important part of
> the explanation of belief. (p. 5)

Given distinctions made in previous sections it becomes fairly easy
to see that there is both something importantly right about this as well
as something even more importantly wrong. It is entirely correct to
insist that, for someone engaged in inquiries of our second and third
kinds, it is not sufficient or even relevant to point out that, were these
acoustic disturbances to be construed as providing premises, this or that
conclusion must then follow necessarily. Yet to go on to suggest that
there are no objective and absolute logical connections, that the content
of premises never dictates lines on which the argument, because correctly
or incorrectly, *ought* or *ought not* to go, is altogether ruinous.

Yet that is precisely what Bloor does proceed to do in his final
servings of the speciality of the house, "A Naturalistic Approach to
Mathematics." He writes: "A more controversial question is whether
sociology can touch the very heart of mathematical knowledge. Can
it explain the logical necessity of a step in reasoning or why a proof
is in fact a proof?" (p. 74). It soon emerges that the desired sociological
explanation of logical necessity is to be one construed as showing that
in reality there is no such thing. Where Hume thought to reveal that
there are no necessities in the world around us, only projections of
our own internal impressions, Bloor aspires to provide that what the
uninstructed see as objective, logical necessities are in truth no more
than relative, social, and psychological.

"Do not the facts," Bloor asks, "refute the claim that logical compulsion is social in nature?" (p. 94). Apparently not. For in the fol-

lowing two chapters—"Can there be an Alternative Mathematics?" and "Negotiation in Logical and Mathematical Thought"—we have an account of pure mathematical investigation that is by the later Wittgenstein out of the middle John Stuart Mill. This is supposed to establish the conclusion that "logical necessity is a species of moral obligation" (p. 141). Thus "Mill's *Logic* furnished the fundamental idea that physical situations provide models for the steps in mathematical reasonings." But "Mill's theory . . . does not explain why mathematical conclusions seem as if they could not possibly be other than they are" (p. 92). What is missing, according to Bloor, is a recognition that "the compelling character of our reasoning is a form of social compulsion"; and he proposes to provide "A more sophisticated understanding . . . of just what the compulsion of a logical or mathematical argument amounts to" (p. 117).

Perhaps this is the moment to bring forward both the record of a previous conviction and evidence of an unfortunate association. In 1974, in *Science Studies* and under the strange title "Popper's Mystification of Objective Knowledge," Bloor concluded:

> To appraise an argument for validity is to apply the standards of a social group. It cannot be other, or more, than this because we have no access to other standards. . . . The objectivity of knowledge resides in its being the set of beliefs of a social group. This is why and how it transcends the individual and constrains him. . . . The authority of truth is the authority of society. (pp. 75–76)

But now, first and more narrowly, is Bloor's sociology so committed to metaphysical collectivism that it has to exclude as inconceivable the possibility that some dissenting minority of one may be seized of an item of objective truth? (Consider the historical heresies entertained by Winston Smith in George Orwell's last appalling nightmare, *1984*). If the only possibility of objective knowledge does indeed lie "in its being the set of beliefs of a social group," and if propositions and arguments are not true or false, valid or invalid, altogether independently of whether anyone acutally recognizes them to be so, then, certainly, there is no standing ground for any dissident individual.

Next, is Bloor really prepared to stand by what appears to be the inescapable implication of his words—that "objective knowledge" can only be defined as nothing else but "the set of beliefs of a social group"? The crucial question to press is whether Bloor's sociology of knowledge, and in particular of mathematical knowledge, can admit that there actually is some knowledge, including some mathematical knowledge, and not just "whatever men take to be knowledge," and hence some truth, including some mathematical truth, and not merely what any social group to which anyone may happen to belong might endorse as being the truth.

How, we must be allowed to interject, are these groups themselves supposed to interpret their own claims, and what is the basis of their own pretensions to authority? It is, it seems, one more problem from the ancient stable of Plato's *Euthyphro*: "Is it good because the Gods command it, or do the Gods command it because it is good?"[7]

Putting pretty much the same objection in a slightly different way, the crux lies in the "merely" and the "nothing but." Where these and other more or less synonymous words and phrases are intruded, what may well have started as a modest disclaimer concerning proper limitations upon the interests and competencies of a particular learned profession, becomes transmogrified into a piece of wildly deflationary metaphysics, an absolute weapon for the destruction of the very ideas of knowledge and truth. And this includes—though it is usually felt to be tiresome bad form to say this—sociological knowledge and sociological truth.[8]

Certainly there may be social pressures to accept that *p* does or does not follow necessarily from *q*, and it is of course with these that the sociologist of belief must professionally be most concerned. But can we not also on another occasion, and in another universe of discourse, say, and say truly and in knowledge, that it does or does not indeed follow necessarily? For—make no mistake about this—if we cannot, if the sociology of knowledge really has to be construed as showing that logical necessity is nothing but a misconception of some sort of social necessity, and if this sociology of knowledge is, as Bloor quite certainly believes, integral to the whole scientific enterprise, then that enterprise surely is, as so many others before have made it, self-refuting.

For the notion of logical necessity is not peculiar and essential to mathematical knowledge only. It is irremovably indispensable to all rational discourse and all valid argument in any and every sphere whatsoever.

4. Beating back the sociological imperialists

Bloor as a sociologist is most emphatically not content to confine himself to questions falling within the third or even the second of the categories distinguished in section 2 above. Instead he has imperialist longings in him, hankering to annex all the territories of the first category and to replace the lay by sociological conceptions of knowledge and truth. The first sentence of chapter 1, "The Strong Programme of the Sociology of Knowledge," puts Bloor's master question: "Can the sociology of knowledge investigate and explain the very content and nature of scientific knowledge?" (p. 1). Clearly it is, as the Latin grammarians used to say, a question expecting the answer "yes."

Equally clearly, Bloor does not either want or expect us, whenever the word "know" appears in his book, systematically to interpret this in some peculiar sense. Certainly he does say, on the following page, that "knowledge for the sociologist is whatever men take to be knowledge." Yet we cannot construe the word in this way on its every occurrence: for instance, all the boldness of the "bold attempt" would be lost were we to be required to read the expression "scientific knowledge" in Bloor's initial challenge in so feeble a sense.

(i) Bloor, therefore, is only in part following an example set by Peter Berger and Thomas Luckmann. Bold-as-brass, they entitle what has become a standard textbook, *The Social Construction of Reality: A Treatise in the Sociology of Knowledge.*[9] Nevertheless it is not, they explain in their introduction, reality that is supposed to be socially constructed, but rather people's beliefs about that reality. Nor again is it knowledge in particular that is to be sociologized. It is, quite indiscriminately, beliefs of any and every possible cognitive status. It is in this lack of scruple about the beliefs to which he is prepared to award the title "knowledge" that Bloor follows Berger and Luckmann. I have already cited what is, from so secular a pen, the most scandalous illustration: "Durkheim's classic study 'The Elementary Forms of the Religious Life' shows how a sociologist can penetrate to the very depths of a form of knowledge" (p. 2).

Berger and Luckmann continue:

> To speak of question marks, however, may give a clue to the peculiar manner in which these terms appear in a sociological context. . . . Sociological interest in questions of "reality" is . . . initially justified by the fact of their social relativity. What is "real" to a Tibetan monk may not be "real" to an American businessman. The "knowledge" of a criminal differs from the "knowledge" of the criminologist. The need for a "sociology of knowledge" is thus already given with the observable differences between societies in terms of what is taken for granted . . . in them. (p. 15)

This, no doubt, is all very well. Yet we must be prepared for disaster the moment those crucial quotes are either overlooked or omitted or misconstrued. Of course the environments of the Tibetan monk and the American businessman, and, to a lesser extent, of the criminal and the criminologist, are different. But what is socially relative is not the reality of these environments themselves, but the beliefs that people have about them, not the reality of these environments themselves, but—as some sociologically minded people would say—the (believed or perceived) "realities" of those who, shall we say, occupy those environments.

Before returning to challenge the bad practice of describing as knowledge what neither is nor is even believed to be knowledge, there are two points to be made about the distinction and the interrelations between reality and (perceived) "reality." First, even when everyone remembers to insert the quotes, it is lamentably easy to misconstrue their significance. Intended to express a noncommittal detachment, they are in fact—almost as often as not—misread or misheard as an index of the commitment of dissent.

Second, like it or lump it, it is entirely impossible for sociologists or psychologists, or anyone else, to study only the (believed or perceived) "realities" while maintaining a scrupulously noncommittal stance about all the factual realities of the environment of their subjects. For although everyone always has to act on the basis of what they believe their situations to be, their conduct, and these beliefs themselves, cannot be made intelligible without some reference to what actually is happening in the universe around them. Their plans, their intentions, and their decisions are no doubt all elements in their "reality." The outcome, however, is in large part determined by the facts not of this (perceived) "reality," but of actual, without prefix or suffix, external reality.

To understand, for instance, how A Squadron came to be annihilated in an ambush it is necessary to know not only where the commander believed the enemy antitank guns to be and why, but also—as he until too late did not—where they actually were. Again, in order to understand the conduct of both the criminals and the criminologists we certainly need to know what they believe their situations to be and why. Yet we must not be so blinkered in a sociological purism as to insist on not knowing what these situations actually were, and how much or how little our subjects were affected by these actual situations.

(ii) The example Berger and Luckmann set, an example that with greater or lesser degrees of frankness and consistency seems to be followed by almost all their colleagues studying the sociology of "knowledge," or the social construction of "reality," must be drawn from Lewis Carroll's White Knight. For they persist in employing ordinary words, yet insist that these are on no account to be understood in any ordinary way. The White Knight's confession, it will be remembered, went:

> But I was thinking of a plan
> To dye one's whiskers green,
> And always use so large a fan
> That they could not be seen.

Yet this persistence in describing as knowledge what neither is nor is believed to be knowledge is a more serious, and more dangerous, matter than so lighthearted a comparison will suggest: the fan in this case is neither sufficiently large, nor sufficiently opaque, nor employed with sufficient regularity, to do the job. The crux is that, as of all people psychologists and social scientists should be most aware, we are creatures of convention, hag-ridden by habit: above all in learning a language we acquire enormously complicated structures of very strong habit. The commoner the word, the more frequent its employment, the more we reinforce thereby those habits that determine the present usage and hence the present meaning of that word.

So it is grotesque to think that we can change the meaning of familiar words, especially the commonest, and ensure that we ourselves and everybody else will from this time forward follow the appropriate new usage by simply deciding and prescribing what the new meaning is to be. It just is not possible to extinguish old habits and to break old associations, and to establish others not merely different but often more or less contrary, instantly and by simply telling ourselves and others that this is what we propose to do and want done. It is a difficult task to replace one set of habits by another, and one that, if attempted, is bound to take time and effort. It will be satisfactorily accomplished, if at all, only after many failures and backslidings into the old ways.

In the meantime there will be much confusion and many mistakes. People will be apt to make the mistake that words and expressions in their prescribed new usages carry all and only their former implications. They will be inclined to overlook the implications, and the objections, that would be perfectly obvious to them had what is said been said in some more ordinarily familiar way. These aptnesses and these inclinations are in fact forever being exploited by users of euphemism and of in-group jargon. They often enable people to get away with murder, sometimes quite literally.[10]

Nor are philosophers and philosophy immune. For example, in *A Discourse on the Method* Descartes proposes to redefine that very common and familiar word "thinking" to mean not ratiocination but being conscious. That was at the beginning of part IV. A few pages later, in part V, he addresses the question of how we might determine that "machines which bore a resemblance to our body and imitated our actions as far as it was morally possible to do . . . were not real men." Yet even Descartes has already, and so soon, forgotten that we are all supposed to be, essentially, "thinking substances," but specifically in his proposed new sense of "thinking." Hence "the two very certain tests" he actually offers are tests not of consciousness but of rationality.[11] He thus loses the right to be hailed as the discoverer of the modern philosophical Problem of Other Minds.

If only Bloor had been alive to such fundamental realities of, shall we say, the psychology of language, then he would not, he could not, have persisted in so much indiscriminate misapplication and discrediting of the word "know," as well as of various other words and expressions similarly and properly peculiar to the first of the three different universes of discourse distinguished in section 2 above. In that case he might, and surely would, have been able to cleave consistently to his early insight: "Whether all belief is to be judged true or false has nothing to do with whether it has a cause" (p. 14).

But as it is, and as we have seen, Bloor keeps lapsing into the flat incompatible assumption that the second and third of our universes of discourse are always and necessarily rivals to the first, and hence "that sociology along with psychology can furnish an adequate approach to the nature of mathematical knowledge and logical thought" (p. 7). Let us conclude this review by reconsidering in the present context one passage quoted earlier:

> When men behave rationally or logically it is tempting to say that their actions are governed by the requirements of reasonableness or logic. The explanation of why a man draws the conclusion he does from a set of premises may appear to reside in the principles of logical inference themselves. (p. 5)

Certainly it is wrong to think of the rational justification for drawing some conclusion as providing any sort of explanation why noises semantically interpretable as expressing that conclusion have been emitted from the organism. Yet it is, if anything, far more, and far more ruinously, wrong to go on to take it that the causal impotence of evidencing reasons shows that there is no objective and socially independent truth about what does or does not follow from what. Bloor continues: "Logic, it may seem, constitutes a set of connections between premises and conclusions and men's minds can trace out these connections. . . . Like an engine on rails, the rails themselves dictate where it will go" (p. 5).

It does not merely seem to be, but actually is the case that there are logical connections between premises and validly deduced conclusions, and that we all can and do trace out some such connections. But in order to hold fast to this essential it is not necessary to follow those who have suggested that there is no room hereabouts for psychological explanations. On the contrary, the emission of whatever (semantically interpretable) noises are emitted when—as we would put it within another universe of discourse—some conclusion is drawn, has indeed to be causally explained. The explanations to be found will, presumably, in the main and in the first instance, refer to all the habits which define the usage and hence the meanings of all the various terms involved. It is going to be quite a job! For, in the words of *Tractatus* 4.002 (Authorized Version)[12]: "Colloquial language is a part of the human organism and is not less complicated than it."

Notes

1. From his apologetic speech to the Thirteenth Congress of the Communist Party of the Soviet Union, in 1924.

2. George Orwell, *1984* (London: Secker and Warburg, 1949), pp. 271–72.

3. Compare chapter 5, section 2.

4. Compare subsection 5 (ii) of chapter 5.

5. For an effective mnemonic to ensure continuing possession of this truth, see section 1 of chapter 5.

6. Compare section 3 of chapter 5.

7. In strict accuracy the *Euthyphro* (9C ff.) treats holiness rather than goodness. For discussion of this and related passages in such other classical sources as Hobbes and Leibniz, compare Antony Flew, *An Introduction to Western Philosophy* (London: Thames and Hudson, Revised Edition, 1989), pp. 26–34.

8. Compare, again, section 2 of chapter 5.

9. First published in the United States in 1966, but since 1971 available as a Penguin University Book.

10. Compare, for example, George Orwell's essay "Politics and the Eng-

lish Language," especially its treatment of the reporting by National Socialists and Marxist-Leninists and their sympathizers of approved killings. This essay is reprinted in volume 4 of the *Collected Essays* (Harmondsworth: Penguin Books, 1970), pp. 156–70.

11. E. S. Haldane and G. R. T. Ross, trans., *The Collected Works of Descartes* (Cambridge: Cambridge University Press, 1911), vol. 1, p. 116. By the way, has anyone written a history of the Problem of Other Minds; and to whom should we credit the invention of that problem?

12. Ludwig Wittgenstein, *Tractatus Logico-Philosophicus* (London: Kegan Paul, Trench, Tribner, 1922). This original translation by C. K. Ogden, apparently approved by the author before publication, possesses merits and defects, when compared with its successor, that parallel those of the King James Bible when compared with the Revised Version.

7

Mental Health, Mental Disease, Mental Illness: "The Medical Model"

> The mentally ill, far from being guilty persons who merit punishment, are sick people whose miserable state deserves all the consideration due to suffering humanity
>
> Philippe Pinel (1745–1826)

In the version printed by *The Listener* on November 6, 1980, Ian Kennedy begins the first of his 1980 Reith Lectures with a satisfactorily arresting paragraph. Reith Lectures, by the way, are members of a series of lectures delivered annually on radio under the auspices of the British Broadcasting Corporation in honor of its first director general. *The Listener* was a journal, founded and run by the BBC, mainly for the purpose of printing some of the talks previously transmitted.

Kennedy's satisfactorily arresting paragraph read,

> Six years ago the American Psychiatric Association took a vote and decided homosexuality was not an illness. So, since 1974, it hasn't been an illness. How extraordinary, you may think, to decide what an illness is, by taking a vote. What exactly is going on here? (p. 600).

1. An engagement with a Reith Lecturer

It is a good question, and equally good whether the "here" is construed as referring to those proceedings of the American Psychiatric Association (APA) or to these Reith Lectures. In the second understanding, Kennedy's answer as a Reith Lecturer is immediate and explicit: "I've set as my task the unmasking of medicine." And, although his nerve then weakens a little with the disclaimer, "It isn't that I think there's something sinister behind the mask," the second paragraph still concludes, "The first step on the way to understanding modern medicine, looking behind the mask, is to unravel the rhetoric of medicine" (p. 600).

In the latter understanding, Kennedy's answer is implicit first in his second sentence: "So, since 1974, it hasn't been an illness." For this comment shows that he is taking that conference resolution as a piece of pure legislation, an authoritative decision laying down what the law is to be. Certainly this must have been at least part of the story. For, just as the general American Medical Association publishes its *Standard Nomenclature of Diseases and Operations,* so too the APA maintains a more particular *Diagnostic and Statistical Manual of Mental Disorder.* One intended consequence, therefore, of the conference resolution must have been corresponding deletions from future editions of that handbook. Nevertheless another and larger part of the story has to have been belated public recognition that homosexuality as such is not, and never was, a kind of illness: an illness, that is, on all fours with pneumonia, yellow fever, or leprosy. In this aspect the APA decision becomes like that of a Debates Union resolving "That there is no God," rather than like that of a legislature passing a law criminalizing, or decriminalizing, some class of actions. And, of course, it is this recognition resolution that is needed to provide, and that does in fact provide, the rationale required for the operational decision to revise the *Diagnostic Manual* and the practice based thereon.

(i) Kennedy now sets himself "to unravel the rhetoric of medicine." It is, as soon appears, a task for which his defective conceptual equipment is quite insufficient. He starts by assuming that those plain persons, his listeners, will insist that " 'Illness' . . . is a technical term, a term of scientific exactitude. Whether someone has an illness, is ill, is a matter of objective fact" (p. 600). Certainly, whether someone feels ill, is suffering from pain, or has been in any way incapacitated, is indeed "a matter of objective fact." But, equally certainly none of the words employed in the previous sentence, nor the terms "illness" and even "disease," are in their primary and original usages technical. I need no expert to tell me that I feel terrible, that I have a splitting headache, and that when I try to get up and walk I collapse into a helpless heap on the floor. By contrast, I do need a doctor, first, to diagnose to which of all the various syndromes distinguished and labelled by medical researchers my condition of illness is to be attributed, and, second, to prescribe a treatment enabling me to escape disease and to get back to health.

Accepting his own false suggestion that all the key words here are technical, Kennedy next considers what he characterizes as "the strangely disquieting insight that illness involves not merely the existence of certain facts; it involves a judgement on those facts." In his usage, which happens to be flat contrary to that of an earlier generation of philosophers, judging is a matter of deciding, not what the facts are, but what is to be done. Thus he continues, "And it is doctors who do the judging. A choice exists whether to categorize particular circumstances as amounting to an illness. Power is vested in the doctor, and the power is not insignificant. . . . Medical practice is, above all, a political enterprise, one in which judgments about people are made."

It becomes important, then, to discover whether there are boundaries to this word, this concept "illness." Can it be applied willy-nilly on the say-so of the doctor, or are there limits to his power? To determine this Kennedy begins by citing some conditions about which there is unanimous agreement—leprosy, cancer, appendicitis: "'We all agree these are illnesses, because we accept two propositions. The first is that there is a normal state in which the appendix is not inflamed, and breathing is easy while resting. Secondly, it is appropriate to judge someone who deviates from this norm as ill."

We have to examine the two explicit assumptions in turn: "Take the first. . . . This seems simple enough. It isn't of course. For a start, it's *only* our convention to call such deviations illness. Others in other cultures may view such conditions entirely differently" (p. 600, emphasis added). It is one mark of the defective conceptual equipment afore-mentioned that Kennedy—along with two or three other recent Reith Lecturers—never thinks to question two further, unstated assumptions. He does not, that is, doubt either, first, that we may validly deduce the absence of objective knowledge from the subsistence of disagree-ment and from nothing else besides, or, second, that, from premises asserting only that something is in some group a matter of accepted convention, a similarly compulsive argument goes straight through to the conclusion that that is *only,* that that is *merely,* that that is *noth-ing but,* the (arbitrary) convention of that group.[1]

However, "in our society," Kennedy continues, "We cleave to sci-ence and the scientific principle of a demonstrable state of normality and a causative agent which brings about an abnormality. . . . What is the state we should regard as normal?" Here he does indicate what is, I shall be contending, the correct answer: "We think in terms of a machine which has a design, which is the norm, and which malfunc-tions when it does not perform according to the design." Indeed we do. For, although most of us have come to believe that no organism ever was in fact designed, that all—like Topsy—"just growed," still every biologist since the Founding Father Aristotle has had to insist that organisms, and perhaps still more the parts of organisms, must be thought of in a teleological way. The challenge facing evolutionists has always been to explain how such overwhelming observed appearances of design could possibly have come about if not through the actual operation of intention and intelligence.[2]

There are, as Kennedy sees it, two shortcomings in any such bio-logical ideal of the normal: "One weakness is that it is crude. We like to think of ourselves as more than machines. We have emotions, moods, and feelings which affect our physical states. A further weakness is that we may not all agree on the design, the blueprint, against which to measure our performance or our state" (p. 600). Under the first head it has at once to be admitted that those various psychological attri-butes and potentialities that distinguish rational animals from the rules may give rise to special, possibly even insuperable, difficulties. We might, that is to say, find that an account of (physical) health developed on these lines could not be satisfactorily transposed to cover its supposed analogue, mental health.

Under the second head it must first be said again that the (alleged) impossibility of achieving unanimous assent constitutes no kind of refutation. Fresh interest and instruction are to be found in Kennedy's illustration: "For example, women have the capacity to bear children. In the old days, it was considered part of the design for women that they bore children. A woman who did not bear children departed from this design. . . . You'll recall that Julius Caesar urged his wife to touch Antony so as to be cured of her barrenness" (p. 600). The crucial distinction, here characteristically and ruinously collapsed, is, in Aristotelian terms, that between potentiality and actuality. Applied particularly it is the distinction between simply being capable of bearing children and actually bearing them: the Caesar of history would not have attributed either a disease or any other sort of physical disorder to a Vestal Virgin who had in fact remained, as she was most imperatively bound to remain, a virgin and childless, while Calpurnia's trouble was that—her own longings and all her husband's no doubt strenuously faithful services notwithstanding—she had succeeded neither in conceiving or in bringing forth. It is the physical condition resulting in this abnormal incapacity that, both today and "in the old days," has to be scored either as a disease or an illness or as some other defection from perfect health and fitness.

The final adversative clause in the last sentence of the previous paragraph should suggest, what will be argued more fully later, that, if we are going to define both health and the various kinds of defection from it along the lines suggested by Kennedy, then we shall have to dig a deep divide. It will run between, on the one hand, terms of this present semitechnical and properly value-neutral sort, and, on the other hand, various everyday words in their ordinary usages. These everyday words carry the implication that the conditions to which they are applied are at least presumptively bad for and/or unwelcome to their patients—hence anyone relieving those conditions will typically be both serving the interests and observing the wishes of these patients.

The best program so far proposed for making and maintaining

such a chasm is to be found in an article "On the Distinction between Disease and Illness" published by Christopher Boorse in *Philosophy and Public Affairs* (1975):

> It is a disease, the theoretical concept, that applies indifferently to organisms of all species. . . . It is to be analyzed in biological rather than ethical terms. The point is that illnesses are merely a subclass of diseases, namely those diseases that have certain normative features. . . . An illness must be, first, a reasonably serious disease with incapacitating effects that make it undesirable. . . . Secondly, to call a disease an illness is to view its owner as deserving special treatment and diminished moral accountability (p. 56, emphasis original).

Boorse writes as if he were doing no more than explicating a distinction already embodied in established usage. In the title of the present paper, for instance, we have not a "Distinction" but "The Distinction." Certainly, it requires no praeternaturally sensitive ear to insist that the syndromes distinguished and labelled by medical researchers should be rated diseases rather than illnesses, and to refuse to tolerate the describing of so very tolerable an affliction as athlete's foot as an illness. No doubt Boorse is also right in his claim that medical textbooks count every kind of physiological order as a disease, that they include among the diseased both the victims of gunshot wounds and persons born blind as well as the syphilitic. But that, as he himself appreciates, is not lay usage. More seriously, even the professionals appear inclined to construe the terms "health," "disease," and "disorder" as all essentially prescriptive. Again, Boorse himself notes and protests this fact: "With few exceptions, clinicians and philosophers are agreed that health is an essentially evaluative notion. According to this consensus view, a value-free science of health is impossible" (p. 50). I therefore suggest that Boorse is being rather too modest, that the truth is that he is recommending a highly desirable measure of conceptual reform; and, furthermore, that this is a measure possessing the great practical political merit of going with other than against the grain of our linguistic habits.

*   *   *

(ii) In the paragraph following next after the one that ended with the misinterpreted reference to *Julius Caesar,* Kennedy draws his moral:

> The point is clear. What is the normal state against which to measure abnormality is a product of social and cultural values and expectations. It is not some static objectively identifiable fact. . . . So, if illness has as its first criterion some deviation from the norm, some abnormality, it too will vary and change in its meaning (p. 600).

Certainly, if the criteria for the application of some term are changed, then its meaning must alter correspondingly. But the crucial and crucially disputatious contention here, surely, reformulated in Boorse's clearer and more incisive words, is that health and disease are essentially evaluative notions, "that a value-free science of health is impossible." It is important to realize that this contention is false, that there can be and are nonprescriptive theoretical ideals. Consider, for example, the status of the First Law of Motion in classical mechanics or of the Principle of Population in the theoretical scheme of Thomas Robert Malthus.[3] Both lay down ideal norms, all deviations from which have to be explained—explained by reference to "impressed forces" in the former case, and by the operation of various "positive and preventive checks" in the latter. But no one (one hopes) is rooting either for the removal of all impressing forces or for the liquidation of all checks on population growth.

It is in the same way possible to develop a completely detached, objective, nonprescriptive ideal norm of health, an ideal norm defined in terms of the fulfilling of the functions that organs and organisms appear to have, yet have not, been designed to fulfill. And, whatever may be the truth about even professional usage in a human context, these in fact are the concepts already applied to the brutes. No one is so free from the taint of speciesism that they would either intend or interpret the "diseased" label under a specimen of *drosophila melanogaster* to imply an imperative need for treatment and cure.

As examples of diagnoses supposedly varying with variations in the socially accepted ideal norm of health Kennedy cites "some of those accused of witchcraft by Cotton Mather in 17th-century Massachusetts." Forgetting—as so many do—how the evidence against these unfortunates was fabricated, Kennedy takes it for granted that they must all have had something in common, in addition, that is, to their defining collective characteristic of having been successfully charged with the (surely impossible) offense of witchcraft. Indeed he takes it for granted that there must actually have been something wrong with the lot of them. They would, he goes on, "probably now be described as epileptics, or as suffering from Huntington's chorea, and seen as ill and certainly not as evil" (p. 600).

Running through these and other examples Kennedy detects "the theme of responsibility." He continues:

> As our views of each person's power to exercise dominion over his life changes, so will our concept of the borders between illness and evil. For evil is seen as a product of someone's choice, and thus something he may be held responsible for. Illness, by contrast, is something which overtakes him; and, once ill, he is absolved from the ordinary responsibilities of everyday life (p. 600).

In welcoming the second two of these three propositions as both basic and substantially true we may be distracted to overlook the falsity of the first. (By the way, the third requires some amendment: to allow for the fact that illness absolves and excuses only and precisely to the extent that it incapacitates or handicaps. It is not the case that just any illness properly provides total absolution. This is something that people are perhaps more apt to forget in talking of mental than of physical illness.)

The reason the first of these three propositions is false is that Kennedy is collapsing the distinction between connotation and denotation. What may change with changing beliefs about the extent of our capacities is the accepted denotation rather than the connotation of the key words. The fact that some people are discovered to have been incapacitated, in some dimension in which it was previously believed that they were not, is a reason, though not by itself a sufficient reason, for conceding that they were patients of some illness. But that same fact is no reason at all, not even an insufficient reason, for introducing some fresh sense or fresh criteria for the terms "health" and "illness." So we shall, or we should, shift the frontier between the populations labelled "the ill" and "the healthy" in step with our discoveries about peoples' capacities and incapacities. Yet in doing this we shall not, most emphatically, be changing the membership qualifications for those two expanding and contracting clubs.

(iii) From all this Kennedy infers, "Illness, a central concept of medicine . . . is a matter of social and political judgment" (pp. 600–601); or, in what he appears to read as an alternative and equivalent formulation, "Illness is an indeterminate concept, the product of social political and moral values which, as we have seen, fluctuate" (p. 601). The implications of this, we are assured, will strike us immediately: "If 'illness' is a judgment, the practice of medicine can be understood in terms of power. He who makes the judgment wields the power" (p. 601).

That final statement just quoted must be unexceptionable, if only Kennedy were not so inclined to assume that the truth of such, shall we say, sociological remarks must exclude that of all other kinds. In this he keeps bad company with all those fashionable "sociologists of knowledge" who mistake what their deliberately misnamed discipline is always and necessarily discrediting. The surely inescapable consequence would be that no belief falling within their compass can truly constitute an item of knowledge. But, of course, the expression of a medical judgment can perfectly well be, at one and the same time, both an assertion of some objective scientific truth and part of an exercise of a life or death therapeutic power. Take, for example, the utterance, in some context that would guarantee their truth, of the arresting words: "If we do not operate at once, the patient will be dead before dusk!"

The same failure to appreciate that two not necessarily exclusive descriptions may both be applicable simultaneously is found again in Kennedy's treatment of Smith's alleged malingering: "Or the doctor may say, 'There's nothing the matter with you, Smith.' His notes may read: 'Another malingerer!' It involves a judgment that Smith ought to be working and that the doctor is not going to aid him in avoiding this responsibility. Another doctor could just as well decide otherwise" (p. 601).

At this point we have a use for the distinction between the different locutionary and illocutionary forces of one and the same utterance, or speech-act.[4]

Roughly speaking, the former is what is said while the latter is what is done by saying it. It was this distinction—or rather, this was one of the distinctions—that John Rex collapsed into a screaming chaos of confusion when, with reference to an Aunt Sally psychometrician, he wrote: "What he does when he rates individuals or groups of individuals on a scale of measured intelligence is to say and to predict that one group of individuals rather than another should have privileges. It is of little use, therefore, that a writer like Eysenck should protest that there is a total disjunction between his scientific observations and his moral views. Scientific observations have political implications."[5]

Suppose someone says, "This person has an IQ of 140 on the Binet scale." Then, what and all that they are maintaining, the entire locutionary force of their words, is the proposition thus conventionally expressed. By itself, as Eysenck was so right to say, this carries no prescriptive implications. However, when that same proposition is uttered in some suitable context, the actual uttering of it may have the elocutionary force of recommending the allocation of a privilege, or, for that matter, of a handicap. For us the moral of this is that Kennedy has no business to infer from the premise that a doctor's uttering, in such and such a context, the proposition "Smith is malingering" has this or that elocutionary force to the conclusion that that, and that alone, is also the locutionary force of the uttering.

Not only is this inference invalid, its conclusion is also false. "What sort of term is 'malingering'?" Kennedy asks. His reply is: "It involves a judgment that Smith ought to be working. . . . Another doctor could just as well decide otherwise." More than enough has been said to demonstrate that Kennedy interprets this as implying that the proposition "Smith is malingering" is what he would call a judgment and nothing else whatsoever but. This bold thesis is, nevertheless, quite grotesquely wrong. For to malinger is precisely to try to escape uncongenial tasks by pretending to be, in some relevant way, incapacitated. So, whatever else a doctor may be either saying or suggesting or doing when he says that someone is malingering, he most certainly is saying, whether honestly or dishonestly, whether truly or falsely, whether with or without warrant, that that person is not in fact, as she or he pretends to be, incapacitated. And that is a plain, or sometimes a not so plain, matter of neutrally descriptive fact.

(iv) Having satisfied himself that assertions of the presence or absence of illness are nothing but value judgments, and that they do not even in part characterize the conditions of the patient, Kennedy seeks a fresh stamping ground:

> So far I have concentrated on the term "illness." Let me now consider the concept of health. "Health," if it is to have any useful meaning, must refer to more than the mere absence of illness. It must have a positive quality. It must refer to all those factors which combine to represent man's aspirations and expectations. . . . This is captured in the World Health Organization's definition of health as "not the mere absence of disease, but total physical, mental and social well-being." (p. 602)

Kennedy's proposal is burdened by two fundamental faults. In the first place, there is no justification for the initial assumption that any useful and important notion must be essentially positive, notwithstanding that this seductive assumption was once harbored by Immanuel Kant. "The above definition of freedom is *negative*," Kant wrote of one disfavored candidate, "and consequently unfruitful as a way of grasping its essence."[6] The truth is—and both freedom and health provide illuminating illustrative instances—that often it is the ostensibly negative notion that "wears the trousers"; that "commonly enough the 'negative' (looking) word marks the (positive) abnormality, while the 'positive' word, *if* it exists, merely serves to rule out the suggestion of that abnormality."[7]

In the second place, it is preposterous to follow the world Health Organization in so redefining "health" that the word becomes synonymous with the expression "the supreme good for man." Since health has been traditionally and, surely, correctly acknowledged to be one, albeit only one, main element in that supreme good, this silly maneuver must leave all its executants looking for some raw new verbal recruits to undertake the job performed previously, to everyone's complete satisfaction, by the old-time hooray word "health."

Neither of these two objections occurs to Kennedy. Instead he notices that many doctors are among those who join in ridiculing such over-ambitious and all-embracing definitions. They object on the grounds that the scope of their own qualifications is limited: "We cannot do anything about these things. We've got enough on our hands dealing with the illnesses about us" (p. 602).

In view of all that Kennedy has already had to say about the alleged irrelevance of what we might uninstructedly have dignifed with the title "medical science," it is scarcely surprising that this modest professional objection leaves him unmoved. However—after concluding that, as just now redefined, "health is far too important to be left entirely to doctors"—he proceeds to distinguish disease from illness on lines similar to those indicated above.

Of course Kennedy does not really believe either that there is no such thing as medical science, or that, whether or not there is, it is irrelevant to the diagnosis of disease and the treatment of illness. Or, at any rate, he does not believe either of these nonsenses consistently and all the time. His trouble, and ours, is that, having grasped or half-grasped a few sociological and philosophical insights, he has succumbed to the very usual temptation to apply newly acquired notions where there is no purchase for them. Confusion is then worse confounded by his seeming inability to entertain the possibility that something might be either both this and that, or else in part this and in part that: that a single speech-act, for instance, might be both an exercise of power and an assertion of scientific fact; or that the meaning of a statement might be both in part neutrally descriptive and in part engaged prescriptive. The upshot is that Kennedy becomes committed to making and defending claims that he too finds, in his rather infrequent cooler moments, altogether unbelievable.

2. Mental illness and the medical model

In the whole length of section 1 there has been precious little direct mention of anything mental, as opposed to physical. Yet everything said there remains relevant to the announced topic of the present chapter. It is significant that the example from which Kennedy began, as well as others cited later, are instances of disputatious conditions which, if they are to be described in a medical vocabulary, will have to be characterized as defections from *mental* health, *mental* diseases, that is, or *mental* illnesses, or, most generally, *mental* disorders. Indeed there is much internal evidence suggesting that Kennedy has swallowed the thesis of *The Myth of Mental Illness* whole, and then extended it to embrace the physical also.[8]

(i) Much more important is the fact that this entire chapter is intended to defend what has come to be called, usually with a slight sniff, the medical model. The nub of this matter, happily epitomized in the masthead motto from Phillippe Pinel,[9] is that our paradigms are and must be (physical) health, (physical) disease, and (physical) illness. It is and can be only and precisely in so far as there are some crucial similarities between conditions typically so described and other conditions that those other conditions may properly and ingenuously be labelled either mental health or mental disease. An examination of the physical paradigms, and some sorting out of the commonest confusions surrounding them, is therefore essential to the main business in hand.

I said that I propose to defend the medical model, so interpreted. But there will be nothing defensive about this defense. Quite the reverse. For it is, and should upon all hands be seen to be, a scandal that there are nowadays many persons enjoying the high status and high salaries normally and rightly accorded to qualified and practising doctors who, sometimes somewhat superciliously at that, repudiate the very idea that there actually are mental illnesses—illnesses that it is their professional duty to treat and, hopefully, to cure. Maybe there are not, and the great Pinel and all his successors were, or are, mistaken. Certainly these despisers of the medical model are among those who are in the best position to know whether or not that is so. But if it is and there are indeed no mental illnesses, then the true moral is that both the APA and its several sister societies must go forthwith into an honorable, voluntary liquidation. It will not do, notwithstanding that it is—they tell me—rather widely done, to continue to luxuriate in the high status and high salaries aforementioned while in return practicing what is thus brazenly confessed to be a kind of not-medicine directed at not-illnesses. Such persons need to be reminded that, in earlier and in this respect better days, it used to be customary for those who lost their faith to relinquish Holy Orders.

I have spoken carefully if strongly of "the medical model, so interpreted." The point is that several of those writing about, and against, what they have called the medical model have in fact directed their attacks at something else, though frequently believing that those attacks also disposed of the pretended priority of the physical paradigm. One patient defender lists five such attacking theses, all entirely different from and independent of one another, and none constituting a head-on challenge to the fundamental here propounded.[10]

Another remarkable source and instance of confusion is to specify what is to be defended as "the medical model" in a vocabulary far removed from traditionally Hippocratic concerns. It has, for example, been said to involve three things. First, "There is an underlying *cause,* and consequently maladaptive behaviors cannot be treated directly because they are products of these causes." Second, "Changed behavior is not really important unless the 'real' trouble has been dealt with. . . ." Third, "The distinction between what the subject does, his behavior, and what the clinician expects, or knows to be there, is blurred, and failure to find the expected cause merely confirms the severity of the problem."[11] In a later volume of *Case Studies in Behavior Modification.* the same authors define "maladaptive behavior." It is "behavior that is considered inappropriate by those key people in a person's life who control reinforcers."[12] But if this is what those Erewhonian "straighteners" are proposing to "cure" then it is not illness, which is primarily a problem for the sick person. They are instead proposing to "cure" deviant conduct, which is a problem, where there is a problem at all, only for those shadowy and slightly sinister key figures "who control reinforcers."[13]

It is, indeed, radically misguided to introduce the term "behavior" into the present context. For this introduction overrides and obscures two distinctions that are fundamental, respectively, to medicine in general and to psychological medicine in particular: between what is or is not conduct, subject to the will, and between those "behaviors" that are and those that are not conventionally meaningful speech-acts.

Fortunately there is no call now to push any further in explorations of such fully realized possibilities of confusion and cross-purposes. Sufficient to reiterate the fundamental principle: it is and can be only and precisely in so far as there are crucial similarities between central and typical cases of (physical) health, (physical) disease, or (physical) illness, on the one hand, and, on the other, certain other conditions, that we shall be able ingenuously and straightforwardly to describe those other conditions as *mental* health, *mental* disease, or *mental* illness.

(ii) Developing suggestions put earlier, let us now distinguish two interpretations of the word "health," interpretations corresponding to the distinction already made between disease and illness. One is (to be) neutral and detached, and negatively defined in terms of the absence of diseases, and also—in so far as these are distinguished from diseases—of wounds, congenital defects, and other similar disorders. The other is the everyday sense, again defined negatively, but this time in terms of the absence of illness and of other such disorderly conditions understood as presumptively bad for the patients themselves. (By the way: the adverb "presumptively" is inserted, as it was once before, in order to take care of awkward cases of persons whose illnesses are welcome to them because they provide a let out. We do not want to have to say that severe asthma, for instance, whenever it ensures exemption for unpatriotic draftees, is not an illness.)

The main thing to emphasize about this proposal is that it opens up possibilities of incongruity: defections from health in the first, and scientifically neutral, understanding will not always and necessarily be congruous with defections from health in a lay understanding, nor yet the other way about. A number of trivial diseases do not make their patients ill. It is also at least conceptually possible that someone could feel very ill indeed, and in some dramatic way incapacitated, without there being any independently detectable physiological disorder to which this illness could be attributed. The first important practical consequence of this possibility of incongruity is that we shall need to be on guard against moves to treat and to "cure" conditions that are unhealthy in the first sense, but not in the second, the layperson's, and of course, the other way about.

Next we have to notice that in both senses of "healthy" the healthy may be statistically quite abnormal. This truth is, when we are thinking about illness, sufficiently obvious, but it is perhaps not quite so obvious that it is possible to construct a conception of an ideal specimen on the basis of a study of actual specimens, all of which may be in fact quite lamentably imperfect. A good proof-example, albeit of an artefact rather than an organism, is provided by the Norden bombsight. Apparently German technical intelligence in World War II, working with nothing but shattered specimens extracted from crashed American bombers, succeeded in reconstructing the design, complete down to the last detail.

One might well be too embarrassed to insist upon points so simple and so luminous were it not for the fact that, especially in the context of the mental, they are constantly neglected, even by people who ought to know better. For example, the neglect was systematic in an otherwise most painstaking, conscientious study of subject that surely above all others demanded the hammering reiteration of such distinctions. Nowhere in *Russia's Political Hospitals*[14] is there any sustained attempt to spell out the criteria for either mental disease or mental illness; nowhere is there any explicit statement of the difference between statistical normality, which is indeed socially relative, and the other sort, which is not.

(iii) Again developing suggestions put earlier, I propose that we should in its purely scientific understanding construe the term "health" by reference to the functions that the organism or its organs look as if they had been designed to fulfill. This is no arbitrary proposal. For the compact edition of the *Oxford English Dictionary* gives the definition: "Soundness of body; that condition in which its functions are duly and efficiently discharged." Disease in the relevant sense is, correspondingly, "A condition of the body, or of some part or organ of the body, in which its functions are disturbed or deranged; a morbid physical condition; a departure from the state of health especially when caused by a structural change." (Let us, instead of being petulant about the circularity introduced with the word "morbid," simply notice, without further comment, that this dictionary definition embraces wounds and those other disorders that laypersons would not ordinarily call diseases.)

The key concept is that of function, and what we have to attend to is not actuality but potentiality. The tongue of a Trappist is not diseased merely because during a penitential fast it is employed neither in tasting nor talking. My rose bushes are not diseased simply because they are not taking in water that is not there. It will be time to begin asking questions about disease if, when the Trappist eventually tries to exercise his tongue, he finds that he cannot, and if, when the bushes are inundated by a cloudburst, still no water enters the system.

Another far more important point comes out when those two examples are compared further. In so far as both show that what matters here is potentiality rather than actuality, they are the same. But in other respects they are crucially different. Suppose that water is supplied to my rose bushes, and that none is then absorbed. That will constitute a sufficient reason for inferring that there must be something organically wrong, although what is organically wrong will not necessarily be a disease. Contrast with this the case of the fasting Trappist. He is a person and not a plant. So the fact that he does not eat when food is provided is no more sufficient to show that there is something organically wrong than is the fact that he refrains from making passes at pretty girls. In his case, but not in the case of the plants, there is room for questions about what he can do if he wants and what he could do if he tried. Indeed it is essential to the description of this particular example that there actually is a gap between what he is doing and what he could be doing if he chose. For anyone who suggests that a dumb eunuch is fitted for a Trappist vocation is altogether failing to grasp what monasticism is about.

The fundamental reality giving purchase to such questions is universally familiar and altogether inescapable. Yet it is a reality that professing social and psychological scientists are often in the last degree reluctant to admit. The truth is that we are all, as rational animals, creatures that can, and cannot but, make choices. The theoretical and practical implications of this ineluctable reality are not only of enormous human interest but also, and in consequence, intensely controversial. So I will try first simply to point to the facts without employing any theoretically loaded terms. The facts are that in the happy bloom of health our bodies are partly, although always only partly, subject to our wills, and that there is a categorical difference between the claim that I moved my arm (without recourse to any extra-bodily apparatus) and the claim that my arm moved (without my moving it). Let us, in order to save words later, and in prudence following the grain of long-established verbal habits, distinguish movement of the former kind as movings, while reserving the word "motions" for movements of the second kind. Non-movings and non-motions will, of course, in both kinds constitute the limiting of special case: remaining stock still is, for present purposes, just as much a form of action as leaping to your feet.

Once this difference between movings and motions has been pointed out, with every care to eschew premature theoretical commitment, then it becomes altogether obvious and undeniable that we are all most immediately acquainted with innumerable specimens of both kinds. It is just not on to attempt to conceal the subsistence of a difference between, on the one hand, the case of, say, my liver, which however hard I try I cannot move at all except by shifting my whole torso, and, on the other hand, my hands, which I can move about whenever and however the fancy takes me. Nor is it possible to pretend that we are not forever, throughout all our waking hours, confronted with alternative possibilities of moving: when we are moving ourselves or any part of ourselves in one way, then we always could have moved ourselves or that part of ourselves in some other way; when we are contemplating any such moving, then there always is and has to be at least one alternative —if not another moving then simply not moving.

If the unreality of choice, as thus ostensibly defined and most directly and certainly known, really is a presupposition of the possibility of any psychological or sociological science, then the implication emerges totally clear: there could and can be no scientific psychology, no scientific sociology. No wonder that so many psychopersons and sociopersons, convinced that this presupposition does indeed obtain, will say or do almost anything in order to hush-up or to divert attention from the most central peculiarity of the nature of man! (I offer the shamefully trendy coinages "psychoperson" and "socioperson" to satisfy two long felt wants: a single word embracing practitioners of all the would-be scientific psychological disciplines—psychology, psychoanalysis, psychiatry, and so on, and another similar single word embracing practitioners of all the aspiring social sciences—sociology, social anthropology, demography, and so on.)

I shall find occasion later to pay brief attention to one or two of the commonest misconceptions encouraging the belief that psychological and sociological enquiry shows this most manifest fact of our nature not to be a fact at all. But it has to be said at once that the fundamental distinctions just now drawn are not to be disposed of by objecting that there are marginal cases that do not fit easily into either of two mutually exclusive categories, or that the differences pointed are to be discounted as mere differences of degree. Such objections can be, indeed are, made against almost every distinction of human concern. They should be dismissed. No doubt there are marginal cases. But, so long as the decisive majority is not marginal, we can and must insist on the difference between those that are centrally and paradigmatically of one kind and those that are, equally centrally and paradigmatically, of the other kind. Nor is it right to sneer at all differences of degree as *mere* differences of degree. The difference between this and that is, for present purposes, a difference of degree if and only if there is a spectrum of actual or possible cases shading by almost imperceptible steps from this to that. Are we therefore to disrespect as *merely* matters of degree the differences between sanity and insanity, age and youth, or riches and poverty?[15]

Suppose then that we take it as given that there is such a thing as being able to move or not to move at will, and that, in a most fundamental sense just now ostensibly explained, every agent could have done other than they did or did not do. How does this bear upon issues of the nature of health, construed as a theoretical ideal? In this way: to say that disease in a person is "a condition of the body, or of some part or organ of the body, in which its functions are disturbed or deranged" is to provoke the question whether these functions do or do not include, besides mere motions, some movings or abstentions from movings.

The response to this gets us to the heart of the matter. For the concept of capability, of what we can or cannot do if we try, is central to the notion of (physical) health—at least in its primary application to human beings. For a man to be fit is not for him to do, but only to be able to do, whatever it is that he is fit to do. Certainly, to be fit to do what a sick or otherwise unfit man cannot do, does in fact always require the actual or potential proper functionings of organs that never are subject to the will. Nevertheless the criterion of the fit man's fitness is not the propriety of these actual or hypothetical motions but rather his capacities for not necessarily proper movings and not movings. So, if a definition of "disease" in terms of the disturbance or derangement of functions is to be retained, we shall have to take it that the function of whatever is normally subject to our wills precisely is to be in this normal way thus subject, while at least the prime function of those organs not subject to our wills must be, correspondingly, to ensure the continuing efficiency and due subordination of those organs that are normally so subordinate. Death, as the end of all fitness or anything, is the ultimate limiting case of total malfunctioning.

In this perspective it becomes obvious that and why we cannot go on to apply the same idea to the whole organism, insisting with Aristotle, that we too, like the organs of which we are composed, must have a function.[16]

The question now arises how health, disease, and disorder—in these theoretical and purely scientific understandings—relate to health, illness, and other conditions construed as being of necessity either presumptively good or presumptively bad for the persons so endowed or so afflicted. When and why do defections from health, in this understanding, constitute suitable cases for treatment?

In *An Introduction to the Principles of Morals and Legislation* (VI, 7) Jeremy Bentham wrote, "Health is the absence of disease, and consequently of all those kinds of pain which are among the symptoms of disease. A man may be said to be in a state of health when he is not conscious of any uneasy sensations, the primary seat of which can be anywhere in his body." It was characteristic of Bentham, yet it is wrong, to present "uneasy sensations" as the heart of the matter. For it is entirely possible to suffer an illness, even a fatal illness, without feeling (seriously) ill. Happily, this seems to have been the case with David Hume's terminal condition—"a wasting disease of the bowels." One hopes that, with the help of modern techniques of anaesthesia and sedation, the same is becoming true of more and more actual illnesses. Certainly it is usual for patients of an illness to feel ill, especially if that illness is allowed to take its course, and certainly that is presumptively bad for them. Nevertheless the crux remains, surely, not pain but incapacitation.

The reason why medical treatment is desirable is at the same time the reason why it is necessary. For although patients might have been able to avoid getting into their present conditions, those conditions themselves are conditions of incapacitation, and, as such, are precisely not of a kind that their patients are able to escape immediately, unaided, of their own volition. This again—though the point seems to elude many psychiatrists called to give expert testimony[17]—is the reason why so many jurisdictions now rule that no one is to be held criminally responsible for any behavior, or for any failure to act, which is the inevitable result of some disease.

(iv) Much of what has been, and is, put down as some sort of defection from mental health does not satisfy this essential condition. But it is perverse to take this as a proof that there is no viable concept of mental health. Yet exactly that is done in a much reprinted and much respected work, *Social Science and Social Pathology:*

> For . . . the psychopath makes nonsense of every attempt to distinguish the sick from the healthy delinquent by the presence or absence of a psychiatric syndrome, or by symptoms of mental disorder which are independent of his objectionable behavior. In his case no such symptoms can be diagnosed because it is just the absence of them which causes him to be classed as psychopathic. He is in fact, par excellence, and without any shame or qualification, the model of the circular process by which mental abnormality is inferred from antisocial behaviour while anti-social behavior is explained by mental abnormality."[18]

Yes, indeed: the astringent conclusions of the second two sentences are as sound as they were characteristic of their author. Yet they constitute no warrant whatsoever for the first statement. Certainly, where there neither is nor is going to be any incapacitation there can be no ill health, whether physical or mental. So what really follows is that the correct next question for the author, accepting that such psychopaths are not in fact sick, becomes this: whether they should, after all, be punished as mainline criminals, whether they should be treated as if they were patients of some illness dangerous to others, or whether they should be handled in some new third way yet to be constructed. For us the question is whether there is room anywhere for a kind of sickness to be distinguished as mental.

There have been, I suggest, various legitimate concepts here, at least two of which can find proper application. Their differences are determined by differences in the interpretation of the distinguishing adjective. Plato, who was the first major figure to develop a notion of psychological health, construed the key Greek word *psyche* as referring to a sort of incorporeal substance, taking all the behavior that distinguishes men as rational agents as the manifesting work of these themselves unobservable entities—entities that are, he thought, what men ultimately and essently are. This provided, at any rate in theory, a satisfying clearcut principle for separating the sphere of psychological from that of physical medicine. However, though much loose talk about the putative activities and interactions of the Unconscious and the Preconscious and the Conscious, of the Ego and the Id and the Superego, does encourage interpretation along such Platonic lines, it is at least doubtful whether any contemporary psychiatrists—with the possible exceptions of some Roman Catholics and Catholicizing Jungians—really intend their theoretical notions to be read in so substantial a way.

Turning quickly from Plato to the modern period, we find mental disorder generally understood as an affliction of the intellect. Thus Philippe Pinel, who did so much to have the demented cared for as the victims of a kind of sickness, once wrote: "The storms of the revolution stirred up corresponding tempests in the passions of men, and overwhelmed not a few in a total ruin of their distinguished birthright of reason." He proceeded to provide a memorable illustration—the unfortunate patient who believed that he had been first guillotined and then afterwards reconstituted—if that is the appropriate word—with someone else's head.[19]

A different yet possibly complementary conception is to be found in its sharpest form in the early Freud's handling of hysteria. The disease gave rise to symptomatic tics and paralyses. The warrant for speaking of a disease or an illness was that these constitute incapacitations: the inability to prevent certain motions in the one case, and the inability in the other to effectuate any movings. The warrant for introducing the epithet "mental" was that, absent any presently discernible organic lesions, there were supposed to be psychological causes, in particular unconscious motives, unconscious purposes, and unconscious intentions.

3. An engagement with Thomas Szasz

It is now over thirty years since *The Myth of Mental Illness* was first published, and the bombardment of explosive books that the author, Dr. Thomas Szasz, then began has perhaps slackened but not yet ceased. That bombardment has, surely, done a power of good. This good has been to show how much that has been put down as mental illness (and treated as such, even compulsorily) is falsely so described. Nevertheless I must now, and by no means for the first time, argue that Szasz is mistaken in his contention that there can be no application for any concept of mental illness.

(i) Szasz begins by picking Freud's handling of hysteria as his paradigm and suggesting, if not in this way outright saying, that most of what the lay person would think of as more or less gross insanity results from neurological disorder. In chapter 1, "Charcot's Contribution to the Problem of Hysteria," it looks as if Szasz is going to adopt a bold, uncompromising radical stance: patients classified by Charcot and his successors as mentally sick were and are, with whatever justification, in fact malingering. Szasz quotes Freud:

First of all Charcot's work restored dignity to the subject; gradually
the sneering attitude, which the hysteric could reckon on meeting when
she told her story, was given up; *she was no longer a malingerer,
since Charcot had thrown the whole weight of his authority on the
side of the reality and objectivity of hysterical phenomena* (p. 25).

But later, taking a hint from the passages which he himself itali-
cized in this quotation, Szasz allows the properly crucial issue of fact
to drop out of view. The development begins in his chapter 2, "The
Logic of Classification and the Problem of Malingering." At first it
is tacitly recognized that the patients are not, after all, malingerers: "The
new rules are: 'Persons *disabled* by phenomena which only look like
illnesses of the body (i.e. hysteria) should be classified as ill' " (p. 41,
italics added). But then we read, a few pages further on: "With Freud
and psychoanalysis . . . hysteria was . . . viewed as unconscious malingering" (p. 46). Before this second chapter is out we have met an American psychoanalyst arguing that "malingering is always the sign of a
disease often more severe than neurotic disorder." This psychoanalyst
then adds the studiously preposterous comment: "It is a disease which
to diagnose requires particularly keen diagnostic acumen" (p. 48). By
the end of chapter 7, "Hysteria and Language," the development is
complete. There is now no longer any question asked as to whether
patients are or are not in fact incapacitated:

> From the standpoint of our present analysis the entire change in
> renaming certain illness-like forms of behavior from "malingering" to
> "hysteria" (and "mental illness") can be understood as nothing but
> a linguistic change . . . for the purpose of achieving a new type of
> action-orientedness. . . . The verbal change as first advocated by
> Charcot, served to command those dealing with "hysterics" to aban-
> don their moral-condemnatory attitude toward them and to adopt
> instead a solicitous and benevolent attitude, such as befitted the
> physician vis-a-vis his patient (p. 133).

Consistent with this development, which must surely have provided the
main inspiration for the corresponding item in the Kennedy manifesto,
is the apparent failure to note, in discussing a quoted description of

the notorious Ganser syndrome, categorical claims that the patients were in fact in the appropriate dimensions authentically incapacitated (pp. 250–51).

Insofar as the issue here is indeed whether we are or are not dealing with conscious and deliberate malingerers, the philosopher in a professional capacity can at best hope to contribute only a few clarifying observations before handing the investigation over to the medically qualified, suggesting perhaps that they might get many invaluable tips for testing out of the memoirs of doctors who have served their time in the armed forces. But if Szasz is after all prepared to live with the admissions of genuine disability made in chapter 2, then it has to be emphasized that there is no mileage to be gotten here out of the constantly reiterated assertion that such supposed mental sickness cannot be referred to any discernible neurological disorder. For sickness, like illness, can be identified without appeal to sophisticated medical science, while the point of adding the qualification "mental" simply is to indicate a psychological rather than a physiological aetiology.

(ii) It remains only to list one or two of the confusions that may have misled Szasz, and which surely mislead others, to deny, neglect, or minimize fundamental distinctions of the kind adumbrated above. The first confusion involves the first Freudian conception of the unconscious. We need to notice, what scarcely ever has been noticed, that in introducing talk of unconscious motives, unconscious purposes, and unconscious what have you, Freud made not one but two new conceptual moves. The obvious change was to permit the attribution of motives, purposes, and what have you to persons unaware of the fact—or who even vehemently and honestly deny—that they are so endowed. The much less obvious yet at least equally important change was to permit us to say that these unconscious motives or whatever give rise to bits of behavior that are, in my terms, motions rather than movings.[20] In so far as this is correct, only the most perverse Freudians could speak of unconscious malingering. For it is a necessary truth about your genuine malingerers that they willfully pretend to be incapacitated in ways in which actually they are not, whereas an unconscious malingerer would, presumably, be genuinely incapacitated without (consciously) intending so to be—that is to say, no sort of malingerer at all.

Second, all the human sciences—psychological, sociological, and historical—labor to show that and how, in the light of the perceived circumstances and of their own background and past development, people would not have been expected to do other than they did. It is all too easy and too common to infer from whatever successes may be achieved through the investigations of these sciences that, in reality, no one ever has any choice. Though perennially and powerfully tempting, this inference is, nevertheless, altogether fallacious. Put as a pithy paradox the truth is that ordinarily we can only say that someone had no (real) choice, that they could not have done other than they did, when we are sure that, in the more fundamental senses ostensibly defined in section 2 (iii) above, they had and they did.

Consider, if I may license myself to redeploy two favorite illustrations, first, Luther before the Diet of Worms, and second, the unfortunate businessman receiving from the Godfather an offer he could not refuse. Certainly those acquainted with Luther might have known that he would in fact stand there, and that it would appear to him, in the everyday interpretation of those words, that "I can no other. So help me God." Yet none of this constitutes reason for drawing the abusive conclusion that Luther remained there erect and stationary because, and only because, he had fallen victim to a sudden paralysis.

The situation is the same with the man challenged by the Mafia gunman: "I shall within thirty seconds have either your signature or your brains on this paper." When we say that such a man had no choice what we mean is not that he had no choice, but that he had no tolerable choice. An agent who acts under compulsion, however severe that compulsion, remains nonetheless an agent. He could, as some would, defy that compulusion. It is entirely different with the errant Mafioso, instantly gunned down from behind. He does not act under compulsion since in the moment of death he ceases forever both to be and to act.

Any client of that second misconception—the first one about the presuppositions of the human sciences—is bound to be reluctant to acknowledge the realities of choice. A third misconception, which is similarly sure to sustain a similar reluctance, consists in the conviction that full determination by causes is incompatible with choice. Although this may well be true in the sense of "cause" in which the effects caused are not human actions, it is certainly false in the sense of "cause" in which we speak of the causes of that very different and peculiar type of effect.

Most of us are not all the time inquiring into the causes of our own conduct. We are told:

> But that is no reason for thinking that if you did preoccupy yourself with these causes you would not find them at work. You may remember that Sir Francis Galton was so much impressed with this possibility that for some time he kept account in a notebook of the occasions on which he made important choices with a full measure of this feeling of freedom; then shortly after each choice he turned his eye backward in search of constraints that might have been acting on him stealthily. He found it so easy to bring such constraining factors to light that he surrendered to the determinist view.[21]

Oddly enough Szasz did once hold the secret of this knot in his hands, yet still did nothing to disentangle it. Thus he remarks: "It should be kept in mind . . . that my desire to see a play is the 'cause' of my going to the theatre in a sense very different from that in which we speak of 'causal laws' in physics" (p. 88). So it should, and so it is. The unexploited secret is, in a nutshell, that whereas physical causes necessitate, the other sort of causes—call them personal causes—do not. For such personal causes, to borrow a phrase from Leibniz, incline yet do not necessitate.

Given the sufficient (physical) causes of, say, an explosion or an eclipse, then of course it follows necessarily from the statement that these are their sufficient causes that those effects will in fact occur. Furthermore, it is also the case that these cause events must physically (as opposed to logically) necessitate those effect events, that these must make the occurrence of those as a matter of fact inevitable, and their nonoccurrence correspondingly impossible. With personal causes the case is altogether different. When, for instance, you give me or I give you cause to celebrate we may each thereby make it likely or predictable or intelligible that the other will in fact celebrate. Yet there is no question of ineluctable necessity or absolute impossibility save in the inescapable need to choose. For to refuse to choose is itself to choose to refuse.

4. A Parthian shot

If, as has been suggested, there can be no necessitating causes of any item of behavior that is at the same time an action, then we are all of us always as agents (physically) uncaused causes. Those who crave the putative profundities of what Marx and Engels and their followers used to rate as classical German philosophy should delight to admit a new member to the club of those distinctively human characteristics that religion is supposed to alienate from man on to its actually nonexistent God.[22] Certainly there will be others who will see here the most striking of all examples of men making gods or God in a human image. For is not the God of traditional theism the Uncaused Cause of all things?

Notes

1. See chapter 6, above, and compare Antony Flew, *An Introduction to Western Philosophy,* rev. ed. (London: Thames and Hudson, 1989), pp. 83 55 and 487.

2. See chapters 1 and 2, above, and, for an account of what was and was not original to Darwin, compare Antony Flew, *Darwinian Evolution* (London: Granada/Paladin, 1984).

3. See, for instance, Antony Flew, *A Rational Animal: Philosophical Essays on the Nature of Man* (Oxford: Clarendon, 1978), chapter 2.

4. See J. L. Austin, *How to Do Things with Words* (Oxford: Clarendon, 1962).

5. "Nature versus Nurture: The Significance of the Revived Debate," in K. Richardson and D. Spears, eds., *Race, Culture and Intelligence* (Harmondsworth: Penguin Books, 1973), pp. 168–69.

6. *The Groundwork of the Metaphysic of Morals,* translated by H. J. Paton as *The Moral Law* (London: Hutchinson, 1948), p. 114.

7. J. L. Austin, *Philosophical Papers* (Oxford: Clarendon, 1961), pp. 45–

51, italics original.

8. Thomas Szasz, *The Myth of Mental Illness* (New York: Dell, 1961).

9. A facsimile of the 1806 first English edition of Philippe Pinel, *A Treatise on Insanity,* was published by Hafner of New York in 1962.

10. See the note on page 62 of Christopher Boorse, "What a Theory of Mental Health Should Be," *Journal of the Theory of Social Behavior* (1976).

11. L. P. Ullman and L. Krasner, *Studies in Behavior Modification* (New York: Holt, Rinehart and Winston, 1965), p. 5, italics original.

12. L. P. Ullman and L. Krasner, *Case Studies in Behavior Modification* (New York: Hold, Rinehart and Winston, 1966), p. 20.

13. Everyone who has had dealings at the lower levels with what Tom Lehrer taught the less stuffy among us to call Edbiz, must be all too familiar with the practice of treating those presenting disciplinary problems to their teachers as if they themselves necessarily "have a problem." (The truth is that, while such troublemakers necessarily are, they do not necessarily themselves have, a problem.)

14. S. Block and P. Reddaway, *Russia's Political Hospitals* (London: Futura, 1978). The most relevant passages are on pp. 23–27, 62, 67, 160, 165–66, and 248–55.

15. Compare, for instance, my *Thinking Straight* (Buffalo, N.Y.: Prometheus Books, 1975), sections 7 to 13 ff.

16. *Nicomachean Ethics,* 1 (7) 11–16: 1097b29–1098a20.

17. See, for instance, H. Fingarette, *The Meaning of Criminal Insanity* (Berkeley, Los Angeles, and London: California University Press, 1972), pp. 97–120, and compare my *Crime or Disease* (London: Macmillan, 1973).

18. B. Wootton, *Social Science and Social Pathology* (London: Allen and Unwin, 1967), p. 250.

19. Pinel, *A Treatise on Insanity,* pp. 9 and 69.

20. See, first, subsection 6(iii) of chapter 2 above, and compare section 5 of chapter 5.

21. B. Blanshard, "The Case for Determinism," in S. Hook, ed., *Determinism and Freedom in the Age of Modern Science* (New York: New York University Press, 1958), p. 6.

22. See Ludwig Feuerbach, *The Essence of Christianity,* trans. George Eliot (New York: Harper, 1957). Yes, the translator was also the author of *Middlemarch.* And yes, this book, first published in 1841, was the original spring from which flowed all the talk about alienation in Karl Marx, *The Economic and Philosophical Manuscripts of 1844,* a flow that was later to become torrential.

Part Three

Scientific Socialism?

8

Communism:
The Philosophical Foundations

1. A German philosopher

"Karl Marx was a German philosopher." It is with this seminal sentence that Leszek Kolakowski begins his great work, *The Main Currents of Marxism: Its Rise, Growth and Dissolution* (Oxford: Clarendon, 1978). Both the two terms in the predicate expression are crucial. It is most illuminating to think of Marx as originally a philosopher, even though nothing in his vastly voluminous works makes any significant contribution to philosophy in any academic understanding of that term.[1] It is also essential to recognize that for both Marx and Engels philosophy was always primarily, indeed almost exclusively, what they and their successors called classical German philosophy. This was a tradition seen as achieving its climactic fulfillment in the work of Hegel, and one that they themselves identified as a main stimulus to their own thinking. Thus Engels, in *Ludwig Feuerbach and the End of Classical German Philosophy,* claimed, "The German working-class movement is the inheritor of German classical philosophy."[2]

So we have to presume that neither Marx nor Engels ever studied Locke's *Essay concerning Human Understanding* or the philosophical works of Hume. Certainly, even if the founding fathers of Marxism were in any way acquainted with these books, they never realized that they needed to come to terms with challenges contained therein. For both men were to all appearance totally innocent of Hume's fundamental distinction between propositions stating, or purporting to state, only "the relations of ideas," and propositions stating, or purporting to state, "matters of fact and real existence."[3]

Never having addressed themselves to Locke's naturalistic account of the origins and development of our conceptual equipment, and never having been subjected to probings by what among English-speaking philosophers is now nicknamed "Hume's Fork," Marx and Engels were at no time forced to appreciate that substantial discoveries of "matters of fact and real existence" cannot be made by studying only particular ideas and "the relations of ideas." Nor, it seems, did they ever make the crucial distinction between logical and physical necessity. The former belongs to the world of language and discourse, the world of the relations of ideas and of propositions, whereas the latter is a matter of fact and real existence in the universe around us. Much of the prophetic writing of Marx and Engels must in consequence fall under the ban imposed by part III of the concluding section XII in Hume's *Enquiry Concerning Human Understanding.*[4]

Apologists have attempted to brush Kolakowski's insightful contention aside. Thus Ralph Miliband wrote in a critical notice: "Marx was not, in fact, a 'German philosopher' . . . no 'philosopher' of the kind Kolakowski has in mind could have written *Capital,* or would have felt any need to write it."[5] Again, in a slighter review, Tony Benn claimed that "unlike many other philosophers . . . Marx began by a deep study of the real world itself—in order to understand how it worked and why, and then drew his own conclusions."[6]

But there is abundant evidence to show that Benn's biographical claim is false. It is indeed the direct reverse of the truth. For all the social and political doctrines peculiarly associated with Marx, all those enormously influential doctrines that were presented most dramatically in 1848 in the *Communist Manifesto*—the doctrines, that is to say, of an inexorable yet always conflict-torn historical development, a development bound in the not impossibly remote future to find its blessed consummation in the revolutionary triumph of the class to end all classes—all these conclusions were originally derived, by what Marx himself described as a philosophical analysis, not from "a deep study of the real world itself," but from a priori maneuvers with various abstract concepts.

These seminal, revolutionary ideas, and all the massively important would-be factual contentions in which they are embodied were, therefore, not the final product of long years of labor poring over blue books in the Reading Room of the British Museum, but instead themselves provided the original incentive to embark upon those political and economic studies that eventually, in 1867, resulted in the publication of the first volume of *Capital*—this being as much of his long promised *magnum opus* as Marx himself could ever be brought to complete. Not only were all the major Marxist contentions presented in the *Communist Manifesto,* years before Marx first applied for his reader's card, but they are also to be found in his earlier books and manuscripts.

In fact it was in 1845, before he had even thought of moving to London, that Marx signed a contract to compose the great book that was supposed to be going to provide empirical confirmation for revelatory conclusions already drawn by a priori analysis. Characteristically Marx proceeded to spend the remarkably—authors might say enviably—generous advance. But no book was produced under that contract, and the wretched publisher got nothing for his money. The whole revealing story of how long and how persistently Engels had to labor to induce Marx actually to create that confirmatory book is best told in the most salutary and least devout of all the now numerous biographies.[7]

2. Dialectical materialism and dialectical logic

In the nineteen thirties and forties what was meant by the expression "Marxist philosophy"—in the narrower, academic understanding of the word "philosophy"—was dialectical materialism.[8] The authoritative primary text, to which all Communist parties in communion with Moscow used to refer, was J. V. Stalin's *Dialectical and Historical Materialism.*

In the British Isles this was often supplemented by David Guest, *Dialectical Materialism* (London: Lawrence and Wishart, 1939), a work published only after the author was during the Spanish Civil War killed in action. Much later, following Khrushchev's secret speech to the Twentieth Congress, some "New Left" fellow travellers, laboring to escape the now abusive epithet "Stalinist," began to contend that the *Economic and Philosophical Manuscripts of 1844* were the true foundation documents of Marxist philosophy, and, hence, that its key word was not "dialectics" but "alienation."

In that now remote earlier period, before the Twentieth Congress, standard expositions typically started by contrasting dialectical materialism with the mechanical materialism of the seventeenth and eighteenth centuries. That, it was alleged, did not recognize development in the universe whereas dialectical materialism put heavy emphasis upon development, thus, supposedly, providing a kind of justification for transforming capitalist into socialist and, ultimately, communist societies. Here it was *de rigueur* to quote Stalin: "Contrary to metaphysics, dialectics holds that nature is not a state of rest and immutability, strangulation and immutability, but a state of continuous movement and change . . . where something is always arising and developing, and something always disintegrating and dying away."

At this point well-girded unbelievers ought to raise and to press awkward questions: "Who were these 'mechanical materialists of the seventeenth and eighteenth centuries,' who somehow contrived not to 'recognize development in the universe'?"; "Who are the twentieth-century metaphysicians who, in the spirit of the pre-Socratic Parmenides of Elea, allegedly assert that there is no such thing as change or motion?"; and "Why is a general emphasis upon development—as something which *is* in fact always occurring—thought somehow to justify the particular change from capitalism to communism as one which actually will and/or *ought* to occur?"[9]

To emphasize "development in the universe," even with the specific purpose of justifying the changing of capitalist society into a communist one, could scarcely constitute an appropriate or sufficient principle of division between dialectical materialism and materialism without prefix or suffix. Nor should we carry things much further forward if we, like Engels in *Anti-Dühring*,[10] were to add to the emphasis upon change and development an insistence upon universal connectedness—"the altogetherness of everything."

There is, of course, more to it than this, if little better. For the Marxist dialectic maintains that development is somehow realized by the unity and struggle of opposites. In the oft-quoted words of Lenin: "The unity (coincidence, identity, equal action) of opposites is conditional, temporary, transitory, relative. The struggle of mutually exclusive opposites is absolute, just as development and motion are absolute."

Some light is perhaps thrown on these dark sayings when later we are told, first, that, according to Marx, material development itself follows the process of thesis-antithesis-synthesis, and, hence, that whereas Hegel's dialectics were idealistic, those of Marx were materialistic. One supposed consequence is that Marxists are supposed to have developed what is called "Dialectical Logic." This maintains that the principle of contradiction is in error, since the change and development characteristic of all things implies that they somehow contain and embrace contradiction.

To all this stuff the most fundamental and overwhelming objection is one that has perhaps never been put better than it was by Herr Eugen Dühring, in the very *Course of Philosophy* against which Engels directed that most famous polemic, *Anti-Dühring:* "Contradiction is a category which can only appertain to a combination of thoughts, but not to reality. There are no contradictions in things, or, to put it in another way, contradiction applied to reality is itself the apex of absurdity."

Engels quotes these two sentences in the first paragraph of the first of the two chapters specifically devoted to this subject. He then complains: "This is practically all we are told about dialectics in the *Course of Philosophy*" (p. 134). Though no doubt a very short way with dissent, it surely is at any rate sufficient for the nonspecialist. For Dühring was absolutely right to insist that it is radically and irredeemably wrongheaded thus to collapse the fundamental distinction between, on the one hand, (verbal) contradictions, which can obtain only between propositions asserted, and, on the other hand, (physical) conflicts and tensions, which can occur only between animals or inanimate objects or other phenomena of the nonlinguistic world. A little more, however, should perhaps be said, not about "dialectical logic," but about dialectical materialism as supposedly somehow scientific. There can be no question that Engels himself approached dialectical materialism through the natural sciences. Thus, in the unfinished manuscript eventually published as *The Dialectics of Nature,* he maintained that, whereas "the laws of dialectics" were by Hegel developed "as mere laws of *thought,*" his own concern was to show that they "are really laws of development of nature, and therefore are valid also for theoretical natural sciences."[11]

Three of these putative dialectical laws of nature are listed in the first paragraph of chapter 2, "Dialectics"; (a) "The law of transformation of quantity into quality and *vice versa*"; (b) "The law of the interpenetration of opposites"; and (c) "The law of the negation of the negation." After this Engels proceeded to list what he saw as some of "the most striking individual illustrations from nature" of the operation of these putative laws. For wherever Engels looked he found such illustrations, some perhaps more impressively persuasive than others, but all always serving as further perceived confirmations for his theories.

To anyone who has ever been to school with Popper this itself provides sufficient reason for suspicion.[12] For the semantic content of these "dialectical laws" is so elusive and so indeterminate that prejudiced ingenuity will have little difficulty in interpreting anything whatever that is found actually to happen as constituting the $n + 1^{\text{th}}$ confirming instance.

To possess the logical form of a law of nature a proposition must imply that, under conditions of such and such a sort, it is physically necessary that conceivable events of one kind must occur, and physically impossible that conceivable events of another kind could occur. And, since every proposition is equivalent to the negation of its own negation ($p \equiv \sim \sim p$), the extent and content of what is asserted by asserting any proposition is precisely proportionate to the extent and content of what is denied by denying that proposition. We have, therefore, to conclude, first, that until and unless our dialecticians can specify some sorts of conceivable phenomena that their "dialectical laws" preclude as physically impossible, those "laws" will remain perfectly vacuous, and that, second, if and when such sorts of conceivable but practically precluded phenomena have been specified, the substance and importance of the resulting laws must be precisely proportionate to the extent and nature of what is thereby precluded.

Communists make much of the necessities and impossibilities involved in laws of nature, and especially of the (in Popper's sense[13]) historicist laws of historical development that they believe were discovered by the founding fathers of their faith. Since, as we shall be seeing later, its revelation of the alleged inevitabilities supposedly guaranteed by those historicist laws has been and remains the chief attraction of their system, that is scarcely surprising.

3. The faulty philosophical foundations

As was pointed out previously, it is a straightforward matter of established biographical fact that all the distinctive essentials of Marxism were originally derived, not from "a deep study of the world itself," but from a priori maneuvers with various abstract concepts, maneuvers that appear to have been completed in 1844. This might not have mattered much: if only the resulting system of ideas had happened to correspond fairly closely to the realities, or if only Marx himself had been prepared openmindedly to investigate how far, or even whether, it truly did. But neither of these alternative protases comes anywhere near the truth. Here we are concerned solely with the second. Perhaps the most significant indication that, about all the issues that they perceived as fundamental, the minds of Marx and Engels were from then on entirely closed is that no one seems to be able to point to any passage in all the voluminous collected works in which either of them recognizes anything as constituting a serious difficulty for what in their correspondence they always described as "our view" or "our theory."

There were, I suggest, two main reasons for this closure of their minds. First: all the most personally meaningful activities and associations of both Marx and Engels were based upon the intellectual system (not first but) most vividly and most compellingly proclaimed in the *Communist Manifesto*. So both of them found it all too easy to yield to temptations to suppress or to distort any apparently irreconcilable facts. Consider, for instance, what Marx wrote to Engels in a letter dated August 15, 1857, a letter that has for us a double interest, in that it also reveals that for Marx himself dialectics was in large part a tactic of obfuscation:

> I took the risk of prognosticating in this way, as I was compelled to substitute for you as correspondent at the *Tribune*. . . . It is possible I may be discredited. But in that case it will still be possible to pull through with the help of a bit of dialectics. It goes without saying that I phrased my forecasts in such a way that I would prove to be right also in the opposite case.

The second reason for the closure of minds was that Marx was a German philosopher, or in deference to such giants of earlier generations as Leibniz and Albertus Magnus, perhaps we should say that he was a young, post-Hegelian, German philosopher. As such Marx never learnt the lessons Locke and Hume had to teach. Above all Marx seems always to have taken it absolutely for granted that the main lines of future historical development can be discovered by analyzing concepts, that such abstract analysis can yield some knowledge of necessary and therefore inexorable historicist laws of historical development. Certainly much of the appeal of Marxism always has been, and still remains, that it is believed to provide (not a philosophical but) a scientific proof that—as crude Comrade Khrushchev used to say—"Communism is at the end of all the roads in the world: we shall bury you."

In the *Economic and Philosophical Manuscripts of 1844,* Marx complains that the classical economists fail to bring out how "apparently accidental circumstances" are nothing but "the expression of a necessary development." The climactic end of that "necessary development" is proclaimed in the final sentences of the first section of the *Communist Manifesto*: "What the bourgeoisie, therefore, produces, above all, is its own gravediggers. Its fall and the victory of the proletariat are equally inevitable." Six years later, in an article on "The English Middle Class" for the *New York Daily Tribune* for August 1, 1854, Marx allowed that, "though temporary defeat may await the working classes, great social and economical laws are in operation which must eventually ensure their triumph."

In 1867, in the original German preface to the first volume of *Capital*, the book so long awaited as the philosopher prophet's promised proof, Marx explains "why England is used as the chief illustration in the development of my theoretical ideas." Everything discovered there will eventually be just as applicable elsewhere:

> Intrinsically, it is not a question of the higher or lower degree of development of the social antagonisms that result from the natural laws of capitalist production. It is a question of these laws themselves, of these tendencies working with iron necessity towards inevitable results. The country that is more developed industrially only shows, to the less developed, the image of its own future.

The only accounts of the Last Days that Marx himself was prepared to provide were studiously sketchy and abstract. Yet, surely, they should still be sufficient to make his prophecies altogether incredible. It was in their day all very well for the Saints and for the Fathers to develop a Christian historicism: beginning with the creation of the universe itself and of Adam, the man made in God's image; continuing to the predestined and foreseen Fall; on to the Incarnation; and culminating in the final establishment of God's Kingdom upon Earth. For in that scheme the particular species of our species-being was from the beginning created by the Almighty with an all-seeing eye to its eventual and truly human destiny. We were created, in the splendid words of the old Scottish *Prayer Book,* "to glorify God and to enjoy him forever." In that scheme the inexpugnable guarantee that the Kingdom will indeed come, never thereafter to be undermined or overthrown, lay in the absolute power and promise of Omnipotence.

How different it is with the secular substitute, the true People's Democratic Republic of Marx. Here the existence of God and his providence have been contemptuously denied. Supposedly we are all atheists now, altogether rejecting religion as an obsolete illusion. It is, in the words of the *Manifesto,* nothing but "the cry of the hard-pressed creature, the heart of the heartless world, the soul of the soulless circumstance, the laudanum of the masses."

How then can we fail to see the massive implausibility of this Marxist eschatology, indeed its internal incoherence? The whole continuing human life-process has perhaps never before been presented in so harsh a light. For instance, the *Communist Manifesto* proper begins, "The history of all hitherto existing society is the history of class struggles," and "law, morality, religion," along with everything else once thought to stand between humanity and the abyss, are nothing but feeble fig leaves miserably failing to conceal unlovely class interests. Yet this long succession of savage struggles is, we are assured, bound to end—and to end pretty soon too—in the annihilating victory of a class to end all classes; a victory to be followed without fail, again in pretty short order, by the establishment of a conflict-free utopia; a utopia in which, harried by no class or other group conflicts, "the free development of each will be a condition of the free development of all."

So how, we should now ask, does the atheist Marx come by his secular revelation? It was, to borrow what should be the famous and revealing words of Engels, by "the philosophic path." Moses Hess was the first to teach communism by that path, and a year or two later Marx made his own way along the same route.[14] This framework of the philosophical ideas of Hegel and his immediate successors is of the greatest importance. For, although the historicism of his historical materialism has been and is by aficionados presented always as scientific socialism, the laborious empirical researches of Marx were in fact undertaken in order to illustrate, to confirm, and to fill out what he considered had been in all essentials already provided by a kind of philosophical arguments. It is in this light that we may best hope to understand certain besetting errors and deficiencies of the Marxist system.

Three features of this long-neglected background are especially relevant. The first is the hardest to characterize. Feuerbach was pointing to it when he said that all speculative philosophers are priests in disguise, and that all the classical German creations—Hegel's Idea, Fichte's Ego, and Schelling's Absolute—were simply substitutes for the Deity, reduced to a more abstract form. The whole climate of opinion was suffused with a profound, providential Christian or post-Christian conviction that in the end all manner of things will be well, a usually unstated and therefore never examined or abandoned assumption that, ultimately, the universe is not indifferent to human concerns.

The two further features are inseparably connected. There was, second, an equally profound and equally unexamined assumption that *a priori* reasoning can discover necessary truths about both the structure of the universe and our true and proper life within it. Third, such rationalist reasoning—reasoning that is rationalist in the technical philosopher's sense, in contrast to empiricist—is typically all-the-balls-in-the-air juggling with terms referring to abstract and indeterminate collectivities.

To indicate the atmosphere it is best to begin by quoting here one or two sentences from Hegel's Inaugural Lecture at Heidelberg, noting that in a passing moment of infidel insight Marx himself spoke of the drunken speculations of this master wizard:

> We shall see . . . that in other European countries . . . philosophy, excepting in name, has sunk even from memory, and that it is in the German nation that it has been retained as a peculiar possession. We have received the higher call of Nature to preserve this holy flame, just as the Eumolpidae in Athens had the conservation of the Eleusinian mysteries, the inhabitants of the island of Samothrace the preservation of a higher divine service.

There is now no escaping what, for anyone raised in the English-speaking philosophical world, is bound to be an excruciating experience. Perhaps this exericse can best be seen as a sort of intellectual inoculation: an injection of a small shot of the virus or the bacillus in order to build up antibodies, lest worse befall. What we have to do now is briefly to immerse ourselves into those intoxicated verbalizings that the Founding Fathers presented and accepted as proving the principles of their new "scientific socialism." To parody a later and funnier Marx, "These arguments may appear to possess no force at all. Yet don't be misled. For they do not possess any force at all."

In the introduction to the unwritten *Critique of Hegel's Philosophy of Law* Marx characteristically conjures up the barely embryonic German proletariat in order to provide an answer to his question: "So where is the positive possibility of German emancipation?" The answer, he asserts, lies:

in the formation of a class with *radical* claims, a class which is the dissolution of all classes, a sphere which has a universal character because of its universal suffering and which lays claim to no *particular right* because the wrong it suffers is not a *particular wrong* but *wrong in general;* a sphere of society which can no longer lay claim to a *historical* title, but merely to a *human* one, which does not stand in one-sided opposition to all the consequences but in all-sided opposition to the premises of the German political system; and finally a sphere which cannot emancipate itself without emancipating itself from—and thereby emancipating—all the other spheres of society, which is, in a word, the total loss of humanity and which can therefore redeem itself only through the *total redemption of humanity.* This dissolution of society as a particular class is the proletariat.[15]

So now, no doubt, we know. And, as if that outburst of drunken pontification was not already too much, here from the *Economic and Philosophical Manuscripts of 1844* is something even more abstract, more arbitrary, more technical and—if that is possible—even less concrete and down to earth:

Communism is the *positive* suppression of *private property* as *human self-estrangement,* and hence the true *appropriation* of the *human* essence through and for man; it is the complete restoration of man to himself as a *social,* i..e. *human,* being, a restoration which has become conscious and which takes place within the entire wealth of previous states of development. This communism, as fully developed naturalism, equals humanism, and as fully developed humanism equals naturalism; it is the *genuine* resolution of the conflict between man and nature, and between man and man, the true resolution of the conflict between existence and being, between objectification and self-affirmation, between freedom and necessity, between individual and species. It is the solution of the riddle of history and knows itself to be the solution. The entire movement of history is therefore both the *actual* act of creation of communism—the birth of its empirical existence —and, for its thinking consciousness, the *comprehended* and *known* movement of its *becoming.*[16]

To achieve as much or as little understanding of such passages as is in fact possible, it would be necessary to make an enormous investment of time and study in Hegel and in other immediate predecessors and contemporaries of Marx, and in the predecessors of those predecessors.[17] The first four chapters of the first volume of Kolakowski's three-decker treatise would serve only as a compressed introduction to some of the main primary sources. Fortunately it is sufficient to realize what no amount of background study ever would or could discover. It would not and could not in any of these writings discover any distinction of physical from logical necessity. Nor would it discover any instructions on how the key terms are to be empirically cashed. For instance, no amount of immersion in the intellectual milieu of the young Marx would leave us any better able than we are now to set about constructing sociologically viable indices either of German emancipation or of human self-estrangement.

The thinking of Marx is here so remote from the concrete, the particular, and the individual that we may be accused of idle frivolity or of a deficiency of historical imagination for pressing questions on how we are supposed to determine how far any of these putative processes have or have not progressed. Still, braving these charges, what observable characteristics will distinguish the blessedly dealienated from those still afflicted with that exotic metaphysical disease self-estrangement—a disease everywhere endemic before and until the wholesale nationalization of "all the means of production, distribution, and exchange"? And what instructions are to be given to the field workers if our research is to determine whether, in this or that actual society of flesh and blood human beings, the conflicts "between existence and being . . . between objectification and self-affirmation, between freedom and necessity, between individual and species" have been or are being *genuinely* resolved?

The fact that no answer to such questions is provided by and within the theory both makes that theory, because in principle unfalsifiable, unscientific, and at the same time makes it endlessly attractive to those who are or aspire to become members of some despotic Leninist elite.[18] Of course it would be entirely possible to give a clear, precise and scientifically useful sense to "alienation" or to any of the other key terms. So the fact that this seems never to have been done by any of our Marxist or Marxisant sociologists shows how far they are from actually being the truth-concerned and critical social scientists they pretend to be.

We could, for instance, suggest that the alienation is perhaps a condition afflicting some or all assembly line workers in (privately owned) mass production industries, the condition displayed in Charles Chaplin's film *Modern Times* or in René Clair's *A Nous la Liberté*. Given this it would not be impossibly hard to assemble measures that together would constitute an Alienation Index. But, of course, committed Marxists are not going to do this. For they cannot fail to fear that, in any understanding that allows their claims about alienation to be in principle falsifiable, it might become possible to demonstrate that these claims are in fact false.

For instance, Fiat built in the former Soviet Union a motor plant physically identical with one owned and operated by the same firm in Italy. Suppose that some Marxist sociologists had unexpectedly shown their scientiific good faith by constructing a viable Alienation Index. Then we might have, if ever *glasnost* had gone so far as to permit such independent and external study of Soviet realities, once and for all settled the long disputed question whether the full implementation of the old original clause 4 of the constitution of the British Labour Party—demanding the public ownership of "all the means of production, distribution and exchange"—really would be, if not a panacea for all the ills to which the flesh is heir, then at any rate a cure for this particular and particularly elusive and intractable condition of alienation. But, of course, this sustained reluctance either to require or to permit the claim that total socialism constitutes the sovereign remedy for alienation to be first precisely and unambiguously formulated and then put to decisive experimental tests should itself be recognized as revealing. For it shows that what we have here is not now, and perhaps never has been, a truth-concerned conjecture. Instead alienation even if it was not always has certainly become an indefinite description of an indeterminate condition, a condition postulated to serve as the elusive yet all-pervasive disease for which socialism—its original promise to provide both emancipation and abundance so visibly and so catastrophically unfulfilled—may still continue to be promoted as the sole and sovereign remedy.

Notes

1. The fact that a joint composition by Marx and Engels first published only decades after their deaths—*The German Ideology*—was adopted a few years ago as a set-book for certain British school examinations in philosophy has to be seen realistically: not as a belated admission of the authors' stature as philosophers comparable with the authors of the other works prescribed— Descartes, Hume, and Mill, but instead as one more example of that servile fawning upon power to which George Orwell saw intellectuals as occupationally inclined.

2. *Selected Works of Karl Marx and Friedrich Engels* (Moscow: Foreign Languages Publishing House, 1951), vol. 2, p. 361. In "Three Sources and Three Component Parts of Marxism" Lenin wrote similarly: "The doctrine of Marx . . . is the legitimate successor of the best that was created by humanity in the nineteenth century. . . . German philosophy, English political economy and French socialism."

3. Compare my "Prophecy or Philosophy? Historicism or History?" in R. Duncan and C. Wilson, eds., *Marx Refuted* (Bath: Ashgrove, 1987), pp. 68–88.

4. The final paragraph begins: "When we run over libraries, persuaded of these principles, what havoc must we make?" Then, referring to the sort of work to which the embargo applies, it concludes: "Commit it then to the flames, for it can contain nothing but sophistry and illusion."

5. *Political Studies* 29, no. 1 (1981): 117.

6. *New Society* (London) for November 3, 1983.

7. Leopold Schwartzschild, *The Red Prussian* (London: Pickwick, second edition, 1986).

8. The outstanding critical study, unlikely ever to be superseded as a treatment of the period it covers, is the Jesuit Father Gustav Wetter's *Dialectical Materialism: A Historical and Systematic Survey of Philosophy in the Soviet Union* (New York: Praeger, 1958).

9. Compare David McLellan, *Marx before Marxism* (Harmondsworth: Penguin, revised edition 1972), p. 657: "It was precisely this gap between what is and what ought to be that Marx considered to have been bridged by the Hegelian philosophy." Those wishing to learn the truth about this controverted topic should study W. W. Hudson, ed., *The Is/Ought Question* (London: Macmillan, 1969).

10. Friedrich Engels, *Herr Eugen Dühring's Revolution in Science (Anti-Dühring)*, translated by Emile Burns (London: Lawrence and Wishart, 1934).

11. Friedrich Engels, *The Dialectics of Nature*, trans. Clemens Dutt (New York: International, 1940), pp. 26–27. This edition contains a preface and notes by J. B. S. Haldane, who was at the time both Britain's leading geneticist and a member of the national executive of the local Communist Party. He suggested that Einstein's low opinion of the work should be disregarded on the ground that Einstein probably saw only the admittedly worthless essay on electricity. So compare the appendix to Sidney Hook, *Dialectical Materialism and Scientific Method* (Manchester: Committee on Science and Freedom, 1955), which prints a letter from Einstein saying that Edward Bernstein showed him the entire manuscript.

12. See, for instance, K. R. Popper, *Conjectures and Refutations: The Growth of Scientific Knowledge* (London: Routledge and Kegan Paul, 1963), especially chapter 1.

13. See K. R. Popper, *The Poverty of Historicism* (London: Routledge and Kegan Paul, 1957), and compare my "Popper and Historicist Necessities," in *Philosophy* (1990): 53–64.

14. See, for instance, McClellan, *Marx before Marxism*, passim. In his *Karl Marx: His Life and Thought* (London: Granada Paladin, 1976), McClellan cites a remark supposedly made by Louis Philippe in 1845: "We must purge Paris of German philosophers" (p. 135).

15. In *Early Writings*, trans. R. Livingstone and G. Berton, introduced by L. Colletti (Harmondsworth: Penguin, 1975), p. 236, emphasis original.

16. Ibid., p. 348, emphasis original.

17. Anyone insisting upon such explorations will find the best guide in S. Hook, *From Hegel to Marx* (Ann Arbor, Mich.: Michigan University Press, new edition, 1962).

18. See, for instance, M. Voslensky, *Nomenklatura: Anatomy of the Soviet Ruling Class* (London: The Bodley Head, 1984).

9

Comparing Marx with Darwin

Darwin's book is very important and it suits me well that it supports the class struggle in history from the point of view of natural science.

Karl Marx
letter to Ferdinand Lassalle, January 16, 1861

Just as Darwin discovered the law of development of organic nature, so Marx discovered the law of development of human history.

Friedrich Engels
Obituary address, March 17, 1883

Does Darwin's account of the evolutionary origin of species by natural selection really constitute confirmation for the revolutionary revelations of the *Communist Manifesto*,[1] and can we accept the claim that Marx was, in his different field, a scientist of the same stature as Darwin?

1. Confirmation for "our theory"?

Darwin's account of evolutionary origins certainly provides powerful reinforcement for some positions that Marx and Engels shared with most other secular materialists.[2] But, equally certainly, it does not reinforce what is peculiar to and distinctive of Marxism, what in their correspondence Marx and Engels distinguished as "our view" or "our theory." As we saw in chapter 8, that theory, first and most famously published in the *Communist Manifesto* of 1848, can most relevantly be characterized as apocalyptic historicist prophecy based upon an all-embracing, supposedly scientific, philosophy of history.

In this characterization the word "historicist" is being employed in Popper's sense. A historicist is thus someone who proclaims supposed inexorable natural laws of historical development. The specimen Popper himself produces to exemplify his understanding of historicism is taken from the preface to *Capital:* "When a society has discovered the natural law that determines its own movement, even then it can neither overleap the natural phases of its evolution, nor shuffle them out of the world by a stroke of the pen."[3]

The expression "philosophy of history" is used here to refer not to the analysis of concepts employed by historians but to the attempt to discern patterns in the succession of events. In this understanding perhaps the first available specimen of the species is the account given by Plato in Book VIII of *The Republic* of the supposedly natural and normal process of Greek constitutional degeneration—from the ideal city state ruled by Platonic philosopher kings to timocracy, from timocracy to oligarchy, from oligarchy to democracy, and from democracy to dictatorship. But it is only with the rise of Christianity that we begin to find philosophy of history encompassing all mankind. The story is now the story of the unfolding of God's plan: Creation, the brief Age of Innocence, the Fall, the Incarnation, the Second Coming, and the Kingdom of God on Earth.

Secular developments are seen within this all-embracing divine framework. For instance, in the late third and early fourth century of the Christian era, Eusebius of Caesarea composed *Praeparatio Evangelica,* purporting to show that the history of the pre-Christian world should be regarded as a process designed to culminate in the Incarnation. Jewish religion, Greek philosophy, and the dominion of Rome constituted the seedbed in which the Christian revelation could be expressed and accepted. Had the second person of the Trinity become incarnate at any very different time or in any very different place, then the world would not have been ready.

To any question why all these earlier historical developments taken together should be regarded as designed to culminate in the Incarnation Eusebius has, given the Christian Revelation, a simple and utterly decisive answer. The reason why they should be so regarded is because they were. To the further question "How can he be so sure about the consummation of the whole historical process in the Kingdom of God on Earth?" his answer, on the same Christian assumptions, can be equally simple and equally decisive. Eusebius can be so sure because he has God's promise, and no power in all the universe can say God nay: "Who is he that saith, and it cometh to pass, when the Lord commandeth it not?" (Lamentations, 3, 37).

Marx and Engels expound a philosophy of history that is at several points reminiscent of the Eusebian scheme. It is indeed, as Soviet spokespersons so loved to say, no accident that it is. For Marx and Engels were, or had been, young Hegelians. And Hegel's own philosophy of history was a recasting of what had traditionally been accepted among Christians. When Marx and Engels, as they put it, "stood Hegel on his head or, rather, stood him right way up" they may have replaced an idealist by a materialist. Yet they still had a Hegel.

Consider, for instance, how the promised eventual establishment of the Kingdom of God on Earth is replaced by the promised coming total triumph of the class to end all classes, and how, at least in later editions, the Fall in the Garden of Eden makes way for the unexplained lapse from primitive communism into a property-owning, and hence, supposedly, class-divided society. Notice too how Marx and Engels—like Alfred Hitchcock in each of his movies—find a place in the plot for themselves: "A small section of the ruling class cuts itself adrift, and joins the revolutionary class, the class that holds the future in its hands" (p. 92). But here the crucial message of redemption is brought not by one element of the triune Godhead but by the proletarians' Ph.D. and his associates: "A portion of the bourgeoisie goes over to the proletariat, and in particular, a portion of the bourgeois idealists, who have raised themselves to the level of comprehending theoretically the historical movement as a whole" (p. 91).

Suppose now that we ask Marx and Engels questions paralleling those previously put to Eusebius. For it is with total confidence that they assert of the enemy class: "Its fall and the victory of the proletariat are equally inevitable"; and so "In place of the old bourgeois society, with its classes and class antagonisms, we shall have an association, in which the free development of each is the condition for the free development of all?" (pp. 94 and 105).

It is, of course, this bold and enormously confident historicist prophecy, reiterated in so many works, that has been the main source of the widespread appeal of "our view." And, until the beginning of the recent progressive economic and political collapse of the former Soviet Union and its satellites and dependencies, it continued to be. Thus in the nineteenth century a very typical Russian convert exclaimed: "The knowledge that we feeble individuals were backed by a mighty historical process filled one with ecstasy and established such a firm foundation for the individual's activities that, it seemed, all the hardships of the struggle could be overcome."[4] In the fifties, sixties, and perhaps especially the seventies of our century it was not difficult to see Marxism-Leninism as constituting the irresistible, or at any rate the not to be effectively resisted, wave of the future.[5]

The confidence placed by Marx himself in such historicist contentions about the allegedly inexorable destinies of bourgeoisie and proletariat appears originally to have been founded upon nothing more concrete than a piece of high Hegelian philosophical analysis, an exercise of the kind of which two sobering specimens were quoted in chapter 8. The *Manifesto,* however, does develop a sketchy and precarious sociological argument: "The advance of industry, whose involuntary promoter is the bourgeoisie, replaces the isolation of the labourers, due to competition, by their revolutionary combination, due to association. The development of Modern Industry, therefore, cuts from under its feet the very foundations on which the bourgeoisie produces and appropriates products" (pp. 93–94).

For the rest of his life the most important academic work of Marx, work from which he continually allowed himself to be distracted and diverted, consisted in attempts to build solid empirical foundations for these historicist contentions, contentions so essential to "our view."[6] Marx signed his first contract to produce the book building these necessary foundations in 1845. Although he accepted, and retained, a remarkably substantial advance, he never delivered the promised manuscript of a *Critique of National Economy and Politics* to the publisher who had paid him. *Capital: A Critical Analysis of Capitalist Production* (volume 1) eventually appeared only in 1867. That was as much of his magnum opus as Marx himself ever prepared for publication and actually published. He died in 1883.

It was therefore left to Engels to transcribe from a mountain of notebooks, and systematically to revise and arrange, the materials that were in 1885 and 1894 eventually published as, respectively, volumes 2 and 3. Finally, at the behest of Engels, Karl Kautsky assembled and edited a mass of further manuscripts. These he published in three volumes between 1905 and 1910 under the title *Theories of Surplus Value*, which together are accounted volume 4 of *Capital*.

Whether with or without its necessary empirical foundations, "our view" was aggressively and often successfully marketed as "scientific socialism." Throughout the nineteenth century and for many years thereafter the two most widely read works in the whole Marx-Engels literature were the *Communist Manifesto* and the opuscule that Engels excerpted from his *Anti-Dühring*, namely *Socialism: Utopian and Scientific*.

To understand the intended contrast notice a passage found among the Marx papers only after his death. It was originally intended to go into *The Civil War in France*, his account of the 1871 Paris Commune, but has been crossed out. Referring to Fourier, Cabet, Owen, and other utopian socialists seen off at the end of the *Communist Manifesto*, Marx wrote:

> They attempted to compensate for the missing historical preconditions of the movement with fantastic pictures and plans of a new society. . . . From that moment on, when the working-class movement became a reality, the fantastic utopians disappeared: not because the working class abandoned the objective for which these utopians had reached, but because the true means had been found for its realization. . . . Still, both the ultimate aims announced by the utopians (i.e. the end of the system of wage-labour and class domination) are also the ultimate aims of the Paris Revolution and the International. Only the means are different.[7]

So does Darwin's account of the evolutionary origin of species by natural selection really constitute confirmation for the revolutionary revelations of the *Communist Manifesto*? Certainly not! Of course, if you believe that we are creatures designed by Omnipotence in order to fulfill his purposes, and if you also believe that the establishment of the Kingdom of God is one of those purposes, then it is not at all unreasonable for you to put your faith in the ultimate fulfilment of this eschatological promise. But for anyone who has rejected God and divine creation in favor of a Darwinian account of origins—an account, that is, of the evolution of species through a blind natural selection, from among unplanned variations, of those fittest simply to survive in a no-holds-barred struggle for existence—it is another matter altogether.

For such a person to insist that somehow a new kind of secular and scientific providence exists and is bound to have its way, and hence that the annihilating victory of a desperate and ever more impoverished proletariat is absolutely guaranteed to produce a conflict-free utopia, is absolutely grotesque. Yet there can be no doubt that, for instance, the second clause of the concluding sentence of the main body of the *Manifesto* is intended to express, not a tricky tautology, but a straightforward and substantial revelation: "In the place of the old . . . society . . . we shall have an association in which the free development of each is the condition for the free development of all" (p. 105).[8]

2. A "law of development of human history"?

The claim first made by Engels beside the grave of Marx continues to be made. It was, for instance, repeated by Lenin. Thus as early as 1894, in his second publication, Lenin wrote: "It will now be clear that the comparison with Darwin is perfectly accurate."[9] And in 1968 the official philosopher to the Communist Party of Great Britain (Muscovite) deployed an even bolder because more specific contention: "The methodology by which Marx arrived at his theory of social development is exactly the same as that employed by Darwin in establishing the theory of the evolution of species by natural selection."[10]

So let us proceed to compare and contrast the methods of Marx and Darwin. This comparison will surely show that it was because Engels was so right in his insistence in the second part of his obituary speech that his friend had been before all else a revolutionary that he was so wrong to conclude the first part with the claim: "*So war dieser Mann der Wissenschaft*" ("That was this man of science").

Abundant biographical evidence reveals Marx to have commenced and continued his researches in order to find empirical and scientific warrant for the historicist prophecies. These prophecies, as was said earlier, were by Marx and Engels originally founded upon the most arbitrarily a priori Hegelianism: the two leaders had, like Moses Hess, been of the few who had "taken the philosophical road to Communism." But if revolutionary troops—the poor, bloody infantry of the class struggle—were to be assembled and encouraged by assurances of inevitable victory and inevitable utopia, then those assurances had to be presented as scientifically based.

Marx and Engels had the same compelling reason to offer their revelation as *scientific* socialism as Mrs. Mary Baker Eddy had for presenting hers as Christian *Science*.[11] So in the *Manifesto*—a document in every other respect antithetical to *Science and Health*—they were, as it were, writing a monster post-dated check drawn on an account in the Bank of Scientific Knowledge, an account into which they had not so far been able to deposit substantial funds.

No one should make the mistake of dismissing any suggested hypothesis as unscientific simply on the grounds either that its antecedents are in some way disreputable or that those putting it forward were persuaded of its truth even before any proper testing had begun. It is not only great mathematicians who persist in following with unshakable conviction hunches that they eventually prove correct. Kepler himself began his calculations believing with his whole heart and mind that the planetary orbits must be circular, while his own grounds for so believing were entirely metaphysical and nonobservational. In the end, though the end was long delayed, he was persuaded, or persuaded himself, to try ellipses as the next closest and hence in his view the next best thing, which, thanks to our good fortune in being able to stand on his shoulders, we know to have been the right answer.

Our first objection is, therefore, neither that the main economic-historical hypotheses of Marx originated in disreputable philosophy, nor that he was most stubbornly committed to them on the basis of evidence which at least at first it would be an understatement to describe as merely insufficient. These are, certainly, grounds for unease. But, for the reasons given, they cannot alone be decisive. The decisive objection here is that those hypotheses that he himself saw as most crucial and most distinctive are in Popper's sense historicist, and that every historicist hypothesis could have been known to be false already, previous to any further and more particular investigation.

In a letter to Weydemeyer dated March 5, 1852, Marx tells us very clearly what he saw to be most crucial and most distinctive in his own pretended scientific achievement, although he is too discreet to reveal what he considered to be the grounds of this pretended knowledge:

> What I did that was new was to prove: 1) that the *existence of classes* is only bound up with *particular, historic phases in the development of production;* 2) that the class struggle necessarily leads to the *dictatorship of the proletariat;* and 3) that this dictatorship only constitutes the transition to the *abolition of all classes* and to a classless society.

The second two assertions are, it is manifest, historicist. That is to say, they assert laws of historical development stating that certain things are going to happen necessarily and unavoidably, and irrespective of anything and everything anyone does or might do in hopes of preventing such outcomes.

Against historicism in this understanding there is an objection more fundamental and more elementary than anything urged in Popper's own famous critique.[12] Because we are agents who as such could do otherwise than we do, there neither are nor can be any natural laws determining human action: there is, in other words, a flagrant conceptual incompatibility between the notions of action and of the impossibility of all alternatives to that action. Furthermore, it can and must be suggested, both these two opposite and incompatible notions are and could only be explained and understood by reference to our most familiar experience of being able to do some things but not others. How, that is to say, could any of us even know the meanings of the relevant terms without being directly acquainted with specimens of both the two categorically different alternatives that those two (sorts of) terms (and expressions) are employed to pick out?[13]

It would, no doubt, be overambitious to maintain that Darwin saw all the implications of this human peculiarity of choice. But it would be far more wrong not to insist that, whereas Darwin in drawing a lesson from Malthus did appreciate that choice makes a vital difference, Marx seems never even to have begun explicitly to question the possibility of finding natural laws determining human action.[14] And if these are indeed a will o'-the-wisp, then how much more implausible are his own pretended revelations of laws of historical development?

3. Social science or revolutionary rhetoric?

That first objection was a matter of error pure and simple. The rest are all more scandalous and less venial. They raise questions about academic and political good faith. It should be obvious that anyone who with any pretensions to rationality is sincerely pursuing any objective, whether that objective is the truth about some subject of theoretical inquiry or the attainment of some objectives of practical policy, will be concerned to monitor their success or failure in these pursuits and equally concerned to adapt their tactics to the lessons of that success or failure.

(i) Such sincere and rational concern is also bound to manifest itself in lucid and unambiguous expression. For how, where there is obscurity or ambiguity, can we hope to settle the questions whether assertions were true or policies effective? Among the best *Maxims* of the Marquis de Vauvenargues are: "Obscurity is the kingdom of error"; and "For the philosopher clarity is a matter of good faith." But not for the philosopher only.

It is in the harsh light of these fundamental and, once well and truly stated, incontestable principles that we have to interpret the often deplored fact that nowhere in all the enormous bulk of the collected works of Marx and Engels is there any systematic, unambiguous, and tolerably full statement of what "our view" was. Here as in other places the contrast with Darwin is, of course, absolute. Years before he ventured to publish anything on evolution by natural selection Darwin had for his private purposes written that "sketch of my species theory," which he then took all necessary steps to ensure should appear immediately after his death were he to die before he was ready for publication.

Deeply damaging passages in the Marx-Engels correspondence show that Marx was, to put it mildly, not consistently concerned through such monitoring to discover and make clear either the truth of the propositions he asserted or the truth about the actual or likely effects of the policies he labored to promote. In examining this correspondence we have always to remember too that what was eventually published is what remained after extensive excision by Engels and further cuts by Laura and Eleanor Marx.[15]

Perhaps the most revealing of all the damaging passages in that remainder is one that, although quoted already in chapter 8, has to be quoted again in the present context. It comes from a letter to Engels dated August 15, 1857, and of course it has no parallel anywhere in the Darwin papers. To anyone enjoying any familiarity with those papers it is simply inconceivable that Darwin could ever have written in a similar sense.

> I took the risk of prognosticating in this way, as I was compelled to substitute for you as correspondent at the *Tribune*. . . . It is possible I may be discredited. But in that case it will still be possible to pull through with the help of a bit of dialectics. It goes without saying that I phrased my forecasts in such a way that I would prove to be right also in the opposite case.

Can we, should we, refrain from repeating that tribute from Engels: "*So war dieser Mann der Wissenschaft*"? Another example of calculated obscurity is perhaps still more significant, since it refers not to an item of occasional journalism but to the presentation of findings in what was supposed to be a major contribution to social science.

Engels foresaw objections to the discussion of surplus value in what was to become the first volume of *Capital* and wrote to Marx: "I marvel that you have not taken this into consideration already, for it will *quite certainly* be held up to you at once and it is better to dispose of it in advance."[16] To this the response from Marx was:

> If I have to *silence* all such objections in *advance,* I should ruin the whole dialectical method of development. On the contrary, this method has the advantage of continually *setting* traps for these fellows which provoke them to untimely demonstrations of their asininity.[17]

(ii) Obscurity or ambiguity of statement, and subsequent further obfuscation, are in the present context important mainly as means of avoiding the admission that a statement has been falsified (shown to be false). Darwin, by contrast, was constantly scrupulous to recognize and to try to meet every relevant objection. When, as was the case with Lord Kelvin's estimates of the youth of the earth, there was at the time no satisfactory answer available, then Darwin honestly recognized and recorded the difficulty, and—once he had satisfied himself both that and what future discoveries might save the situation, and that his was by far the most plausible theory in the running anywhere—left that difficulty to the future to meet.

What more or what else could we ask of any scientist? Darwin, indeed, is a very paradigm of complete good faith and single-mindedness in the pursuit of truth. Sigmund Freud was later to commend "the great Darwin" because "he made a golden rule for himself, writing down with particular care observations which seemed unfavourable to his theory, having become convinced that just these would be inclined to slip out of recollection."[18]

With Marx, I fear, we have a very different story and a very different man. Two examples of his ways of dealing with falsifying fact will have to suffice. But both the two chosen are of the highest intrinsic interest and importance. Both help to show that Marx was, as Engels insisted, first and always a revolutionary, albeit, as Engels neither said nor perhaps ever noticed, a revolutionary for revolution's sake rather than for the sake of whatever reliefs to man's estate revolution might rationally be expected to bring. It was, surely, this which led him to commit these and other malpractices with falsifying fact.

First, then, consider what is customarily called the "immiseration thesis." In the *Manifesto* this is asserted in what would appear to be a strictly self-contradictory form: "The modern labourer, instead of rising with the progress of industry, sinks deeper and deeper below the conditions of existence of his own class" (p. 93). (Anyone who lived through successive British national income and price policies during the sixties and seventies is bound here to recall the legendary cry of trades union spokesmen: that, while it stands to reason that everyone should get at least the average increase, some groups and, in particular—surprise, surprise!—that represented by the speaker, must get a lot more than the average.)

On this occasion, however, eschewing all such logic-chopping around that particular formulation, we have to understand only that and why Marx and Engels needed to maintain a strong immiseration thesis. For their revolutionary purposes they had to insist that the proletariat must inevitably grow progressively more numerous and poorer, while the capitalists must, equally inevitably and at the same time, grow fewer and richer. How else could they sustain their cherished historicist prophecy: "What the bourgeoisie, therefore, produces, above all, is its own grave-diggers. Its fall and the victory of the proletariat are equally inevitable" (p. 94)?

Given this transcendent revolutionary purpose there is no escape into any of those weakening, even if in the end still false, "interpretations" so beloved of devout defenders never willing to admit their gurus to have been just plumb wrong. It is no use saying that—actually—Marx and Engels meant relative not absolute immiseration, or that it is only one or other kind of tendency and not a historicist law, and so on. They have either to pack it in or to brazen it out.

Precisely and only because he was primarily a revolutionary agitator rather than an academic social scientist Marx, when it came to the crunch, always chose the second alternative. Thus in the first volume of *Capital* most official British data are cited as near as possible up to the date of publication: that concerning public health up to 1865; the reports of factory inspectors up to 1866; and so on. Yet Marx refrains from citing the run of statistics revealing the rise in real wages after 1850. When a second German edition was issued in 1873 he seized the opportunity to make other revisions and corrections, but added not a word about real wages. Just before his death Marx prepared a third edition issued posthumously by Engels in 1883. On this crucial matter, still silence. Nor did the materials left for volumes 2 and 3 break the silence. "That silence," as Bertram Wolfe comments, "speaks louder than words."[19]

When Marx felt compelled to admit the fact of rising real wages he tried to minimize its extent, while resolutely refusing to recognize the falsificatory relevance of any such rises to his cherished theories. In volume 1 of *Capital,* for instance, we read that, "Between 1849 and 1859, a rise of wages practically insignificant, though accompanied by falling prices of corn, took place in the English agricultural districts" (p. 638). But two years before the first publication of this volume, in an address to the General Council of the International, Marx had written:

> Having premised so much, I proceed to state that from 1849 to 1859 there took place a *rise of about 40 per cent* in the average rate of the agricultural wages of Great Britain. I could give you ample details of proof of my assertion, but for the present think it sufficient to refer you to the conscientious and critical paper read in 1860 by the late Mr. John C. Murton at the London Society of Arts on "The Forces used in Agriculture."[20]

(iii) The second major example of Marx's methods for disposing of falsifying fact in the interests of revolutionary propaganda is provided by what he presented as a history of the Paris Commune. In his two-edged tribute, *Marx as Politician,* David Felix says, "*The Civil War in France,* argued with his superb disdain for the facts," was "the last of Marx's polemical masterpieces."[21] Judging by measures of political influence, rather than by the standards of historical scholarship, it is indeed an extraordinary achievement. For it succeeded in persuading almost everyone—friend and foe alike—that the Commune constituted the first Communist coup, providing a paradigm case of the exercise of a "dictatorship of the proletariat," something Marx himself privately insisted, both before and after the event, that it neither was nor could have been.

Thus in the Second Address of the *General Council of the International on the Franco-Prussian War,* drafted by Marx between the sixth and the ninth of September 1870, he solemnly warned the Paris proletariat not to succumb to any temptation to try to overthrow the new Republican Government of National Defense:

> The French working class finds itself in an extremely difficult position. Any attempt to overthrow the new government, when the enemy is now almost knocking on the gates of Paris, would be an act of desperate folly. The French workingmen must do their duty as citizens, but they must not let themselves be dominated by the national memory of 1792. . . . It is not their task to repeat the past, but to build the future. Let them quietly and with determination utilize the means which republican freedom gives them to carry on systematically and thoroughly the organization of their own class.

Subsequently Marx continued to do everything he could to discourage those susceptible to his influence from attempting to overthrow that new republican government. But then, after such an attempt had been made, he began to claim the entire enterprise as an achievement of the International. Thus in a letter to Kugelmann dated April 12, 1871, Marx described "this present insurrection of Paris . . . this storming of the heavens by the Parisians" as "the most glorious deed of our party since the June insurrection" of 1848.[22]

But that, as Marx knew perfectly well, was altogether false. For the majority of the leaders of the Paris Commune were not members of the French section of the International. In so far as the leadership was socialist at all it consisted of Blanquists and Proudhonists, only a minority of whom were members of the International. With the possible exception of the Hungarian-Jewish refugee Leo Frankel, not one was a Marxist. Even at the lower levels of the leadership the one committed Marxist was Serailler, the very man whom, according to a letter to Engels dated September 6, 1870, Marx despatched to Paris in order so to "arrange matters" with the International there that they should not commit the aforementioned "act of desperate folly."[23] When many years later, in a letter to Danela Nieuwenhuis dated February 22, 1881, Marx uttered his last words on the Paris Commune they were:

> Apart from the fact that this was merely the rising of a town under exceptional conditions, the majority of the Commune was in no sense socialist, nor could it be. With a small amount of common sense, they could have reached a compromise with Versailles useful to the whole mass of the people.

One clearcut and memorable example of that "superb disdain for the facts" shown by Marx in *The Civil War in France* is his assertion that all elected councillors and appointed functionaries had "to do their jobs at workingmen's wages." For the truth is that the six-thousand-franc annual wage that the deputies of the Commune voted for themselves and set as a maximum for state officials was over ten times that being paid the rank and file of the National Guard for defending the Commune—namely thirty sous, or one and a half francs, per day.

4. Ignoring the realities of socialism

It was only after taking up residence in London and beginning a really thorough study of the classical economists that Marx was led to recognize "the Asiatic mode of production" as a form of political economy radically different from anything for which he and Engels had previously provided. Adam Smith had noted similarities between imperial China and "several other governments of Asia." James Mill in his *History of British India* identified the "Asiatic model of government" as a general institutional type, and he rejected attempts to assimilate it to feudalism. His son, John Stuart Mill, accepts this identification right from the earliest pages of his *Principles of Political Economy,* a work first published in 1848, the same year as the *Manifesto.* We know that between 1850 and the summer of 1853 Marx studied both *The Wealth of Nations* and these two works by the Mills, as well as Prescott's *Conquest of Mexico* and *Conquest of Peru,* and—what had been a prime source for the economists—Francois Bernier's *Travels in the Mogul Empire: A.D. 1656–1668.*

Having seized on the notion of "Asiatic society" (Richard Jones) or "Oriental society" (J. S. Mill) as a quite distinctive social form, Marx employed it in his articles for the *New York Daily Tribune,* as well as in early drafts for *Capital.* But, in part no doubt because, as we have remarked, there was at no time any precise, full, yet compassable statement of "our view," he never frankly faces the question of how, if at all, that theoretical scheme can be squared with or adjusted to the admission of this further kind of social system.

He ought to have seen this as a problem right from the beginning. For even though attention was concentrated on the final transformation in the series, the *Manifesto* had provided for a serial evolution of species of social systems: ancient society developing into feudalism, the bourgeois or capitalist order emerging from the womb of feudalism, and then the final stage in which the class to end all classes shatters capitalism and establishes the classless socialist utopia. To fit in a primal state of primitive communism is not too difficult. But to attempt to intrude a fifth kind of social order within the original four-part series might be thought to be rather like trying to squeeze other inhabited worlds into a scheme that had already embraced a unique incarnation at the very center of the physical universe and its history.

The opening words of the *Manifesto* had been: "The history of all hitherto existing society is the history of class struggles." It was easy to amend that by adding the qualification "written," thus making room for an Age of (propertyless) Innocence prior to the (appropriative) Fall. It is a very different thing to meet the challenge to find classes and class struggles in the indisputably post-lapsarian "Asiatic system." It is very different and, for Marx, very difficult, because this challenge is at one and the same time a challenge to his theoretical and to his practical commitments. The way in which he in fact met or, rather, failed to meet it constitutes a sinister indication that, even on the most charitable judgment, neither Marx nor Engels can be allowed to have been unambiguously and unreservedly committed to libertarian and humanitarian ends.

It is easy to indicate how the sociological principles of Marx required him to respond to this theoretical challenge. As Wittfogel argues in his massive study *Oriental Despotism,* Marx "should have designated the functional bureaucracy as the ruling class."[24] But even if he had taken this road Marx would quickly have found himself in what would have been, from his point of view, a cul-de-sac. For under oriental despotism this ruling class is so dominant that it can and does prevent all organization by any possible rivals: "The history of hydraulic society suggests that class struggle, far from being a chronic disease of all mankind, is the luxury of multi-centred and open societies" (p. 329).

Even granting this, you may ask, why should Marx not have met all such objections by simply conceding that his claims about class conflict applied only to those Western societies in which he and his readers were most interested? The sixty-four-thousand-dollar answer is that the centralized, totally socialist state proclaimed in the *Manifesto*—that supposedly quite new form of social order for which Marx was working all his life—would be sure to be, or very soon become, a kind of oriental despotism; and, so far from the state machinery of such a social system tending to wither away, historic experience shows oriental despotism to be an extraordinarily persistent form, with no strong inherent tendencies either towards decay and dissolution or towards development into some different and perhaps more pluralist system (ibid., passim).

There is no call and no place here for us to deploy much argument in support of these conclusions. For the ambivalent and evasive attitudes of Lenin himself, the official suppression of all discussion of the concept of oriental despotism under what until the middle eighties had been becoming the ever more numerous established Marxist-Leninist regimes, combine to show that both the "New Tsars" and the "New Mandarins" realized how well it applied. They not only saw but also insisted that socialism in practice—"actually existing socialism"—was and remains incompatible with individualistic dissent and democratic pluralism.

Consider, for instance, the statement issued in 1971 by the Institute of Marxism-Leninism in Moscow. With its eyes then mainly on Chile and France it sketched a program for achieving, through "United Front" or "Broad Left" tactics, irreversible Communist domination: "Having once acquired political power, the working class implements the liquidation of the private ownership of the means of production. . . . As a result, under socialism, there remains no ground for the existence of any opposition parties counterbalancing the Communist Party."[25]

Marx, of course, did not in his century have such abundant contemporary experience of total and hence necessarily totalitarian socialism. Nevertheless he did have access to information about earlier despotic systems under which the economy was largely or wholly socialist. (Noting that he read Prescott during his studies of the "Asiatic mode of production," one is reminded that the socialist generals who ruled Peru for much of the 1970s called their project "the Inca Plan.")[26]

Even more significant is the fact that Marx was again and again confronted with the charge that socialism, or at any rate socialism as he and Engels understood it, must involve slavery and despotism. Ruge, for instance, with whom Marx collaborated in 1844 on the *German-French Yearbook,* called the socialist dream "a police and slave state." In 1848 the vice president of Louis Blanc's party told Engels, "You are leaning towards despotism." Similar objections were developed later by Proudhon, and by Bakunin in his 1873 book *Statism and Anarchism.*

To such criticism neither Marx nor Engels ever published any reply, although Marx did eventually add extensive annotations to his copy of *Statism and Anarchism.* Since both were as much inclined to engage in polemic as Darwin was reluctant, how can this silence, sustained over thirty years, be otherwise explained than as an indication that neither was able to think up any effective answer, but that, although they did not want potential followers to become persuaded of the correctness of these objections, they themselves were not seriously disturbed? The unlovely practical commitments of Marx thus seduce him into sins against science, not only, as we have seen, into his inhibited treatment of traditional oriental despotism, but also into his refusal to apply what was there to be learnt to reveal the prospect of Marxist socialism realized as a prospect of oriental despotism redivivus. The upshot, therefore, has been to display the hopelessness, not to say the sheer indecency, of any attempt to present Marx as the scientific equal of Darwin.

Notes

1. K. Marx and F. Engels, *The Communist Manifesto,* trans. S. Moore, ed. A. J. P. Taylor (Harmondsworth: Penguin, 1968).

2. Compare, for instance, my *Darwinian Evolution* (London: Granada Paladin, 1984), II 2.

3. K. Marx, *Capital: A Critical Analysis of Capitalist Production,* trans. S. Moore and E. Aveling (Moscow: Foreign Languages Publishing House, 1961).

4. Quoted in R. G. Wesson, *Why Marxism? The Continuing Success of a Failed Theory* (London: Temple Smith, 1976), p. 46.

5. Compare, for instance, a claim quoted above in section 3 of chapter 8, the claim made by Nikita Khrushchev as chairman of the Council of Ministers of the U.S.S.R. in an address to a diplomatic reception in Washington during September 1959.

6. The best source for the whole story is Leopold Schwartzschild, *The Red Prussian* (London: Pickwick, 1986). It is regrettable that this new edition of a work that had appeared in the United Kingdom first in 1948 could not include the updating appendix, which, among other things, told the tale of the seduction of the *"au pair"* Lenchen Demuth, and of how Engels was persuaded falsely to acknowledge paternity of the resulting natural son.

Here is perhaps as good a place as any to record Sir Karl Popper's reactions. In a note first added to the fifth edition of *The Open Society and Its Enemies* (London: Routledge and Kegan Paul, 1966), he wrote:

> Some years after I wrote this book . . . Leopold Schwartzschild's . . . *The Red Prussian* . . . became known to me. . . . It contains documentary evidence, especially from the Marx-Engels correspondence, which shows that Marx was less of a humanitarian, and less of a lover of freedom, than he is made to apear in this book. Schwartzschild describes him as a man who saw in "the proletariat" mainly an instrument for his own personal ambition. Though this may put the matter more harshly than the evidence warrants, it must be admitted that the evidence itself is shattering. (vol. 2, p. 396)

At that time (1965) Popper added nothing about Marx as a supposedly sincere seeker after scientific truth. But after seeing a copy of Schwartzschild (1986), Popper wrote in a letter to me, from which I now quote, with his permission,

I was personally shattered by Schwartzschild's book, but it was only my view of Marx's moral stature which was shattered. The reason that my view of Marx's stature as a scientist was not shattered is very simple. I had not had a *very* high opinion to start with, but I had given him all the benefit of the doubt; and my opinion had *slowly* deteriorated, both while writing the book and after having written it; so slowly that I never clearly noticed it. When I read Schwartzschild there was nothing left to be shattered. (emphasis in original)

7. Quoted at pp. 38–39 of Melvin Lasky, *Utopia and Revolution* (London: Macmillan, 1976), a work most strongly recommended.

8. For an extensive study of the relations and lack of relations between the Utopian longings and the scientific pretensions of Marx, compare Bertram D. Wolfe, *Marxism: One Hundred Years in the Life of a Doctrine* (London: Chapman and Hall, 1967), chapters 17 to 19.

9. V. I. Lenin, *Collected Works* (Moscow: Progress, 1960), vol. 1, p. 142.

10. M. Cornforth, *The Open Philosophy and the Open Society* (London: Lawrence and Wishart, 1968), p. 27.

11. For the latter see H. A. L. Fisher, *Our New Religion* (London: C. A. Watts, 1933).

12. K. R. Popper, *The Poverty of Historicism* (London: Routledge and Kegan Paul, 1957), and compare my *Thinking about Social Thinking* (London: Harper-Collins/Fontana, 1992), chapter 7.

13. For an expansion and defense of this contention, see section 5 of chapter 5 above.

14. Whereas Malthus himself in the *First Essay* mistook the multiplicative power of human populations to be humanly irresistible, Darwin, in applying "the doctrine of Malthus . . . to the whole animal and vegetable kingdom" immediately appreciated that, whereas in the human case there could be "prudential restraint from marriage," in the rest of the "animal and vegetable kingdom" there could not. Compare my *Darwinian Evolution,* III 1.

15. For a summary comment on the nature and purpose of this correspondence, and for the reason why so much of it has survived, see note 13 at pp. 255–56 of David Felix, *Marx as Politician* (Carbondale and Edwardsville, Ill.: Southern Illinois University Press, 1983).

16. *Engels on Capital,* trans. and ed. by Leonard Mins (New York: International Publishers, 1937), p. 125.

17. Ibid., p. 127.

18. S. Freud, *Introductory Lectures on Psychoanalysis,* trans. Joan Riviere

(London: Allen and Unwin, 1922), p. 61.

19. Wolfe, *Marxism* (1967), p. 323.

20. K. Marx, *Value, Price and Profit,* ed. Eleanor Marx Aveling (London: Allen and Unwin, 1899), pp. 24–25, emphasis original. Would a comparable *decline* have been equally insignificant, either theoretically or practically? For further material about the responses and refusals to respond of Mrs. Aveling's father to falsifications of his fundamental and absolutely crucial immiseration thesis compare Schwartzschild 1986, chapter 15, and Thomas Sowell, *Marxism: Philosophy and Economics* (London: Allen and Unwin, 1985), chapter 7.

21. Felix, *Marx as Politician* (1983), p. 175.

22. Wolfe, *Marxism* (1967), part III, and compare Felix, *Marx as Politician* (1983), pp. 166–81.

23. For a somewhat fuller prosopographic study compare, Wolfe, *Marxism* (1967), pp. 131–33.

24. K. A. Wittfogel, *Oriental Despotism: A Comparative Study of Total Power* (New York: Random House, Vintage Edition, 1981), p. 381.

25. Quoted in *The Economist* (June 17, 1972): 23.

26. For a critical review of the available information about the Inca and other proto-socialist societies, compare Igor Shafarevich, *The Socialist Phenomenon* (New York: Harper and Row, 1980). The production of this very useful book was a most remarkable achievement—the author, a mathematician by both training and profession, apparently was throughout working in the Soviet Union.

10

Market Order or Commanded Chaos?

> The ideas of economists and political philosophers, both when they
> are right and when they are wrong, are more powerful than is com-
> monly understood. Indeed the world is ruled by little else. Madmen
> in authority, who hear voices in the air, are distilling their frenzy from
> some academic scribbler of a few years back.
>
> J. M. Keynes[1]

These much quoted words of Lord Keynes are peculiarly appropriate
to the case of Lenin. For the stated and intended aim of Lenin and
the Bolsheviks precisely was to establish, upon the ruins of the empire
of the czars and ultimately throughout the entire world, a political
economy shaped by the seminal ideas of Karl Marx and Friedrich Engels. All the other Soviet-type economies of eastern and central Europe
resulted from the imposition of that Soviet model upon every country
that was in 1945 wholly occupied by the Red Army.

1. The promise of the socialist project

The voices Lenin heard were those of Marx and Engels, and the ideas
that he and the Bolsheviks took from these teachers were those of what

they were pleased to call scientific socialism. For our purposes the best source is *Socialism: Utopian and Scientific.* Originally excerpted from *Herr Eugen Dühring's Revolution in Science (Anti-Dühring)* this substantial pamphlet has been, after the *Communist Manifesto,* the most widely circulated classic of Marxism. Although actually written and published by Engels there is no question that both *Anti-Dühring* as a whole and the particular parts selected to form *Socialism: Utopian and Scientific* constitute authoritative representations of what in their correspondence both collaborators characterized as "our view" or "our theory."

Engels here explains that its foundations are "two great discoveries, the materialistic conception of history and the revelation of the secret of capitalistic production," both of which putative discoveries he then asserts that "we owe to Marx. With these discoveries Socialism became a science."[2] Socialism is, of course, here understood to involve essentially—in the words of the original clause 4 of the constitution of the British Labour Party—the collective ownership of "all the means of production, distribution and exchange." According to the materialistic conception of history aforementioned there comes a time when:

> The proletariat seizes political power and turns the means of production into State property.[3] . . . With this . . . the social anarchy of production gives place to a social regulation of production upon a definite plan, according to the needs of the community.[4] . . . The expansive force of the means of production bursts the bonds that the capitalist mode of production had imposed upon them. Their deliverance from these bonds is the one precondition for an unbroken, constantly accelerated development of the productive forces, and therewith for a practically unlimited increase of production itself.[5]

What Marxists call the capitalist relations of production eventually, it is claimed, constrict the growth of the forces of production, forces that had admittedly, at least during the earlier stages of the development of capitalism, grown as never before. But, with the establishment of the new socialist order, and the consequent shattering of these perceived fetters, there should be nothing to stop the almost infinite expansion of productivity. So in 1919 Lenin was to maintain that:

In the final instance, labour productivity is the most important, decisive circumstance for the history of the new social order. Capitalism has created labour productivity which was unknown under feudalism. Capitalism can be vanquished, and will finally be vanquished, through a new, much higher labour productivity, created by socialism.[6]

Two decades later, in a speech introducing a five-year plan, Stalin insisted, "Not abstract justice but socially necessary labour time justifies socialism."[7] Later still Nikita Khrushchev, as general secretary of the Communist Party of the Soviet Union, with much fanfare, announced a new party program promising that, thanks to the uninhibited and assured growth in productivity, the Soviet people would have achieved Communism "in the main" by 1980, when they would be enjoying "the highest living standard in the world." It has not happened. "Instead, they face the prospect of falling even farther behind the rest of the developed world in this regard."[8]

2. The crucial unasked question

When predictions based upon a theory have been thus decisively falsified, scientific curiosity, and indeed scientific integrity, demand that we should seek out the initial errors and deficiencies which have misled the theorists to commit themselves to such false predictions.

(i) It has often been remarked that the most eloquent tribute ever paid to the incomparable effectiveness of capitalist social arrangements as means for achieving economic growth was that of the *Communist Manifesto*. Yet it is rare to notice that neither Marx nor Engels, either there or elsewhere, either asks or attempts to give an answer to a question that, to anyone proposing to revolutionize these arrangements, ought to have appeared crucial, namely, What was the secret, and how shall we ensure that under our proposed alternative arrangements, that secret is not lost? That never-too-often-repeated tribute reads:

> The bourgeoisie, during its rule of scarce one hundred years, has created more massive and more colossal productive forces than have all preceding generations together. Subjection of Nature's forces to man, machinery, application of chemistry to industry and agriculture, steam-navigation, railways, electric telegraphs, clearing of whole continents for cultivation, canalisation of rivers, whole populations conjured out of the ground—what earlier century had even a presentiment that such productive forces slumbered in the lap of social labour?[9]

But how was it done, we ought to ask. What was and is the secret of this fabulous, unprecedented, undeniable, and undenied triumph? To this the first response—a surprising response from such a hostile source —is that it was all perfectly peaceful and nonviolent:

> The bourgeoisie, by the rapid improvement of all instruments of production, by the immensely facilitated means of communication, draws all, even the most barbarian, nations into civilisation. The cheap prices of its commodities are the heavy artillery with which it batters down all Chinese walls, with which it forces the barbarians' intensely obstinate hatred of foreigners to capitulate. It compels all nations, on pain of extinction, to adopt the bourgeois mode of production. . . . In one word, it creates a world after its own image. (*CM*, p. 225)

So far, so good; indeed, rather too good to be perfectly true history. But we still have to press the question: why did they want, and how did they become able, to do all this? For that, in Communist eyes, most frightful Hydra, "the bourgeoisie," is in fact no science fiction monster, no strange creature from another world, with powers that pass our understanding. It is instead a class or set of ordinary, finite, flesh and blood humans, a class or set consisting of nothing but individuals of our own familiar species. Apparently members of this assemblage have a peculiar and characteristic need, and it was in the course of satisfying this need that "the bourgeoisie" found itself creating "a world after its own image." Thus the *Manifesto* asserts: "The need of a constantly expanding market for its products chases the bourgeoisie over the whole surface of the globe. It must nestle everywhere, settle everywhere, establish connexions everywhere."

*   *   *

(ii) But again, why? The nearest we get to an answer in that document simply pushes the question one stage further back. This interim response is that these producers need to find an ever wider market for their products because they will keep producing ever more of the wretched things. Presumably this is because they are, with an equally stubborn constancy, forever increasing the efficiency of their methods of production. For, we are told:

> The bourgeoisie cannot exist without constantly revolutionising the instruments of production, and thereby the relations of production, and with them the whole relations of society. . . . Constant revolutionising of production, uninterrupted disturbance of all social conditions, everlasting uncertainty, and agitation distinguish the bourgeois epoch from all earlier ones.(*CM*, p. 224).

This "constant revolutionizing of production" is, of course, what Schumpeter was later to characterize as a "gale of creative destruction."[10] About this gale two things must be said at once. The first, obvious and less important, is that we still require some explanation of why constantly to revolutionize "the instruments of production" is supposed to present itself to every individual bourgeois as a compelling need. The second, more important and—once the first point has been put— almost equally obvious, is that it does not. For there are in fact plenty of firms, not protected by monopoly privileges, that nevertheless continue to stay in business for long periods without even trying to effect any revolutions in their methods of production. (Can anyone, for instance, point to any reference in the Marx-Engels correspondence to any such revolution effected in the Manchester mill of that mini-multinational, Ermen and Engels, during all the long years of the managerial involvement of Friedrich Engels?) Much the same can be true even of entire industries.

The importance of that second point is to remind us that all innovation presupposes new ideas and fresh initiatives. In industrial production, for instance, someone has to think of what would in fact be a better, more efficient way of doing whatever it may be. Or, more fundamentally, someone has to invent a new product to be produced or a fresh service that might be provided. After that someone—perhaps, yet not necessarily, someone else but very necessarily someone who is in, or can get into, a position to realize that creative idea—someone has to become both persuaded that it is a winner and persuaded actually to take whatever steps are needed to put it into effect.

Yet even where you do have people both trying to invent such ideas and people able and eager to implement them if and when they become available, there neither is nor can be any guarantee that potential winners will be, first, thought of, then recognized to be such, and, finally, adopted. This very fact, that the occurrence, recognition, and realization of successful human creativity is not guaranteed—neither by God nor by history nor by anything else—constitutes just one more good reason why those who want economic growth should seek and favor social arrangements that will ensure, as far as any such arrangements can, that whoever is in a position to make decisions on investment or disinvestment is subject to the strongest possible incentives to ensure that the senses of those decisions turn out to have been maximally wealth-creating, or maximally wealth-preserving, as the case may be.

Marx and Engels would seem to have been misled by their materialistic conception of history to neglect if not outright to deny the general importance of individual human creativity and, in particular, of the crucial importance for the achievement of economic growth of the incentives and disincentives affecting the makers of investment decisions. For Marx and Engels, to put it no stronger, were very much inclined to think of what they called "the forces of production" as if these were natural forces, natural forces that human actions may perhaps check or release from checks but that otherwise develop and operate spontaneously.

(iii) Perhaps the main reason why Marx and Engels seem never to have recognized the crucial reason for the productive success of competitive capitalism is that—like their disciple Lenin[11]—their purpose in pinning on a label was not so much to understand as to destroy an opponent. There might have been more truth in the first claim made by Engels at the graveside, that Marx was the Darwin of the social sciences, had not his second claim been altogether too correct: that always and "above all Marx remained a revolutionist." For the fact is that, again and again, in all his published writings, scientific truth is sacrificed to revolutionary rhetoric.

Why, for example, is the central concept in *Capital* itself that of value, defined in terms of whatever is from time to time and from place to place the (socially necessary) labor time required to produce that value, rather than that of price, presumably defined similarly as a function of relative scarcity and effective demand? The inadequate answer —and the insufficient excuse for all the excruciating elaboration of consequent complexities—can only be, surely, that this tortuous and tortured exercise is necessary if the supposedly infamous thing, capitalism, is to be exposed as essentially, irreformably, and viciously exploitative.[12] Certainly a truly Weberian value-freedom (*wertfreiheit*) in theoretical economic science can permit no place for any notion of value that is not some sort of function of price,[13] while any system of price determination that refuses to take account of relative scarcity thereby removes all possibility of economic rationality.

Another and perhaps deeper source of Marxist reluctance to recognize the importance of human creativity, and the need for appropriate incentives for economic decision makers, has been mentioned already. It lies in their commitment to materialistic metaphysics. Their materialistic conception of history which was, notoriously, reached by standing Hegel on his head (or, rather, by putting him for the first time on his feet) required Marx and Engels to insist that—this side of the revolution, at any rate—ideas occur or arise and are adopted when and only when the development of the material conditions of production makes their occurrence and adoption timely and even inevitable.

3. Competitive capitalism's open secret

For anyone to whom no such revelatory guarantee has been vouchsafed, the central question is who—what man or assembly of men as Hobbes would have had it—makes the decisions to invest, or to reinvest, or to disinvest.[14] Once this question is answered science requires us to go on to ask under what constraints, and subject to which incentives and disincentives, these key people make their decisions. Under the system Marx and Engels seem to have been among the first to characterize as capitalist, but that Adam Smith knew only as "the natural system of perfect liberty and justice" or "the obvious and simple system of natural liberty,"[15] these decisions to invest or to reinvest or to disinvest are made either by the owners or by the agents of the owners of the capital concerned.

(i) The making of decisions to invest or to reinvest or to disinvest constitutes the role of the enterpriser. This is a different role from that of the manager, although it is one that may at different times be played by the same one man (or assembly of men) who (or which) plays the role of manager. I write "enterpriser" rather than "entrepreneur" because it is long overtime for the language of the people that made the first Industrial Revolution to employ a native word for members of the set that led it. (By Cantor's Axiom for Sets the sole, essential feature of a set is that its members have at least one common characteristic, any kind of characteristic.)

We should not, perhaps, be surprised to find Marx unwilling to make room in *Capital* for a discussion of the role of the enterpriser. For he would have been bound to regard any halfway sympathetic treatment—at least of a capitalist enterpriser—as a treacherous defense of the class enemy. Indeed, and presumably for similar reasons, he showed almost as little understanding of the function of management. He would like to make out that "the labour of supervision and management" consists only in the supervision of labor. But one unexplained reference to "the wages of management both for the commercial and industrial manager" suggests some awareness that sometimes something further might be involved.[16] This awareness could have been stimulated by remarks in letters from Engels. For instance: "Since I have become the boss, everything has become much worse because of the responsibility" (April 27, 1867).

The capitalist answer to the question we have been contending to be crucial is that decisions to invest, to reinvest, or to disinvest are far too important to be entrusted to anyone save those who have the greatest possible individual interest in getting them right—in making them, that is, in such ways that they will turn out to have been maximally wealth-creating, and/or minimally wealth-destroying. In particular they must, therefore, be made either by the immediate owners of the capital to be employed, or misemployed, or else by the directly and immediately and individually responsible agents of those owners. Precisely this is the argument Smith is putting in a never too often quoted but much too frequently misunderstood and misrepresented passage from that first, and greatest, and maybe only masterpiece of development economics, *An Inquiry into the Nature and Causes of the Wealth of Nations:*

> But it is only for the sake of profit that any man employs a capital in the support of Industry. . . . As every individual, therefore, endeavours as much as he can . . . to employ his capital . . . that its produce may be of the greatest value; every individual necessarily labours to render the annual revenue of the society as great as he can. He generally, indeed, neither intends to promote the public interest, nor knows how much he is promoting it. . . . By directing . . . industry in such a manner as its produce may be of the greatest value, he intends only his own gain, and he is in this, as in many other cases, led by an invisible hand to promote an end which was no part of his intentions. Nor is it always the worse for the society that it was no part of it. By pursuing his own interest he frequently promotes that of the society more effectually than when he really intends to promote it. (4 [2])

(ii) I myself first met this material now all of forty years ago, as an undergraduate in the University of Oxford. It was cited in a popular series of lectures given by G. D. H. Cole, then Chichele Professor of Political and Social Theory. Like most of us in his audience then, Cole could see nothing more here than the occasion for a swift passing sneer. This was, after all, merely a piece of apologetics for those obviously outmoded and altogether indefensible arrangements called by Cole laissez-faire capitalism. To such principled secularists as Cole himself, this particular defense was made the more repugnant by what we quite wrongly interpreted as the suggestion that these ongoings are benevolently guided by the invisible hand of an all-wise Providence.

Certainly Cole and the rest of us were right to see in this passage some defense of pluralistic and competitive capitalism. For it does indeed offer, for that and against monopoly socialist alternatives, an argument far more powerful than anything Cole was able to recognize or, I will now add, to meet. But where we were utterly wrong was in suspecting Smith of making some sort of antiscientific appeal to supernatural intervention. On the contrary, this text is a landmark in the history of the growth of the social sciences. For—almost a century before Darwin—Smith was uncovering a mechanism by which something strongly suggesting design could come about without any actual, conscious design, or, rather, without any intention directed towards that particular, ultimate outcome. The truth, as F. A. Hayek has labored to teach us,[17] is that Smith was one of the Scottish founding fathers of social science, men of the Edinburgh Enlightenment concerned above all to show that and how all the basic social institutions, and not the economic only, evolved as unintended consequences of intended human action.

To appreciate this is to realize how mistaken it is to construe Smith's invisible hand as an instrument of supernatural direction. To do this is as preposterous as to interpret Darwin's natural selection as being really supernatural selection. For Smith's invisible hand is no more a hand directed by a rational owner than Darwin's natural selection is selection by supernatural intelligence. It was precisely and only by uncovering the mechanisms operative in the two cases that they both made supernatural intervention superfluous as an explanation. Adam Smith's invisible hand is not a hand, any more than Darwin's natural selection is selection. Or—to put the point in a somewhat more forced and technical way—"invisible" and "natural" are in these two cases just as much alienans adjectives[18] as are "positive" and "people's" in the expressions "positive freedom" and "people's democracy."

Again, it is wrong to accuse Smith, as he so often is accused, of assuming or asserting that the results of the operations of all such unplanned and unintended social mechanisms are always, if only in the long run, providentially happy. The most elegant refutation of this particular accusation is to be found in his treatment of the division of labor. Certainly, he writes, this "is not originally the effect of any human wisdom, which foresees and intends the general opulence to which it gives occasion. It is the necessary though very slow and gradual consequence of a certain propensity in human nature which has in view no such extensive utility; the propensity to truck, barter, and exchange one thing with another" (1 [2]). But Smith then goes on to describe and lament the dehumanizing consequences of extreme developments in this occasion of opulence. It is these purple passages that Marx quotes in *Capital* to support his own polemic on this count,[19] but neither there nor anywhere else does Marx even attempt to show how and why socialism can be relied on to make an end either of the division of labor or of the evils perceived to be consequent upon it.

Having thus disposed of misconceptions about what Smith's contention was, we can now see that he had excellent, down to earth, altogether this-worldly reasons for concluding that, if the object of the exercise is—as the title of his book indicates that for him it was—to maximize gross national product, then the enterpriser role is best filled by the immediate owners of the capital either already at risk or about to be put at risk. For, necessarily, they have obvious, direct, and exactly proportionate personal interests in achieving the most satisfactory combination of maximum security and maximum return on the capital employed. Of course there is no guarantee that all such persons will get all their decisions right. Even those who usually turn out to have spotted winners will sometimes pick losers. It is indeed precisely because things are so difficult, and so apt to come unstuck, that anyone concerned to increase the wealth of nations has such an excellent reason for wanting to have the crucial decisions made, the crucial initiatives taken, always and only by directly and appropriately interested parties.

Also, where and in so far as people are—as Smith nicely has it— "investing their own capitals," the unsuccessful will, to the extent that they have made bad investments, necessarily be deprived of opportunities to make further costly mistakes, while the successful will by a parallel necessity be enabled to proceed to further and, we may hope, greater successes. Smith himself seems never to have emphasized or even seized this corollary point about feedback, although it must be of the last importance in any consideration of alternative ways of providing for the taking of economic initiatives.

4. Spontaneous order or central command?

So what is the alternative to social arrangements by which enterpriser decisions are made by, or immediately on behalf of, the several owners of the capital involved? The first supposedly scientific socialist answer to this question was offered by Engels just before his collaboration with Marx began, and neither of them seems to have vouchsafed anything fuller or more adequate in their later years. Engels starts with a favorite phrase, several times repeated in *Anti-Dühring:*

> The present anarchy of production, which corresponds to the fact that economic relations are being developed without uniform regulation [planning], must give way to the organization of production. Production will not be directed by isolated *entrepreneurs* independent of each other and ignorant of the people's needs; this task will be entrusted to a specific social institution. A central committee of administration, being able to review a broad field of social economy from a higher vantage point, will regulate it in a manner useful to the whole of society, will transfer the means of production into hands appropriate for this purpose, and will be specially concerned to maintain a constant harmony between production and demand.[20]

The most fundamental and ruinous fault in all such socialist thinking is the assumption that the only alternative to command is chaos, the refusal to recognize any regularity or order that has not had to be, and has not been, imposed by orders and regulations. The productive activities of firms in a market economy certainly are anarchic if and in so far as all that is meant by saying this is that these activities are not directed by the commands handed down "from a higher vantage point" by "a central committee of administration." But it is the diametric opposite of the truth to assert that the managements of these several firms, because their activities are not all coordinated and controlled from some central and supreme headquarters, must be in a worse position than such a supreme headquarters, both for discovering and meeting "the people's needs" and for maintaining "a constant harmony between production and demand."

For when and in so far as decisions are made at the level of the individual firm, the information that has to be processed by the local deciders, if their decisions are to be economically rational, is exactly the same information about the prices customers are prepared to pay for the products and about the (local) prices of the factors of production as the information that central planners, if they are to have any hope at all of issuing economically rational directions to all their subordinates, will have somehow first to collect from all the firms under their command, and then to coordinate, collate, and process.

Because for their revolutionary polemical purposes they preferred to devote themselves to developing a theory of value logically independent of any market-determined price Marx and Engels neglected to inquire into the functions of prices in the system they wanted to destroy. Actual market economies, like actual command economies, all in various ways and to a greater or lesser extent defect from their different and opposed ideals. But, ideally, in a market every price of every product or service is a function of the relative scarcity of, and of the effective demand for, that particular product or service.

Prices fulfill three main functions in such an idealized market society. First, they transmit information. Users learn, for instance, that it is necessary to conserve energy because that information is transmitted to them in the shape of higher prices for fuel. The range of information thus transmitted is enormous. It includes information about people's product preferences, about resource availability, and hence about productive possibilities. Market-determined prices thus enable innumerable, widely scattered economic activities to be coordinated without dependence upon any centralized organization for the collection of relevant information and the issuing of appropriate commands.

A second function such prices perform is to provide incentives to adopt the least costly methods of production and to employ available resources for whatever—whether rightly or wrongly—are in fact the uses most highly valued in whatever market is in question. Borrowing a phrase from the vocabulary of advertisers, perhaps the chief "product plus" of such a price system is that the incentive to appropriate action automatically accompanies the information thus transmitted. The third task performed by the price system in an ideal market economy is to determine the (passive) distribution of earned income[21]—by making all rates of pay a function of the relative scarcity of and effective demand for various sorts of labor.

Once we have learnt to appreciate both these three main functions of a market-determined price system and the reasons why investment decisions are more likely to prove wealth-creating—or at least wealth-preserving—if made either by the several owners or by the direct agents of the owners of the capitals employed, it becomes easy to see both that and why the "anarchy of production" in a market economy is bound to do better than the "central committee of administration" in a command economy, both in discovering and meeting "the people's needs" and in maintaining "a constant harmony between production and demand."

5. Some significant failures

Theoretical reasons why we ought not to have expected the prophecies of continuing greater growth in Soviet-type economies (STEs) to be fulfilled have been spelt out at length. It is now time and overtime to indicate, however briefly, one or two of the particular practical consequences of reconstructing and maintaining economies upon devoutly Marxist principles. But in order to form a tolerably detailed picture of what went wrong in the Soviet economy and in the other STEs of Eastern Europe, and why, the reader will have to refer to one or two of the particular studies published by such organizations as the London-based Centre for Research into Communist Economies.

(i) Take agriculture first, since this constitutes perhaps the most striking failure of the socialist system. Apparently "it costs the U.S.S.R. twice as much in real resources to produce a unit of agricultural output as it does in comparable climatic areas in the West. Much of this difference is accounted for by the extraordinarily large expenditure of labour in the U.S.S.R." Thus "the productivity of labor in Western agriculture was found to be some ten times that in the U.S.S.R. Even Soviet statistics agree that labor productivity in the U.S.S.R is only 20 to 25 percent of that in the United States, and that it has been at this relative level for many years."[22] Nor should it be forgotten that, whereas the former Russian Empire became a major exporter of grain, this was no longer true of the U.S.S.R. From time to time it even had to make substantial imports. The ultimate causes of the various grotesque inefficiencies that produced this remarkable reversal are among independent experts scarcely disputed. The state owned all the land and, for all practical purposes, all the capital stock as well. It was this socialist fact that explains

> the difference with which the farmers treat their land and capital stock and, in particular . . . the revealed short-term bias in farm management decision-making. Nobody has a strong incentive to care for the land and capital stock or to try to maximize the returns to these resources over their lifetime. Thus the Soviet government has for ideological reasons denied itself the fruits of the strong incentives to the efficient use of resources that are inherent in private ownership. Moreover, because state ownership of land and capital in the farms means that there is no market and [hence that there are] no market prices for their resources, the government is hard put to know how to allocate them to their best use. It lacks an efficient (economizing) guide to choice.[23]

(ii) In their industrial sectors all the STEs appeared to be extravagant in the use both of energy and of raw materials, which in turn is one, but by no means the only, reason why outputs of pollutants were absolutely and proportionately so much greater than in the market economies. The self-styled German Democratic Republic, for instance, emitted "more than four times as much sulphur dioxide *per capita* as the Federal Republic (and at half the living standard at that!)"[24] This is one of a kind of facts that should be recalled whenever anyone recommends public ownership as necessarily more friendly to the environment than private.

The explanation of this extravagence is not far to seek. In a market economy—it is the tyranny of the bottom line!—firms face more or less immediate bankruptcy if the returns from selling their products do not exceed their costs of production and marketing. The prices such firms pay for raw materials and other factors of production are functions of relative scarcity and effective demand. Management therefore has an urgent incentive to economize in the use of these factors, and to be always on the lookout both for cheaper alternatives and for reductions in the quantities employed. But in a command economy the prime incentive is to obey or to appear to obey the commands, while the resource inputs will be either more or less arbitrarily and unrealistically priced or else simply allocated. Milton Friedman loves to tell the story of the Chinese minister of materials distribution who, about to visit the United States, wanted to discover "who in the United States is responsible for the distribution of materials?"[25] Hence the expert verdict is:

> The main reasons for the lavish use of energy in the Soviet economy and for its manifest difficulties in spurring conservation lie in the *modus operandi* of the economic system itself. Because of the deficiencies of Soviet price-setting, energy has seemed cheap, even to the planners. . . . Oil and gas prices are well below their opportunity costs, and coal prices are still so low that the entire industry operates at a substantial and growing loss. Prices are changed only after long intervals, despite rising costs of production. Far more important, however, is the fact that producing enterprises respond weakly, if at all, to changes in prices. . . . Their fuel supplies are allocated to them . . . through central rationing, and enterprises have been motivated to obtain as much as possible. . . . The success of the firm and the bonuses for its managers have always depended on meeting the plans for output. . . . With such an orientation toward output and its growth, targets for saving energy and other resources have had secondary status and have generally been unmet.[26]

(iii) Another significant weakness in the Soviet economy and in other STEs was the lack of innovation both in developing the technology of production and in introducing new consumption goods. Can anyone point to any kind of such good or, in particular, to any new pharmaceutical product that was developed and marketed first in any of the STEs? General Secretary Brezhnev himself once complained that the managers of industrial enterprises in the U.S.S.R. "shy away from innovation the way the Devil shies away from incense." (This weakness, however, did not afflict the bloated sector supplying the military and the police, a sector which in all these economies was far larger than in almost any market economy, and the demands of which were, of course, always granted absolute priority.[27]) Once again the source of the trouble would appear to be the perverse system of managerial incentives, a system that seems to be inherent in the nature of such a command economy:

> Put most simply, the balance of risks and rewards for innovative behaviour is heavily skewed toward the former, at least from the point of view of the manager. First of all, decisions to install new machinery or processes or to produce new products are tangled in a mass of plans, rules, regulations and directives from above. . . . Even more important, managerial incentives have always been heavily oriented toward meeting monthly, quarterly, annual and now five-year plans for production. . . . The specific rules governing these rewards have been altered many times. . .—itself a factor blunting the efficacy of any incentive system—but always the bulk of a manager's bonus has depended on meeting his plan for output. . . . Installation of new machinery and processes or producing new products disrupts the routine of plant operations. Production lines . . . must be shut down temporarily, workers retrained or redeployed and the inevitable "bugs" in the innovations coped with. By innovating and coping with the inevitable disruptions, the manager risks not meeting his production plan and depriving himself and his employees of bonuses.[28]

Why then should he innovate? In fact he does not. After all, innovation and especially successful innovation is not, and scarcely could be, commanded.

Notes

1. J. M. Keynes, *The General Theory of Employment, Interest and Money* (London: Macmillan, 1936), p. 383.

2. F. Engels, *Socialism: Utopian and Scientific,* trans. E. Aveling (London: G. Allen and Unwin, 1892), p. 44.

3. Ibid., p. 75, emphasis original.

4. Ibid., p. 74.

5. Ibid., p. 80.

6. Quoted in K. C. Thalheim, *Stagnation or Change in Communist Economies* (London: Centre for Research into Communist Economies, 1986), p. 12.

7. Stalin was, as usual, studiously following in the footsteps of both Marx and Lenin in the first as well as the second part of this statement: "The moment anyone started to talk to Marx about morality, he would roar with laughter." And Lenin correctly insisted that there was in the teaching of Marx "not a grain of ethics from beginning to end" since "theoretically, it subordinates the 'ethical standpoint' to the 'principle of causality': in the practice, it reduces to the class struggle." For the references see S. Lukes, *Marxism and Morality* (Oxford: Clarendon 1985), pp. 27 and 21.

8. Gertrude Schroeder, *The System versus Progress* (London: Centre for Research into Communist Economies, 1986), p. 72.

9. K. Marx and F. Engels, *The Communist Manifesto,* reprinted in, for instance, D. McLellan, ed., *Karl Marx: Selected Writings* (Oxford: Oxford University Press, 1977), p. 225. (Hereinafter cited parenthetically in the text as *CM* followed by a page number.)

10. J. Schumpeter, *Capitalism, Socialism and Democracy* (London: Allen and Unwin, 1963), chapter 7.

11. Lenin was fond of quoting G. V. Plekhanov: "First, let's stick the convict's badge on him, and after that we can examine his case." See R. Conquest, *Lenin* (London: Collins Fontana, 1972), p. 40.

12. One testing problem for Marxist casuists must be to explain how, in operating a wholly automated factory, surplus value is to be profitably extracted by *not* buying any labor power at all. A reading of the most relevant chapter 15 in *Capital,* "Machinery and Modern Industry" (in volume 1, part 4, "Production and Relative Surplus-value"), suggests that, controversially, their best bet would be to divert discussion to the more urgent and practical problem of what alternative employment, if any, might be found for workers displaced by automation.

13. For the late Scholastics the just price of anything, and hence presumably its real value, was its actual price in an ideally normal, fully competitive market. See, for instance, R. Roover, "The Concept of the Just Price,"

The Journal of Economic History 18 (1958), and compare Alejandro A. Chafuen, *Christians for Freedom: Late-Scholastic Economics* (San Francisco: Ignatius, 1986).

14. The third alternative of reinvestment is introduced to cover the case in which, perhaps because its market has collapsed or perhaps because its competition has become too formidable, an enterprise can no longer carry on producing what previously it was producing; however, the decision is not to shut down, dismiss the staff, and sell off the plant for what it will fetch, but instead to employ (much) the same equipment and (much) the same workforce to produce something else that will—it is hoped—sell better. When the market for widgets has collapsed, maybe there is still a future for gizmos.

15. A. Smith, *An Inquiry into the Nature and Causes of the Wealth of Nations*, ed. R. H. Campbell and A. S. Skinner (Oxford: Clarendon, 1976), 4 (7) 3 and 4 (9).

16. K. Marx, *Capital*, ed. F. Engels, trans. S. Moore and E. Aveling (Moscow: Foreign Language Publishing House, 1961), vol. 3, chapter 23, pp. 376–82.

17. See, for instance, his *Studies in Philosophy, Politics and Economics* (London: Routledge and Kegan Paul, 1967).

18. See note 12 to chapter 4.

19. Marx, *Capital*, vol. 1, chapter 14, p. 362.

20. Quoted at pp. 256–57 of B. D. Wolfe, *Marxism: One Hundred Years in the Life of a Doctrine* (New York: Dial, 1955).

21. In the ever-proliferating literature of what is curiously distinguished as *social* justice it is assumed, almost always without supporting argument, that all wealth and income ought to be actively (re)distributed. Compare, for instance, my *The Politics of Procrustes: Contradictions of Enforced Equity* (Buffalo, N.Y.: Prometheus Books, 1981).

22. Schroeder, *The System versus Progress* (1986), p. 61.

23. Ibid., pp. 63–64.

24. J. Winiecki, *Economic Prospects: East and West* (London: Centre for Research into Communist Economies, 1987), p. 77, and compare also p. 40.

25. *Market or Plan?* (London: Centre for Research into Communist Economies, 1984), p. 26.

26. Schroeder, *The System versus Progress* (1986), pp. 52–53.

27. Intense militarization would appear to be characteristic of Marxist-Leninist regimes as such. See J. L. Payne, *Why Nations Arm* (Oxford: Blackwell, 1989).

28. Schroeder, *The System versus Progress* (1986), pp. 42–43.

Part Four

Applied Philosophy

11

The Right to Death

The wise man will for reasonable cause make his own exit from life
on his country's behalf, or for the sake of his friends, or if he suffers
intolerable pain, mutilation, or incurable disease.

Zeno of Litium (the Stoic)

Let us start from a phrase in the Declaration of Independence, but
adopting the rather indirect approach of quotation within a quotation.
With his usual shrewd grasp of fundamentals, the small-town lawyer
Abraham Lincoln wrote in 1857:

The authors of that notable instrument . . . did not intend to declare
all men equal in all respects. They did not mean to say that all men
were equal in color, size, intellect, moral developments, or social
capacity. They defined with tolerable distinctness in what respects they
did consider all men created equal—equal in certain "unalienable rights,
among which are life, liberty, and the pursuit of happiness."

1. Two kinds of rights

It is perhaps tempting to digress to support and to belabor the point
that neither Lincoln nor the Founding Fathers believed either that "at

249

birth human infants, regardless of heredity, are as equal as Fords" or that some such repudiation of genetic fact is implied or presupposed by any insistence upon an equality of fundamental human rights.[1] But our present concern is with the actual prescriptive and proscriptive content of these particular norms. For us the crux is that they are all, in M. P. Golding's terminology, *option* as opposed to *welfare* rights: the former forbid interference, within the spheres described, entitling everyone to act or not to act as they see fit, whereas the latter entitle everyone to be supplied with some good, by whom and at whose expense not normally being specified.[2] Hence, with that "peculiar felicity of expression" that led to his being given the drafting job, Thomas Jefferson spoke not of rights to health, education, and welfare—and whatever else might be thought necessary to the *achievement* of happiness, but of rights to life, liberty, and the *pursuit* of happiness—it being up to you whether you do in fact pursue (and to the gods whether, if so, you capture) that prey. An option right is thus a right to be allowed, without interference, to do your own thing. A welfare right is a right to be supplied, by others, with something that is thought to be, and perhaps is, good for you, whether you actually want it or not.

To show that the Founding Fathers were indeed thinking of option rather than welfare rights, it should here be sufficient to cite a passage from Blackstone, one which has the further merit of indicating upon what general feature of our peculiarly human nature such fundamental rights must be grounded. From its first publication in 1765, his *Commentaries on the Laws of England* had a profound influence on all the common-law jurisdictions in North America, an influence that continued well into the federal period. Blackstone wrote:

> The absolute rights of man, considered as a free agent, endowed with discernment to know good from evil, and with the power of choosing those measures which appear to him to be most desirable, are usually summed up in one general appellation, and denominated the natural liberty of mankind. . . . The rights themselves . . . will appear from what has been premised, to be no other, than that *residuum* of natural liberty, which is not required by the laws of society to be sacrificed to the public convenience; or else those civil privileges, which

society has engaged to provide in lieu of the natural liberties so given up by individuals.[3]

But now, if those self-evident fundamental and universal rights are thus option rights, and they surely are, then the right to life must be at the same time and by the same token the right to death: the interference forbidden must be the killing of anyone against that person's will, and that person's entitlement, the entitlement to choose whether or not to go on living as long as nature would permit. In saying this I am not, of course, so rash as to maintain that it is something that all or any of the signers of the Declaration saw and intended. The claim is, rather, that, irrespective of what they or anyone else appreciated in 1775, this does necessarily follow from what they did then so solemnly attest and declare. It is today even more obvious that, if all men are endowed with certain natural and unalienable rights, then all must include all: black and white together. Yet this now so manifest consequence seems for many years to have escaped many people, up to and including justices of the Supreme Court. So a widespread failure to appreciate what may now appear an obvious implication is not sufficient to show it not really an implication at all.

2. The right to life and the right to death

In the lower court decision in the now famous case of Karen Ann Quinlan, Judge Muir denied the plaintiff's request to have the life-sustaining apparatus switched off, indicating that he did not find grounds in the Constitution for any right to die. Insofar as the Declaration of Independence is not part of the Constitution, we might give him the point. Yet, in my very unlegal opinion, if the amendment on which *Roe* v. *Wade*[4] was decided really does warrant what the Supreme Court decided that it did warrant, then it must surely warrant both suicide and assisted suicide. For in abortion what the pregnant woman is killing, or getting her doctor to kill for her, is arguably—notwithstanding that this is not an argument that I myself accept—another person with his or her right to life. So, if it would be a constitutionally unacceptable invasion of privacy to prevent a woman from killing a fetus or getting someone else to kill it for her, then surely it must be a far more un-acceptable incursion to prevent women, or for that matter, men, from either killing themselves or getting someone else to kill them. For in all those secular systems of law in which suicide still is a crime, it is a much less serious crime than murder.

(i) Judge Muir next went on to say that, if he were to grant the re-quest of the plaintiff, then "such authorization would be homicide and a violation of the right to life."[5] Since it was not disputed that Karen Quinlan had on at least three occasions insisted that, should this sort of situation arise, she would not wish to be maintained in the condi-tion in which she then was, Judge Muir's "right to life" becomes one that is at the same time a legal duty. Just that, or substantially that, does seem to be the present position in all those jurisdictions that recognize a right to life. For even where, as in my own country today, suicide itself is not a crime, to assist it still is, while with very few exceptions doctors and others are legally required to employ every available means to prolong life of any kind.

For good measure consider two further statements, one from each side of the Atlantic. The first was made by Mr. James Loucks, presi-dent of the Crozer Chester Medical Center at Chester, Pennsylvania. He had obtained a court order to permit his hospital to force a blood transfusion on a Jehovah's Witness who had previously requested in writing that, out of respect for her religious convictions, the hospital do no such thing. Mr Loucks explained that he and his staff overrode her wishes "out of respect for her rights." The second statement was made by the chairman of a group calling itself the Human Rights So-ciety, set up in the United Kingdom in 1969 to oppose the legalization of voluntary euthanasia. The chairman said, "There are really no such things as rights. You are not entitled to anything in this universe. The function of the Human Rights Society is to tell men their duties."[6]

It has sometimes been suggested that it is contradictory to speak of a right where the exercise of that putative right is compulsory.[7] This is certainly a tempting suggestion, and it may be what led the chair-man of the Human Rights Society thus categorically to deny what his society pretends to defend. But if we are going to allow welfare as well as option rights, then this contradiction seems to arise only with the latter and not the former. If that is correct then we can pass, for instance, article 26 of the 1948 United Nations Universal Declaration of Human Rights: "Everyone has the right to education. . . . Elementary education shall be compulsory." Yet it will still allow us to reject the combination of a right to join a labor union with any corresponding compulsion so to do. For if the exercise of a welfare right is to be made compulsory, then the justification of the compulsion can only be the good, the welfare, of the persons so compelled. Yet, in England at any rate, the spokesmen for the labor unions, and their political creatures in the Labour Party, try to justify forced recruitment on the grounds, not paternalistically, that membership is in the best interests even of those who fail to see this themselves, but indignantly, that all holdouts are freeloaders enjoying the benefits, which it is alleged that the union has brought, without undertaking the burdens of membership.

So, allowing that it can be coherent to speak of a right that its bearers are to be forced to exercise, could there be such a compulsory welfare right to life? The crux here is whether the prolongation of life that it is proposed to impose can plausibly be represented as being good for the actual recipients of this alleged benefit. But perhaps, before tackling that question, it needs to be said that any answer will leave open the different issues raised by considering the good of others. Certainly, while insisting on a universal human option right to life, in the sense explained earlier, and while urging always that it is overtime for this to be recognized and protected by our laws, I am myself ever ready to maintain that such most proper considerations of the good of others make some suicides morally imperative and others morally illicit: the suicide of Wilson, to better the chances of the remaining members of Scott's last expedition, provides an example of the one; and that of the English poetess Sylvia Plath, effected in another room of the house in which she was living with her two young and dependent children, provides an example of the other.

So long as we confine our attentions to what may vaguely but understandably be called normalities, and to the suicides and suicide attempts of the tolerably fit and not old, it is reasonable enough to hold that in general the frustration of such attempts does further the good of the attempters. Indeed, any realistic discussion in this area has to take account of the facts that a great many of what look like attempted suicides are in truth only dramatized appeals for help and that many of those genuine attempters whose attempts are aborted by medical or other interference survive to feel grateful to the interferers. But when we turn to the old, faced perhaps with the prospect of protracted senility, of helpless bedridden incontinence, of lives that will be nothing but a burden both to the liver and to everyone else, then the story is totally different. Here you do have to be some sort of infatuated doctrinaire to maintain an inflexible insistence that life, any life, is good for the liver.

Consider, for instance, what was said with such force and charm by the splendid Doris Portwood in her book *Common-sense Suicide*.[8] It should be enough to report that as a woman over sixty-five she saw herself as making, and encouraging her peers to join with her in making, a distinctive contribution to the women's movement. "How many of us," she asks those peers, "attending a friend or relative in her final days (or weeks, or months, or years) have said, 'It won't happen to me. I'll take care of that.' But did we say it aloud? It is time to say it loud and clear. And often." It is time, she concludes, mischievously mimicking the jargon of her juniors, to "declare our intention to start a meaningful dialogue on common-sense suicide."[9]

Or, again, take a newspaper letter written by Mrs. Margaret Murray, who had two years earlier published an article "declaring my intention to end my own life when increasing helplessness from multiple sclerosis makes it a hopeless, useless burden." This led to the production of a memorable television program. The present letter was a response to the statement by the medical director of St. Christopher's Hospice that "requests to end life are nearly always requests to end pain." That medical director had in that program asserted, "Though I might be helpless and actually fed and washed and have other sordid details attended to, my life had a value and I still had something to give." Dismissing this particular piece of sanctimonious self-deception with the question "Who are these greedy takers?" Mrs. Murray proceeded to deploy three cases:

An eighty-year-old army colonel, who realised he was becoming senile, flung himself in front of an Inter-City express as it went through the village where I live. A few months later a Newbury coroner gave a verdict of "rational suicide" on a retired water bailiff who took his own life because increasing infirmities meant it was no longer worth while to him.

And what of sufferers from Huntington's Chorea, never still a moment and unable to speak clearly enough to be intelligible? One of these unfortunates who is well known to me has tried three times to end her own life.[10]

(ii) The previous subsection dealt with the question whether there could be a right to life, the exercise of which is not allowed to be a matter for the choice of the individual. Such a right, of course, could only be a welfare not an option right. The issue in the present subsection is whether the option right to life, as explicated above, covertly contains an incongruous and unacceptable welfare element. The suggestion is that a right to life that is at the same time and by the same token a right to anticipate the death that would otherwise have occurred later must impose on some other person or persons a corresponding duty to bring about that earlier death: "A person's right to be killed gives rise to someone's (or everyone's) duty toward that person. If anyone can be said to have a right to be killed, someone else must have a duty to cooperate in the killing. . . . The important thing is that someone—a doctor, a nurse, a candystriper, a relative—intervene actively or passively to end the right-holder's life."[11]

This passage is, on the one hand, entirely sound insofar as it is insisting that all rights must impose corresponding duties; however, since all duties do not give rise to corresponding rights, the converse is false. This logical truth constitutes the best reason for saying that welfare rights do not belong in a Universal Declaration of Human Rights. For who are the people who have at all times and in all places been both able and obligated to provide for everyone "social security" (article 22), "periodic holidays with pay" (article 24), "a standard of living . . . including . . . necessary social services, and the right to security in the event of unemployment, sickness, disability, widowhood, old age, or other lack of livelihood in circumstances beyond his control" (article 25 [1]), to say nothing of the provision that that compulsory elementary education aforementioned "shall further the activities of the United Nations for the maintenance of peace" (article 26 [2])?

But the same passage is, on the other hand, entirely wrong insofar as it is trying to draw out the implications of an option right to life. Such rights do necessarily and as such impose corresponding obligations. These obligations rest uniformly and indiscriminately upon everyone else, not just upon some unspecified and unspecifiable subclass of providers, who may or may not in fact be available and able to provide. But these obligations are obligations not to provision but to noninterference. In a jurisdiction, therefore, that recognized and sanctioned the option right to life, the people who decided that they wanted to suicide[12] would, if they needed assistance, have to find it where they could. Their legal right to noninterference imposes no legal duty on anyone else to take positive steps to assist, although, of course, this is quite consistent with its being the case that someone is under a moral obligation so to do. Here as always we have to distinguish questions about what the laws do or would permit or prohibit from questions about what people are morally obliged to do or not to do.

3. Doctors and the right to die

Forty or more years ago, when I first joined the Voluntary Euthanasia Society, the emphasis was on extremes of physical pain. The main policy objective was to get voluntary euthanasia legislation that would establish official machinery to implement the wishes of those terminal patients who urgently and consistently asked for swift release. In response to medical and other developments in the intervening years the emphasis has shifted to irreversible decay into helpless futility and afflictions resulting in prolonged but not especially painful survival at a subhuman level of existence. The chief and most immediate objectives are also different. The Young Turks, at any rate, as well as their more wide-awake and forward-looking seniors, are now pushing for amendment of the Suicide Act and for measures to enable patients and their representatives to ward off unwanted treatment and vexatious life-support, rather than for an act setting up the paraphernalia of panels considering applications and directing that their decisions be implemented.

(i) It is in consequence no longer so true as once it was that "supporters of voluntary euthanasia do not merely want suicide or refusal of treatment or allowing a patient to die. They want the patient dead when he wants to be dead, and they want this accomplished through the physician's agency."[13] In the great majority of cases such as Doris Portwood or Margaret Murray have in mind, the agent would be the patient or, with patients too far gone to act themselves, the spouse or other close relative or friend. Consider, for example, Lael Wertenbaker's *Death of a Man* or Derek Humphry's *Jean's Way:* as both would have wished, the prime agent in the former was the wife and in the latter the husband. The only necessary involvement of the medical profession here is through the providing of advice on instruments, and maybe the instruments themselves, and not insisting on mounting an all-out campaign to revive the patients.

The desired amendment of the United Kingdom Suicide Act 1961, an act that already decriminalizes the deed itself, would replace the present general offense of "aiding, abetting, counseling or procuring the suicide of another" by the limited and in fact very rare one of doing this "with intent to gain or for other selfish or malicious reasons," leaving the courts to decide, as they so often do elsewhere, when the motives of the assistance were indeed discreditable. From a libertarian point of view this suggestion has, as against any voluntary euthanasia legislation, the great advantage of specifying not what is legal but what is illegal.

(ii) Next, and with special but not exclusive reference to the other sort of case, in which it is almost bound to be the doctors who would be either killing or letting die, a few brief and insufficient words about the absolute sanctity of all (human) life and the idea that killing (people) is always wrong. The suggestion is that, if these so often mentioned principles are to stand any chance of being ultimately acceptable, then both need to be amended in at least two ways.

The first amendment is already accepted almost universally when people think of it. It consists in actually inserting the unstated qualification "innocent." The point is to take account of killing in self-defense and of the execution of those who have committed capital offenses. In our terms, people who launch potentially lethal assaults thereby renounce their own claims to the option right to life. Reciprocity is of the essence; just as one person's option right gives rise to the corresponding obligations of all others to respect that right, so, if people violate the rights of others, then that nullifies the obligations of those others to recognize any corresponding rights vested in the violators.

The second amendment consists in adding some indication that what is to be held sacred and inviolate is a person's wish to go on living. This takes account of the enormous, and in almost all contexts crucial, differences between murder and suicide. These are that murderers kill other people against their will, whereas suicides kill themselves, as they themselves wish. It is perverse and preposterous to characterize suicide, and to condemn it, as self-murder. You might as well denounce intramarital sex as own-spouse adultery.

In the present context the importance of this second amendment is that it attends to those particular human essentials that provide the grounds on which all claims to universal human rights must be based. It was to these that Blackstone was referring when, in discussing "the absolute rights of man," he wrote "of man, considered as a free agent, endowed with discernment to know good from evil, and with the power of choosing these measures which appear to him to be most desirable." It was on these same universal features that Thomas Jefferson himself insisted. In Query (XIV) to the *Notes on the State of Virginia* he made various lamentable remarks about blacks, remarks that I shall not repeat and that would today disqualify him from all elective office. For Jefferson, it was notwithstanding all these alleged racial deficiencies that blacks (and Indians) certainly do have what it takes to be endowed with the "rights to life, liberty, and the pursuit of happiness." Again, it was to these same essential features of people as beings capable of choosing values and objectives for themselves, and of having their own reasons for these choices, that Immanuel Kant was referring when he laid down that famous but most confused formula: "Act in such a way that you always treat humanity, whether in your own person or in the person of another, never simply as a means, but always at the same time as an end."[14]

(iii) Finally, it is necessary to relate the right to die to the Hippocratic Oath. That has often been cited as a decisive reason why doctors and other health-care professionals must strive always and by all means to maintain life, irrespective both of the quality of that life and of the wishes of its liver. The argument is still employed sometimes, notwithstanding that nowadays probably only a small minority of doctors even in the liberal democracies do actually swear that oath. (In the Communist countries it was, of course, outlawed—as making doctors servants of their individual patients rather than of society as represented by the state.)

The relevant sentences of the Hippocratic Oath read: "I will use treatments to help the sick according to my ability and judgment, but never with a view to injury and wrongdoing. I will not give anyone a lethal dose if asked to do so, nor will I suggest such a course."[15] It is obvious that, in the area of today's gerontological concerns, the second and subsidiary undertaking may come into conflict with the primary promise to "use treatments to help the sick according to my ability and judgment."

In such situations it is impossible to keep the oath. Happily, there is no doubt which of the incompatibles should then be preserved. For at the heart of the entire Hippocratic tradition is the ideal of the independent professional who—always, of course, within the framework formed by the universal imperatives of moral duty—puts his skills at the service of his patients. So it is quite clear, to me at any rate, that, given a more libertarian system of public law, that service must not only exclude forcing unwanted treatment upon those who have, either directly or indirectly, asked to be left alone, but also include providing instrumental advice on suicide, and maybe the means too, if suicide is the considered wish of their patients.

Notes

1. The quotation is borrowed from Ludwig von Mises, *Theory and History* (New Rochelle, N.Y.: Arlington House, 1969). It derives from Horace M. Kalker's article on behaviorism in the *Encyclopaedia of the Social Sciences* (New York: Macmillan, 1930-5), vol. 2, p. 498.

2. See E. L. Bandman and B. Bandman, eds., *Bioethics and Human Rights* (Boston: Little Brown, 1978), chapter 4.

3. The Cadell and Butterworth edition (London, 1825), pp. 125 and 128.

4. 410 U.S. 113, 93 S A. 705 (1973).

5. In the Opinion of Robert Muir, Jr., in the Matter of Karen Quinlan: An Alleged Incompetent. Super. A. N . J., Chancery Division, Morris Company, C-201-75 (November 10, 1975).

6. The second statement was copied from a report in *The General Practitioner* (London) for November 26, 1978. The first comes from *Reason* (Santa Barbara, Calif.) for September of the same year.

7. See, for instance, Bertram Bandman in Bandman and Bandman, eds., *Bioethics,* chapter 5.

8. New York: Dodd Mead, 1978.

9. Ibid., p. 10.

10. *The Guardian* (London) for January 20, 1979. Mrs. Murray did later succeed in executing her plans to take her own life.

11. Bandman and Bandman, eds., *Bioethics,* p. 141.

12. My employment of either the single word as an intransitive verb or the affected sounding gallicism "suicide themselves" is calculated. For the ordinary English expression "commit suicide" is one of these expressions—first noted in Aristotle's *Nicomachean Ethics,* 1107A 8-13—that "already imply badness." Since I do not hold that suicide is always wrong I deliberately eschew that implication.

13. Bandman and Bandman, eds. *Bioethics,* p. 130.

14. *Groundwork of the Metaphysic of Morals,* in *The Moral Law,* trans. H. J. Paton (London: Hutchinson, 1968), p. 94 (italics removed). For a development of a Kantian rationale for the option rights of the Declaration of Independence, see my *Equality in Liberty and Justice* (London, and New York, Routledge 1989).

15. W. H. S. Jones and E. T. Withington, ed. and trans., *Hippocrates and the Fragments of Heracleitus* (Cambridge, Mass., and London: Harvard University Press, and Heinemann, 1959), I, 298. The translation here is in fact my own.

12

Brainwashing, Deprogramming, and Mental Health

Many people react to my proposed treatment of fetishism and neu-
rosis . . . by exclaiming in horror, "Surely this is nothing but brainwashing." . . . Nobody knows what brainwashing is . . .

H. J. Eysenck[1]

Some years ago a journal enjoying a wide circulation in Britain among
doctors in general practice (GPs) published a news item under the
characteristically arresting headline: "GP warns on the menace of the
Moonies." Between the opening paragraph, addressed to "fellow doctors who are called on to deal with the victims of the cult religion,"
and the conclusion, giving particulars of "the organization set up to
help the families of young people caught up in cult religions," this
anonymous GP is quoted as saying, among other things: "My daughter
was recruited two years ago, when she was only seventeen and on
holiday in America. . . . The whole thing is desperately difficult because I just don't know what to do. Trying to disillusion a convinced
Moonie is as hopeless as trying to convince a devout Catholic that
transubstantiation is rubbish."[2]

True, no doubt, only too true. Certainly I myself do not propose,
either here or elsewhere, to challenge this doctor's implicit assessment

261

of the cognitive status of the teachings either of the Unification or of the Roman Catholic Churches. Remember, after all, the four chapters of part one above! I too should be just as concerned as the anonymous GP, were either of our own two daughters to become converted to any religion at all, whether one of the new "cult religions" or one of the older and, I suppose—odd though this sounds—noncult kind. But the questions for us here and now are altogether different. Why should it be thought that such conversions, however regrettable, present any sort of medical problem, and are there circumstances in which it really is or would be proper for doctors or for psychiatrists, acting in their professional capacities, to try to change the religious or irreligious beliefs of their patients?

1. What is brainwashing?

That same issue of *Pulse* provided the merest hint towards some answer to the first of our two questions. For the news item from which the previous quotations were taken refers readers to a later feature: "How GP's Can Help the Mind-Thief Victims." When, however, we turn to that we find that the psychiatrist author, John Gleisner, confines himself to a significantly more limited question: "How do you cope with a young person who presents in the surgery saying he or she has been brainwashed?" Gleisner's answer refers in the main to one particular case coming to "a therapist who helps disturbed people at a community mental health centre near Manchester." This patient, Christine Nixon, gives her own story elsewhere in the same issue.

(i) This case is very different from that of the anonymous doctor's daughter. The complaint and the problem there arose from and for the father: the daughter was not complaining about her own condition, did not see it as a problem, and had never asked for any kind of help or treatment, whether medical or nonmedical. We thus have opportunity to remark that those who think of themselves as members of helping or caring professions would do well to ask, much more often than they do: "Who is it who actually is complaining, or who actually does see the situation as a problem, and precisely what is *their* complaint, or *their* problem?"

Many problem children, for instance, who nowadays get sent out of class for counselling rather than for punishment, are not problems, or at any rate not perceived problems, for themselves, however serious the all-too-serious problems they impose upon their parents, their teachers, or their peers. Many, too, of those so fashionably categorized as disturbed (passive) might more accurately be described as disturbing (active). Remember the story of the three Boy Scouts assuring their scoutmaster that they had duly performed their good deed for the day:

> "We helped a poor old lady across the road."
> "Surely it didn't need three of you to do that?"
> "She didn't want to go."

By contrast, it appears that Christine Nixon did, albeit with some hesitation, bring herself to make a complaint. She complained that "she had been brainwashed." Both she and Gleisner provided in their articles good reason for accepting his (different) judgment on her condition, a judgment that, we should perhaps notice, contains no conjecture about the causes of that condition. "Christine Nixon," he says, "suffered a complete breakdown after a week's course with the Moonies." Yet for us the next question is, "What is meant by 'brainwashing'; and would such treatment—supposing that this girl and others have in fact been subjected to it—justify the application to them, if necessary under constraint, of other treatments designed to secure the reversal of any conversions originally effected by such means?"

(ii) That this is indeed the question comes out very clearly from a letter, written by a spokesperson for FAIR, "the organisation set up to help the families of young people caught up in cult religions," and published in another British medical journal, *The Nursing Mirror* (July 30, 1979). Under an appropriate headline, "Beware the 'brainwashing' religious cults," this correspondent argues that "without progamming there would be no need of deprogramming!" The letter continues,

> The methods used by these pseudo-religious cults are a dangerous misuse of psychology. . . . There are many reports by . . . experts in mental health of the effects on the mind caused by a cult's programming and the obvious conclusion to be drawn . . . is that deprogramming, carried out properly and sympathetically, is the only possible way of restoring the individuality of a convert and his ability to think and act freely.

There is no need, at least on this occasion, to dispute the hypothetical contention that—were it once granted that certain people had been converted to new systems of belief when physically confined, and by the use of drugs, violence, starvation, sleep-deprivation or other manifestly improper means—then it might well become licit to employ similar, normally unacceptable means in the attempt to restore the, or their, previous condition. Fortunately that difficult question does not in the present case arise. Certainly the enemies of the various minuscule sets that those enemies like to call "cult religions," or "pseudoreligious cults," are very free with vivid, metaphorical charges of soul-snatching, mental rape, mind-thievery, brainwashing, and the like. They appear nevertheless unable or unwilling to spell out any literal, specific, and suitably scandalous content for all this scarifying abuse.

For example, Ferdinand Mount, a journalist more genuinely critical than most, put a key question in *The Spectator* (July 4, 1981): "But is there really a distinction in kind between the Moonies' methods of indoctrination and conversion and the methods of recognized religions?" He got no answer either from FAIR or from anyone else, neither in private nor published in the letters column of his magazine. But I was able to add my own further contribution there: "Like most of those who have attended academic conferences organized and financed by the Moonie cultural foundation, I myself have received many letters of private protest. To every one I have replied with an assertion and a question: the assertion, that the conferences I have attended were all conducted with absolute academic propriety; and the question, what outrageous and peculiar methods of persuasion employed by the Moonies are being denounced as 'brainwashing'?" No correspondent has ever given me a clear and definite answer revealing the basis of the accusation.

There is here, endemic, a crucial equivocation. Where charges are being brought against disfavored religious ultras, the word "brainwashing" is intended to carry implications of well nigh if not altogether irresistible pressures, with suggestions of the cruel and unusual techniques employed by the Chinese Communists on helpless prisoners captured in the Korean War. But when evidence is demanded to justify such charges, we find that the word is once more being construed only in its weaker sense—the sense in which it has become commonplace to speak of anyone accepting any item of unexamined and conventional foolishness as having been brainwashed into that acceptance.

2. Religious conversion: A freshly identified mental illness?

Yet we cannot simply leave things there, with a strong warning about the ambiguity of the term "brainwashing." For in the United States, and to a much lesser extent elsewhere, things have already gone far further. Some people have already made careers out of offering to the anxious families of young converts, in return for substantial fees, their own services as deprogrammers. Consider, for instance, his publisher's advertisement for Ted Patrick's *Let Our Children Go*: "Patrick is the man whose profession is the rescuing of brainwashed youngsters from cults like Hare Krishna and Sun Myung Moon. With their parents' help he snatches them off the street and takes them to a hideout to deprogramme them. He almost always succeeds—he has saved more than 1,000—and the youngsters themselves are intensely grateful. Now he tells us how he does it."[3]

Mr. Patrick himself, who is not by any standards psychiatrically qualified, and who had been operating without the protection of the law, was in September 1980 sentenced by the San Diego Superior Court to one year's imprisonment, five years probation, and a fine of $5,000. According to the *International Herald Tribune* of September 20, 1980, this sentence was for Patrick's part "in the kidnapping of a twenty-five-year-old Tucson waitress whose family feared that she was controlled by a religious zealot." Judge Norbert Ehrenfreund ruled, "We must observe the law that makes it a crime to abduct another human being." Allowing that Patrick had done a deal of good work, the judge insisted nevertheless: "There must be no further deprogramming. That part of his life must exist no longer."

This, however, was by no means the end of the affair. For others have been laboring to secure the protection of the law for the confinement of converts, and for their compulsory subjection to the deprogramming treatment. Some qualified psychiatrists are also arguing that conversions to disfavored minority belief systems fall within their own professional bailiwick, and should therefore be diagnosed and treated by and only by themselves and their colleagues. The effort to obtain legal sanction for forcible deprogramming takes the form of either appeals to existing laws, or moves to introduce new laws, under which converts can or could be made wards of some other members of their families, who then will, or would, with the full backing of the state power, see to it that the convert gets the treatment. This treatment is in fact, to put it mildly, harsh, while everyone, most especially including the patient, must know that, once they have been so confined, there will be no escape either from the legal guardianship or from that harsh treatment until and unless the deprogrammers become persuaded that they have effected a sound and thorough deconversion.

The psychiatric argument is that the original conversion has to be diagnosed as either being, or being the symptom of, a mental illness— a freshly identified syndrome for which someone has suggested the uncomfortable Anglo-Saxon label "faith sickness." Since it is an illness it must be bad for the patient. After all, as Ted Patrick said, when it is all over, "the youngsters themselves are intensely grateful."

By the way: this particular argument does not possess the same force in the present case that it must be allowed to have when deployed to justify the forcible frustration of suicide attempts. For it is, surely, one criterion of the soundness of a deprogramming job that the persons deprogrammed should be content in the belief system to which they have now reverted. Any Englishman of my generation must, therefore, be reminded of the immortal words of Miss Mandy Rice-Davies, when told of men who had denied her assertions about their sexual activities: "Well, they would, wouldn't they?"

3. Suitable cases for treatment?

It is not, of course, surprising that there are some psychiatrists eager to diagnose unpopular belief systems as symptomatic of a "faith sickness," and even more eager to offer their services (suitably remunerated) in order to cure even unwilling patients of this alleged affliction. Certainly these are not the only professional workers ready to welcome every chance to extend the area of application of the skills by which they earn their livings. So we must not be shy of challenging them to make good their contention that these are indeed suitable cases for psychiatric intervention. (After all, what experts are for—as they often need to be reminded—is to determine the least costly means to secure whatever ends their lay employers see fit to choose.[4])

The evidence actually offered is of three kinds. First, it is asserted that the belief systems of all these peculiarly unloved "pseudoreligious cults" are so irrational and so absurd that no sane person could by any open and above-the-board program of persuasion be converted to them. Second, it is claimed that the aforesaid cults have succeeded in developing almost if not quite irresistible techniques of conversion, techniques which, unlike those to which the then newly coined label "brainwashing" was originally applied, do not require the physical confinement or coercion of their subjects. Third, it is maintained that the effect of such improved Mark II brainwashing is to deprive its victims of free will, making them the zombie creatures of the persons or of the organization effecting this transformation.

(i) Proponents of the first of these three contentions reveal no more than the extreme narrowness of their own experience. For anyone having any familiarity with the fabulous variety and extreme preposterousness of the religious beliefs for which otherwise sane and sensible people have been willing to live and even, if required, to die, must realize that there is nothing in any of these freshly formed cults that would entitle unbelievers to draw the comfortable conclusion that their converts cannot but have been won by means incontestably illicit. The suggestion that adhesion to any such belief system constitutes a decisive demonstration of some fundamental unsoundness of mind is reminiscent of nothing so much as that old stubborn, bigoted insistence that any act of or attempt at suicide must be proof positive that—however temporarily—the balance of the agent's mind was disturbed.

(ii) The second contention, being of a less sophisticated logical type than the first, seems to be just plain false. No one has been able to cite any technique of persuasion employed by these tiny modern sects for which it is not possible to find plenty of precedents or parallels in earlier times or in other places. Furthermore, our best evidence indicates that whatever methods are in fact current in the Unification Church remain very far from 100 percent effective.[5]

(iii) The third contention is not of a kind to be expected from psychiatrists or, for that matter, from practitioners of any other psychological discipline.[6] Such persons are all much more likely to feel that their cloth requires them to minimize if not to deny the reality of free will, rather than to promise to restore it to those deprived. Be that as it may, this contention does possess the great merit of direct relevance. For, if it could be made out, it would show these conversions to "pseudoreligious cults" either to be, or to produce, paradigm cases of affliction with mental illness.

Consider first how we must in the present context interpret talk of a loss of free will. Presumably it means that the victims of such a loss are, at least in certain respects, like the victims of a paralysis or of St. Vitus Dance. They cannot, that is to say, as the rest of us can, at will move themselves or certain parts of themselves, or, as the case may be, prevent either certain parts of themselves or even their whole bodies from moving. If, furthermore, these victims are said also to be "zombie creatures of the persons or the organization" that has effected "this transformation" from their previous normal condition of being able at will to move or to prevent the movement of those various parts of themselves, then again what this implies, presumably, is that they are not themselves, at least in certain respects, truly agents. Instead they are, as it were, executing irresistible post-hypnotic suggestions from those dark and sinister persons, or that dark and sinister organization, offstage. (Perhaps there are further implications about glazed eyes and a general woodenness in movement, recalling presentations of "soul-snatched zombies" in horror movies with a Haitian setting. But these extras we may for present purposes ignore.)

If this is indeed the correct reading of the expression "a loss of free will," and certainly no alternative has been offered here, then the conditions of the victims of such a loss must most closely parallel that of several of Freud's early patients—those, that is to say, who were afflicted with tics and paralyses not attributable to any organic lesions or other physical deformations. What sufficiently justified these patients in reporting sick was this incapacitation, their inability either to move or to stop the movements of certain bodily parts normally subject to the will. What warranted speaking of mental rather than physical disease was the facts: that there were no relevant organic lesions or physical deformations, and that the incapacitations could be accounted for in psychological terms, and sometimes perhaps removed by psychotherapy.

But again, allow that these are the correct readings of "a loss of free will," and of the other similar expressions applied to supposedly brainwashed converts to "cult religions." And we must emphasize both that no other readings are suggested and that it is only in these readings that such converts could become suitable cases for psychiatric treatment—especially compulsory psychiatric treatment. Then we also have to notice that no sufficient means is ever given to warrant the application of such expressions to these converts. The complaint—which, typically, is made not by the intended patient but by the intended patient's family—is not that the convert cannot abandon the principles and practices of his or her new "cult religion," but that he or she most stubbornly and persistently refuses so to do. And that, however deplorable, is a totally different matter.

4. What should we mean by "mental illness"?

In the previous sections I have been taking for granted two fundamentals for which extensive argumentative support was provided in chapter 7: first, that ideas of mental health and mental illness ought to be modelled very closely upon ideas of physical health and physical illness, and hence, second, that actual sickness of either kind must involve discomfort and/or incapacitation in the patient. It is only and precisely as consequences of these two fundamentals that we become entitled to draw certain inferences that are in fact persistently and universally drawn and maintained, both within and outside the medical world, even by many who have long since lost their grip upon the premises needed to warrant these accepted conclusions. It is because, and in so far as, sickness is essentially painful and/or incapacitating that some forms of sickness may become acceptable excuses for failures to perform duties, or even for more positive delinquencies.

Again, and much more to the present point, it is only and precisely if sickness is essentially painful and/or incapacitating that the providers of relieving or curative treatment can normally be presumed to be doing something both desired by, and in the interests of, the patient, rather than, for example, simply advancing their own personal ideals or serving the supposed interests of that many-headed monster, Society. Even when the patient genuinely is, in this traditional understanding, sick, whether physically or mentally, the libertarian must scruple to connive in any compulsory therapy, the only exception being where sickness in that particular form constitutes a real and present danger to others.

Once we are fully seized both of these important consequences and of the interpretation of the premises required if we are to be entitled to draw such consequences therefrom, then we can see that we absolutely must not tolerate—at any rate in either a penal or a therapeutic context—any definition of "mental illness" not demanding that its patients must be as such substantially incapacitated or otherwise seriously incommoded. Thus it will not do, notwithstanding that it all too often has been and is done, to define the putative mental illness of psychopathy in terms only of dispositions to act in various antisocial ways, with no reference to any debilitating discomfort or relevant incapacitation in the psychopath. When this is nevertheless done it is, or ought to be, obvious both that psychopathy cannot any longer serve either to excuse or to extenuate such behavior and that any treatments imposed on the psychopath will have to be justified by reference to the good of others rather than in terms of the Hippocratic duties of the psychiatrists to their patients.[7]

Again, if "schizophrenia" is to be defined similarly, in terms of the harboring of "reformist delusions," or of actual conduct offensive to the ruling party and government—conduct perhaps including brave protests against the 1968 reconquest of Czechoslovakia or other more recent manifestations of Soviet imperial policy in Poland, Afghanistan, Ethiopia, Indochina, or wherever—then the "deprogramming" treatments inflicted on such schizophrenics certainly cannot be presumed to be either desired by them or even directly in their interests. It is the more necessary to belabor such points since many of those who played a leading and honorable part in condemning and resisting psychiatric abuses of individual liberty, both in the former U.S.S.R. and in the United States, have been curiously reluctant to engage with the general questions of the nature and scope of mental health or mental sickness. This is true, for instance, of the authors of both *Russia's Political Hospitals* and *New Religions and Mental Health*.[8] Urgently and conscientiously concerned to insist that Soviet dissidents were victims not of "reformist delusions" but of totalitarian tyranny, and that converts to unfashionable and perhaps authentically delusive religious belief systems cannot properly be dealt with as if they were carriers of catastrophically infectious physical diseases, these friends of freedom and dignity have not taken the time to spell out what makes some condition a mental illness, and as such a suitable case for treatment by the mind doctors.

In particular they have failed to explicate the relevance and irrelevance of normality. In the commoner understanding normality is absolutely nothing to the point. Sickness can be quite normal, in the sense that most or even all members of a population are so afflicted, just as open dissidence under total socialism is by the same token very much a sacrificial eccentricity. "Disease," however, as opposed to "sickness" or "illness," may be defined in terms of failure to fulfill natural or normal functions, failure that may well be, in the commoner sense, in fact normal. Most actual specimens of whatever it may be, that is, can be in fact diseased. The compact edition of the *Oxford English Dictionary* explains "health" thus: "Soundness of body; that condition in which its functions are duly and efficiently discharged." "Disease" in the relevant sense becomes, correspondingly, "A condition of the body, or of some part or organ of the body, in which its functions are disturbed or deranged."

Certainly this is a viable notion of disease, and one with which it is possible for pure scientists to work without making any disputatious normative commitments. For certainly it is possible to achieve agreements on the function or functions of some organ, and to achieve this even when all available specimens are, through their inability to fulfill that function or those functions, to be accounted defective.[9] But if we do admit this notion, then we must never forget that it is, and should remain, not categorically imperative but strictly nonnormative. So we have to make a very sharp and very firm distinction between disease, in this neutral and surely scientific understanding, and the committed concepts of sickness and illness, as already elucidated.

We can at this stage best enforce this point by referring to the sex organs. It can scarcely be denied that their biological function is reproductive. Yet by this neutral criterion every homosexual employment of these organs, as well as every heterosexual employment in which effective contraceptive precautions are taken, becomes diseased. I trust that there is no one who, at this late hour, remains prepared to urge that such a disease is a sickness or an illness, and hence that such employments constitute appropriate occasions for Hippocratic intervention —for the sake, of course, of the suffering or incapacitated patients!

Notes

1. *Crime and Personality* (London: Paladin, 1964), p. 181. On the general topic of methods for producing radical conversions, compare William Sargant, *Battle for the Mind: A Physiology of Conversion and Brainwashing* (London: Pan, 1959).

2. *Pulse* (May 16, 1981).

3. Ted Patrick, *Let Our Children Go* (New York: Ballantine, 1977).

4. The traditional maxim of the (top) administrative class of the British Civil Service was that experts should be on tap, but never on top.

5. Anyone who truly wants to know the truth about this particular matter

must now consult Eileen Barker, *The Making of a Moonie: Choice or Brainwashing?* (Oxford, and Cambridge, Mass.: Blackwell, 1984). The same author's *New Religious Movements: A Practical Introduction* (London: HMSO, 1989) covers a wider field.

6. Allow me to present here, in the comparative privacy of a footnote, the shamefully trendy coinage, "psychoperson." This, along with its equally new minted cousin, "socioperson," fills what at least should have been a long-felt want. The former term refers indiscriminately to psychotherapists, psychometrists, and practitioners of all the other psychological disciplines, both theoretical and practical, while the latter correspondingly, and with equally indiscriminate abandon, embraces sociologists, demographers, social anthropologists, social workers, and all others trained in or practicing the actual or aspiring social sciences.

7. Compare Antony Flew, *Crime or Disease?* (London: Macmillan 1973), passim, and, of course, chapter 7 above.

8. S. Block and P. Reddaway, *Russia's Political Hospitals* (London: Futura, 1978) and H. Richardson, ed., *New Religions and Mental Health* (New York and Toronto: Mellen, 1980).

9. Recall, again, the example cited in chapter 7 above. In World War II German technical intelligence, working with nothing but mutilated specimens, succeeded in reconstructing both the blueprints and the operating manual of the U.S. Norden bombsight.

13

Three Concepts of Racism

I want to be a man on the same basis and level as any white citizen—
I want to be as free as the whitest citizen. I want to exercise, and
in full, the same rights as the white American. I want to be eligible
for employment exclusively on the basis of my skills and employability,
and for housing solely on my capacity to pay. I want to have the
same privileges, the same treatment in public places as every other
person.

Ralph Bunche,
the first African-American to serve as, among other things,
U.S. permanent representative at the United Nations

So what is racism? And why should we abominate racists? These two
straight questions ought to be both asked and answered, yet all too
rarely are, before anyone either denounces someone else as a racist or
puts forward policies to combat racism. Instead the word "racist," like
the word "fascist," has for many of those most eager to employ it become
a vehemently emotive term of abuse with precious little determinate
descriptive meaning. It is, for instance, significant that when the (British)
National Union of Students first adopted its now notorious "No
Platform!" policy, it was whomsoever the local militants might choose
to denounce as racists and/or fascists who were to be prevented from
speaking in any institution of tertiary education within the United

274

Kingdom. It is equally significant that the supporters and implementers of this "No Platform!" policy never provided definitions enabling outsiders to determine either whether and of precisely what those to be forcibly silenced were guilty, or why guilt on these counts supposedly deserved to be treated as egregiously heinous.

1. Racism as a sort of bad behavior

Once these two initial questions are put and pressed it becomes obvious that, if racism is to be deservedly condemned as wicked, then it must be a kind of bad behavior, rather than a sort of false or otherwise disfavored belief about matters of supposed fact. This first point remains both true and crucial even after we have gone on to recognize that, with this as with other kinds, there are those who will attempt to justify bad behavior by appealing to various matters of actual or alleged fact.

"Racism" should, therefore, be defined as advantaging or disadvantaging someone, as discriminating in their favor or discriminating against them, for no other or better reason than that they belong to one particular racial set and not another. The reason for writing "sets" is that this word does not carry the unwanted implications of "group," "class," or "community." (By Cantor's Axiom for Sets the sole essential feature of a set is that its members share at least one characteristic, any sort of characteristic.) Those who insist upon talking of blacks or of any other racially defined set as a community are thereby suggesting that those concerned see themselves—and, presumably, that they are to be encouraged to continue seeing themselves—as primarily and distinctively members of a racially defined and hence racially exclusive set. If some set just happens to contain members of only one particular race as, for instance, the sets of all Muslims resident in the United Kingdom just happen to consist almost entirely of Asians, then they will not as such be, what of course in fact they are not, racially exclusive. It is if and only if (iff) some set is actually defined as containing members all of whom are to be of one particular race that all others are necessarily excluded.

In this first and recommended understanding it becomes immediately obvious why racism, a.k.a. (unjust) racial discrimination, is morally wrong. Manifestly, it is morally wrong precisely and only because it is unjust. The injustice consists not in treating people in different ways, and hence unequally, but in treating differently, and hence unequally, people who are themselves, *in all relevant respects,* the same. It would be—it is—preposterous to do what nowadays so often is done, namely, to equate justice for all with equality for all. No system of criminal justice, for instance, could survive a requirement to treat offenders in exactly the same way as nonoffenders![1]

Obviously the crucial term here is "relevant." For the defining characteristics by which one race is to be distinguished from another—skin pigmentation, shape of skull, etc.—are strictly superficial and properly irrelevant to all, or almost all,[2] questions of aptitude and employability. To accord decisive weight to differences in respect of any such strictly surface and trifling physical characteristics, when you are making discriminatory decisions the senses of which matter to the individuals concerned, is as grotesquely unfair as to disqualify competing candidates because they are bald, or blond, or red-headed.

If there is to be realistic and constructive discussion in this area, then it is essential to become and remain clear both about precisely what racism is and about why racism, so defined, is properly to be put down as quite self-evidently wrong. It is vital because nowadays people, policies, and even propositions are continually being rejected and denounced as racist notwithstanding that they are not racist at all—not, that is, in any understanding that makes "racism" a word for a sort of morally wrong behavior. At the same time both persons and policies are being promoted as "antiracist" or "against racism" notwithstanding that, in this first and recommended understanding, those persons and those policies are themselves manifestly racist.

In the United Kingdom, for instance, the Commission for Racial Equality (CRE) proclaims in all its publications that it was "set up by the Race Relations Act 1976 with the duties of working towards the elimination of discrimination and promoting equality of opportunity and good relations between racial groups generally." Yet the CRE has never in any of its annual reports recommended that central government should cease its present practice of awarding grants to remedy, in racially defined minority sets of disadvantaged persons, the sorts of disadvantage also suffered, but without similar remedy, by members of the racial majority.[3] Indeed the CRE itself, as is also revealed in its annual reports, does not scruple to fund or otherwise encourage organizations that define themselves as Conferences of [exclusively] Black Filmmakers or Societies of [exclusively] Asian Lawyers or the like. It should also be recalled, much more often than it is, that the universally condemned charter policies of the Nationalist Party in South Africa were all policies to promote racially separate development in racially exclusive local communities . . . *apartheid* being the Afrikaans for apartness.

2. Racism as a kind of heretical belief

It is difficult if not impossible to find any direct and straightforward explication of what needs to be distinguished as a second, unacceptable concept of racism. Those who employ this second concept still treat "racism" and "racist" as among the fiercest terms of abuse. Yet for them to account for and to denounce people as racists it is certainly enough that those people should hold what, in its policy proclamations,[4] the former Inner London Education Authority (ILEA) delicately described as "negative beliefs." Among such must certainly be any that contradict the following categorical pronouncement by the U.S. Department of Labor, a statement issued in 1965 on its own sheer authority and without any citation of supporting evidence:

> Intelligence potential is distributed among Negro infants in the same proportion and pattern as among Icelanders or Chinese, or any other group. . . . There is absolutely no question of any genetic differential.

It was clearly this second concept that in the seventies misguided all those engaged in the great coast-to-coast hounding of Professor Arthur Jensen of the University of California at Berkeley. The reason given for the consequent calls to "Fire Jensen," or even to "Kill Jensen," was that he was a racist. This charge was taken to be proved by the fact that he had in 1969 published an article on "How Much Can We Boost

IQ and Scholastic Achievement?" in the *Harvard Educational Review.* There Jensen had pointed to statistically significant differences in IQ test performance between blacks and other racially defined sets among the U.S. population. He had gone on to argue that these differences, which are of course average differences between sets, must in large part be genetically determined.[5]

More recently, in 1989 a near-unanimous faculty senate of the City College of the City University of New York denounced their philosopher-colleague Michael Levin, and dissociated themselves from his "abhorrent racist utterances." What he had said, in the final paragraph of an article in a small-circulation Australian monthly, was that, again only on average, blacks in IQ tests score fifteen points—about one standard deviation— lower than whites (and hence lower still than Chinese or Japanese).[6]

Most recent and surely most scandalous of all is the case of Jean Philippe Rushton, a distinguished and highly productive professor of psychology in the University of Western Ontario.[7] His fault was to have indicated, and offered a hypothesis to explain, differences between three vast racial sets—negroids, caucasoids, and orientals—differences reported in the social science literature with respect to some sixty variables. Although as always these were average differences between sets, with some individuals rising way above or falling way below whatever was the average for their set, the caucasoid averages regularly lay between those for the negroids and the orientals.

The wider publicization of this work, which had originally been published in respectably refereed scientific journals, led the then premier of Ontario, David Peterson, to denounce it as "highly questionable, destructive, and offensive to the way Ontario thinks," and to call for Rushton's dismissal. The Toronto *Star* published a cartoon showing Rushton in a Ku Klux Klan hood. Later, in an Easter Sunday editorial, the paper linked "an academic at an Ontario university" with the Holo- caust and the Anti-Christ. Within his university many of Rushton's colleagues began to treat him as a pariah. The first steps were taken in official proceedings towards his dismissal. These were reluctantly reversed only after the University of Western Ontario had been subjected to a barrage of protest from scholars in many countries.

None of these three victims of "antiracist" persecution was even being accused or, so far as is known, ever has been accused, of racially discriminating behavior—of racist behavior, that is to say, in our first and recommended sense of "racist." Their offense in the eyes of their persecutors was the holding and propagation of disfavored beliefs.

To define the word "racism" in this second way, the way in which the persecutors of these academic heretics implicitly define it, is to make racism, in the most literal sense, a heresy. For heretics are as such anathematized not for what they do or fail to do but simply for maintaining what are alleged to be false beliefs, or at any rate beliefs they are for some other reason required not to hold. If that is what racism is to be, then we are left with no warrant for denouncing the racist as wicked. Of what moral fault are heretics supposed to be guilty— always, of course, providing that their convictions result from honest and openminded enquiry?[8]

3. What does not and does follow from such heresies

This is not the place to try to reach a categorical conclusion as to whether or not the genetic contention of the U.S. Department of Labor is true. Anyone wanting to know the present state of the scientific investigations, and how that state has been systematically misrepresented in the U.S. media, should refer to a recent, very thorough and conscientious study by Mark Snyderman and Stanley Rathman.[9] What is very much to the present point is to explore the reasons why so many persons of good will see such a doctrine as one which must on no account be questioned.

It is, surely, because they believe, or believe that others will believe, that racially discriminatory conclusions would be validly derivable from "negative beliefs" contradicting that doctrine. They believe, that is to say, that equality of opportunity for members of different racially defined sets can be justified only to the extent that the distribution of all the relevant genes in the gene pools of those different sets is for practical purposes substantially the same. In the United States these misconceptions seem sometimes to arise from a careless reading of a sentence in the Declaration of Independence: "We hold these truths to be self-evident, that all men are created equal, that they are endowed by their Creator with certain inalienable rights, that among these are life, liberty and the pursuit of happiness." But the signers were certainly not asserting that all individuals or all sets of individuals are endowed with the same innate abilities. Even if they had been, those remarkable men certainly had more sense than to think that such a universal and contingent fact could be self-evident. The equality they held to be self-evident, and in which these rights claims are grounded, is our common humanity, the fact that we all are members of a kind of creatures who can and cannot but form projects and make choices.[10]

Some people are indeed disposed invalidly to derive racially discriminatory conclusions from such heretical beliefs about average differences. There are two favorite fallacies here. Besides the so-called Naturalistic Fallacy of pretending to deduce normative (*ought*) conclusions from neutrally descriptive (*is*) premises,[11] there is that of drawing a conclusion about particular members of some set from propositions stating only the average characteristics of that set as a whole—as if we could validly infer from a statement that the average height of some set of people is five feet and nine inches the conclusion either that all of its members are of that height or that none are either much taller or much shorter. The fallaciousness of these two forms of argument is something all sincere opponents of racism have an interest in appreciating and publicizing. Otherwise they are bound to be anxious about research findings that, to those lacking this appreciation, might appear to license racist discrimination.

It should nevertheless be seen as both imprudent and as obscurantist to attempt to prevent research into possible genetically determined, occupationally relevant differences between different racial sets, or to howl down any reported findings of such research as intolerably "offensive to the way Ontario thinks" or any other jurisdiction now thinks. Such attempts to suppress and such uproars of outrage will only lead contra-suggestible inquirers to suspect that reports that are so unwelcome must be true. ("I never," the diplomat said, "believe anything till it has been officially denied.")

If indeed there actually are, on average, substantial, occupationally or achievement-relevant, genetically determined differences between different racially defined sets, then in the long run it will not be possible in otherwise open societies to conceal this fact. All concerned, therefore, are best advised to take a moral originally pointed against historians proposing to justify their own antiracism by reference to the alleged high cultural achievement of ancient (black) African civilizations:

> I would much prefer equal treatment and political rights to be argued from "the brotherhood of man" than from dubious theses of ancient cultural achievement, for I am appalled at the implication that if Africans had no glorious past behind them they would somehow be ineligible for freedom and fraternity.[12]

From propositions asserting the average IQ, the average height or the average anything else of the members of some set, nothing follows about the actual IQ, the actual height, or the actual anything else of any individual member of that set. That is, incontestably, both true and important. But, by the same token, such propositions do carry implications about those same sets considered collectively. And these implications ought to disturb all those inclined to hold either or both of two very different assumptions: that racial equality—a.k.a. racial justice—requires that all racially defined subsets within the population of a multiracial society be (pretty near) proportionately represented in every field of endeavor and achievement, and/or that that is the distribution which, absent all racist discrimination, we may reasonably expect to find.

The two propositions thus conjoined or disjoined need to be clearly distinguished. Whereas the rejection of racist discrimination requires that all individuals be treated on their individual merits, regardless of the particular racial sets of which they may happen to be members, the ideal expressed by the first of these two propositions is radically collectivist. To realize it would in fact require an enormous structure of racist quotas and racist preferences. And in so far as it is realized all holders of coveted positions become bound to both see themselves and be seen not as individuals who had achieved those positions on their own merits but as the appointed representatives of their own particular racial collectivities.

The second proposition expresses a supposedly factual assumption misguiding most of the activists intending to promote the ideal of a color-blind society, the ideal embodied clearly and unambiguously in the U.S. Civil Rights Acts of 1964 and, much less clearly and unambiguously, in the U.K. Race Relations Act of 1976.[13] This assumption misleads those activists to find always more racist discrimination than there actually is, and then, in consequence, to take steps leading inexorably towards the utterly different, collectivist ideal of racial equality as universal proportionate representation.[14]

Those holding either or both of these two assumptions have excellent reasons to be disturbed by the implications of average differences between different racial sets. For instance, given that a characteristic is normally distributed, as is the case with IQ, then a substantial difference between the averages—say that of a single standard deviation—will produce noticeable differences in the numbers at the extremes. This means we should expect, again absent racist discrimination, and all other things being equal, that the set with the higher average IQ will be comparatively overrepresented in the sorts of occupation and achievement demanding very high IQs. On the same assumption we should also expect that set to be correspondingly underrepresented among those rated as, by whatever are the prevailing standards, educationally subnormal.[15]

4. The relevance of cultural diversity

Section 3 distinguished two very different but often conjoined assumptions: first, "that racial equality—a.k.a. racial justice—requires that all racially defined subsets within the population of a multiracial society be (pretty near) proportionately represented in every field of endeavor and achievement"; and second, "that that is the distribution which, absent all racist discrimination, we may reasonably expect to find." Both assumptions presuppose that there are in fact between these racially defined subsets no substantial differences of any kind relevant to occupation or achievement. Section 2 cited claims that there are indeed some such substantial differences, differences that must in part or in sum be genetically determined. (In fact none of these heretics has ever claimed, what all know to be untrue, that heredity provides the full and complete explanation of all observed differences in IQ.)

Part of the spillover into Britain of the Jensen uproar was the publication of a bestselling paperback entitled *Race, Culture and Intelligence*.[16] In their introduction the editors proclaimed, "In planning this book we have attempted to step back from the debate itself and look at the concepts which underlie it. This involves a close examination of the key ideas—intelligence, race, heredity, environment. . . ." In the event neither of the two editors nor any of the other contributors made any attempt either to define the key word, explaining why in that understanding racists are to be abominated, or to disentangle the notions of race and culture.[17]

The differences are absolutely crucial. For while our races are unequivocally determined by our genes, our cultures, in so far as they actually are necessitatingly determined, must be so determined by our environments. So cultures may be and often have been shared by people of different races, while peoples of the same race may have and often have had different cultures. For instance, in its heyday the Roman Empire was multiracial yet monocultural or, at most, allowing for the divide between the Latin West and the Greek East, bicultural, whereas at its foundation the Dominion of Canada was overwhelmingly caucasoid, yet most emphatically and stubbornly bicultural.

The widespread, unquestioning acceptance of the doctrine that a multiracial society must be multicultural, with the cultural differences corresponding to the racial, should be seen as the offspring of conceptual confusion born of historical ignorance. Those who in this way constantly confound race with culture need to be reminded that it was an essential element in the authentically racist teachings of Adolf Hitler's National-Socialist German Workers' party that German high culture could not have been produced and could not be fully shared by anyone not of the right, supposedly superior race.

Just as there are those who in the name of "antiracism" would have it that there cannot be genetically determined, occupationally relevant differences between different racially defined sets, so there are those who for the same (motivating rather than evidencing) reason insist that there are, there can be, no properly relevant differences between cultures.[18] Thus, in *Race Culture and Intelligence,* Donald Swift, professor of education in the Open University, apparently felt no scruples about maintaining that the politically correct "cannot accept quality distinctions between cultures" (p. 156).

In the traditional sense of the word "culture" only the more elevated activities of a people count as constituting its culture, and in that sense a people could conceivably be without any culture at all.[19] But in the present sense, which is that of the anthropologists and other social scientists, every social set must necessarily have some culture. For now a culture is every kind of acquired preference, loyalty, disposition, social practice, and what have you, and not only of those involved in activities that are, in the traditional understanding, specifically cultural.

We need a further distinction in order to dispose of the outrageous yet nowadays commonplace claims that all cultures are equally good, and that—"in a multiracial society"—all equally must be "affirmed" and encouraged. (It is remarkable that none of those who are so strenuous and persistent in making such claims ever notices the implication that racist and sexist cultures must therefore be just as good as their antitheses!) The distinction we need is that between instrumental and noninstrumental goods. To value something noninstrumentally is to value it as good in itself, irrespective of any possible further consequences of having it, whereas to value something instrumentally is to value it as a means to achieving some other and further end or ends.

To maintain that anything is noninstrumentally valuable is indeed to make a value judgment, which is, no doubt, an inherently contentious move. For it is to say that, regardless of consequences, but all other things being equal, whatever it is that is thus noninstrumentally valued ought to be preferred. But to maintain that something is instrumentally valuable, adding the needed indication of the presumptively good end or ends to which it is alleged in fact to be a means, is to make a purely (would be) factual assertion, an assertion that must therefore be unequivocally true or false. For it is to say, only and precisely, that what is thus instrumentally valuable in fact just *is* an effective means of achieving a certain objective, and all this quite regardless of whether you or I or anyone else either *does want* or *ought to want* that particular objective.

This abstract and philosophical distinction has a completely concrete and practical application, for it enables us conveniently to bypass all those judgments of intrinsic value that a generation rotted with relativism is so reluctant to make. For there can be no doubt that there are certain features of certain cultures that will help and others that will hinder those immersed in those cultures if they wish to pursue a career in some wider society. Take language, for instance, at the same time perhaps the least controversial and certainly the most important case. Whatever may be urged for or against the claims to intrinsic merit of this or that natural language, there can be no question that the instrumentally most valuable for you is that of the country in which you hope to earn your living.

Wherever it is worth anyone's while to distinguish one ethnic or racial set from another there always are, there are almost bound to be, sufficient cultural differences between those sets to account for what are often remarkable, indeed sometimes quite spectacular, differences in their actual achievements. The indispensable source here is *Ethnic America: A History* (New York: Basic, 1981), by the distinguished (and, as it happens, black) economist Thomas Sowell. This book contains an abundance of examples of sometimes spectacular performance differences between different racial or ethnic sets that no hypothesis of hostile or friendly discrimination can possibly explain. How, for instance, could any such hypothesis account for the striking superiority of the track record of blacks immigrating from the West Indies as compared with that of native-born black Americans? (pp. 216–20). Or again: "Back before World War I, a study in New York City showed that German and Jewish school children graduated from high school at a rate more than a hundred times that for Irish or Italian children."[20] Now that really was for the Irish and Italians an achievement in underachievement! Nor, in view of the later rises of both the Irish-Americans and the Italian-Americans, is it plausible to try to diminish this negative achievement by postulating any genetically determined average inferiorities?

5. Racism and antiracism as ideologies

The fullest formulation of the third concept of racism comes from the United Kingdom. It was apparently developed by the Institute of Race Relations (IRR) in London,[21] and has certainly been employed to guide or misguide the policies of many local education authorities (school districts) in the United Kingdom. But it also has a much wider importance. For it provides a systematic ideological justification for various preferential policies that are also being implemented or advocated in the United States and elsewhere. Furthermore, we should notice that the IRR and its revealingly entitled journal, *Race and Class,* continues to receive funding from the World Council of Churches through its Programme to Combat Racism. This third concept is defined as follows[22]:

> There are certain routine practices, customs and procedures in our society whose consequence is that black people have poorer jobs, health, housing and life-chances than do the white majority. . . . These practices and customs are maintained by relations and structures of power, and are justified by centuries-old beliefs and attitudes which hold that black people are essentially inferior to white people—biologically, or culturally, or both. "Racism" is a shorthand term for this combination of discriminatory practices, unequal relations and structures of power, and negative beliefs and attitudes.

The word "black" was previously redefined to include "*both* Afro-Caribbean *and* Asian," while "Afro-Caribbean" was itself extended to include all and only those previously rated black. Obviously, the first purpose of this redefinition is, by collapsing distinctions between different racial sets and thus concealing the very different track records of those sets, to clear the way for the contention that any disadvantage in any racial minority, as compared with the white majority, is to be put down to hostile racial discrimination by that majority.[23] The second purpose is revealingly illuminated by quoting a disclaimer added, so far as I know, only in that collection generally entitled *Race, Sex and Class* from the Inner London Education Authority. (The then political masters of that authority could claim to have anticipated by several years the

Rev. Jesse Jackson's attempt to form a Rainbow Coalition of all who can be persuaded to see themselves as aggrieved victims of oppression):

> Other groups . . . also suffer varying degrees of prejudice and discrimination . . . Chinese, Greek Cypriots, Turkish Cypriots, Turks, Vietnamese, Moroccans . . . Irish . . . Jews. . . . *In using the term "black" in this paper it is not the Authority's intention to exclude any minority group.* (emphasis supplied)

The first objection to this third definition is that it refuses to recognize any racism save that of hostile discrimination by whites against nonwhites. Since for some years British classrooms had contained children of Asians driven from Uganda by the black racist policies of the unspeakable Amin, and since everyone with experience of those multiracial classrooms recalls some cases both of black children insulting whites or Asians as such, and of Asians generally unenthusiastic about blacks, this refusal is bound to raise questions about both the suitability and indeed the sincerity of the consequently proposed policies for "antiracist education." But we need here to take note also of the much more widely important fact that the Programme to Combat Racism launched by the World Council of Churches has from the beginning deliberately maintained a similarly exclusive, "whites only," concern.[24]

The second objection is that this third definition makes racism, at least in the first instance, a characteristic of social institutions rather than of individual behaviors. But the truth is that, in the true sense explained earlier, racism, like the violent causing of gross bodily harm, is essentially intentional. So to speak where intention is absent of either institutionalized racism or institutionalized violence is a perversion,[25] for it is natural to resent intentionally inflicted evils precisely in as much as they are inflicted intentionally. Hence to redefine the word "racism," in a way which makes all comparative disadvantage in all recognized minority groups necessarily a product of what is still inevitably going to be construed as intentionally hostile racist discrimination is—presumably of intent—to cause it to be resented in the way in which it would be, and indeed quite rightly, if it truly was so produced.

The third objection to this third definition is that it refers to eventual consequences rather than original intentions, and to inequalities of outcome rather than inequalities of opportunity. Given this, and given too that for some reason unstated racism is still to be public enemy number one, then sooner or later we are going to be asked to condemn and abandon anything and everything the actual effects of which are that the racial distribution in any social group is substantially different from that in the population as a whole. If there are X percent of blacks and Y percent of Asians in the population as a whole, then there will have to be (at least approximately) X percent of blacks and Y percent of Asians in every profession, class, team, area, or what have you.

That these are indeed the intended implications becomes clearer as we read on in *Race, Sex and Class*. Since the abomination of racism is defined as embracing all, repeat all, "practices, customs and procedures whose consequence is that black people have poorer jobs, health, housing, education and life-chances than do the white majority," it is now:

> necessary to remove those practices and procedures which discriminate against black pupils/students and their families. These include courses, syllabuses, schemes of work, topics, textbooks, materials and methods which ignore or deny the validity of black experience, perspectives and culture; some of the tests and other criteria, including teachers' expectations, which govern access and admission to particular schools or post-school courses, or are used to allocate pupils/students to particular sets, streams, classes, or bands.[26]

The "tests and other criteria" it is thus thought necessary to remove are—note well—not any that in some traditional understanding, discriminate irrelevantly and unfairly. On the contrary: it has become sufficient to simply show that some approved minority set performs worse than the majority. Inferior performance now has to be accepted, not as at best more or less good evidence, but as the decisive criterion for racist discrimination. Similarly, wherever U.S. courts and other "civil rights" enforcement agencies find that some "tests and other criteria" have what they call "disparate impact," they become licensed to infer "institutional discrimination," something which in that country is explicitly allowed to embrace the unintentional.

If and in so far as any institution anywhere does proceed to introduce new "tests and other criteria" deliberately designed to satisfy this pretended "antiracist" requirement, then it will itself be practising, in the true sense first defined, unjust racial discrimination. For such new "tests and other criteria" will have been specifically designed by reference to the racial set membership of those to be subjected thereto. This racist practice—described in the United States as "race norming" to remedy "disparate impact"—is now in that country apparently a commonplace.[27] So far I know of no absolutely clearcut parallel in the United Kingdom. But that, unless we have a sharp change of course, is where we too are set to arrive ultimately.

The inescapable yet extremely paradoxical consequences of the widespread acceptance of the third concept of racism—which, by the way, seems to embrace the second—thus is the progressive replacement of what under that concept is so misleadingly characterized as institutional or institutionalized racism by what really and truly is, under the first and traditional concept, institutionalized racism![28]

Notes

1. For an extended critique of this seemingly ever more popular misconception compare my *The Politics of Procrustes: Contradictions of Enforced Equality* (Buffalo, N.Y.: Prometheus Books, 1981), chapters 2 to 4.

2. The trifling qualification "or almost all" does perhaps need to be included lest we be called upon to condemn some theater director for preferring a black actor for the name part in *Othello* while refusing to hire an otherwise well-qualified but black actress to play Desdemona.

3. See Antony Flew, *A Future for Anti-Racism?* (London: Social Affairs Unit, 1992), and compare Frank Palmer, ed., *Anti-Racism: An Assault on Education and Value* (London: Sherwood, 1986); Russell Lewis, *Anti-Racism: A Mania Exposed* (London: Quartet, 1988); and Ray Honeyford, *Integration or Disintegration?: Towards a Non-Racist Society* (London: Claridge, 1988).

4. These "antiracist and multicultural" policies were propounded in four documents under the general title *Race, Sex and Class,* distributed, at the beginning of the academic year 1983–84, to all teachers employed by ILEA. The subtitles were: *Achievement in Schools; Multi-ethnic Education in Schools;*

A Policy for Equality: Race; and *Anti-Racist Statement and Guidelines.*

5. For Jensen's own story, compare his *Genetics and Education* (London: Methuen, 1972). For another account of this affair, together with accounts of all too many similar persecutions, see Roger Pearson, *Race, Intelligence and Bias in Academe* (Washington, D.C.: Scott Townsend, 1991).

6. See Daniel Seligman, "The Case of Michael Levin," in the *National Review* (May 5, 1989): 39–40.

7. See Barry R. Gross, "The Case of Philippe Rushton," in *Academic Questions* 3, no. 4 (1990): 33–46, and further references given there. In this case and in that of Michael Levin I am drawing also on personal communications.

8. The fulfillment of that proviso must, surely, be the ground for claims to a moral as opposed to a legal right to academic freedoms. For these are to be defended not as rights to proclaim and propagate whatever we fancy, irrespective of all reasoned and evidenced objections, but as freedoms to pursue, and to publish and to teach the results of, sincerely truth-directed critical inquiry. See, for instance, my *Sociology, Equality and Education* (London, and New York: Macmillan, and St. Martins, 1976), chapter 8, or "Academic Freedoms and Academic Purposes," in *Education Today* (December 1990).

9. *The IQ Controversy: The Media and Public Policy* (New Brunswick, N.J., and London: Transaction, 1990). The heresies evidenced here include, generally, anything contradicting Horace Kaller's claim in the article "Behaviourism," in the 1935 edition of the *Encyclopaedia of Social Sciences:* "At birth human infants, regardless of their heredity, are as equal as Fords."

10. For what Mr. Jefferson, who actually drafted the Declaration, himself believed here, see my *The Politics of Procrustes: Contradictions of Enforced Equality* (London, and Buffalo, N.Y.: Temple Smith, and Prometheus Books, 1981), pp. 32–33, while for an explanation and defense of such a grounding compare my *Equality in Liberty and Justice* (London: Routledge, 1989), chapter 2.

11. For discussion of this fallacy, see W. D. Hudson, ed., *The Is/Ought Question* (London, and New York: Macmillan, and St. Martins, 1969).

12. Melvin Lasky, *Africa for Beginners* (London: Weidenfeld and Nicolson, 1962), p. 153n.

13. For a critique of this act, compare my *A Future for Anti-Racism?* (1992).

14. The best account of this development as it has occurred in the United States is provided by Herman Belz, *Equality Transformed: A Quarter Century of Affirmative Action* (New Brunswick, N.J., and London: Transaction, 1992).

15. Compare Jensen, *Genetics and Education* (1972), pp. 241–42, 330–

32, and passim.

16. Ken Richardson and David Spears, eds., *Race, Culture and Intelligence* (Harmondsworth: Penguin, 1972).

17. If only they had then what likes to describe itself as the "Career Teachers Organization," they might not, in *Multi-Ethnic Education* (Birmingham, England: NAS/UWT, no date) have mistaken it to be manifest that multiracial entails multicultural, when, on the contrary, it ought to have been obvious that it does not: "The NAS/UWT accepts the fundamental principle . . . that since we live in a multiracial society, *all* pupils . . . should be taught in such a way as to reflect the multicultural approach to the curriculum" (p. 4).

18. Philosophers are given to warning against deducing an *ought* from an *is* (the Naturalistic Fallacy). But, as Wallace Matson has observed, the stronger contemporary temptation seems to be to move no less invalidly in the opposite direction.

19. Consider, for instance, the unfortunate Ik, whose appalling conditions are described in Colin Turnbull, *The Mountain People* (London: Cape, 1973).

20. Thomas Sowell, *The Economics and Politics of Race* (New York: William Morrow, 1983), p. 38.

21. For information about the character and activities of Dr. Ambalvaner Sivarandan, director of the IRR, see the article "Racial Mischief" in Frank Palmer, ed., *Anti-Racism* (1986).

22. In the documents listed in note 4 above.

23. For available evidence showing that Asian children whose parents originated in India and Pakistan were in fact already performing significantly *better* than whites, and blacks coming from the Caribbean significantly *worse*, see Flew, *A Future for Anti-Racism?* (1992).

24. See, for instance, Bernard Smith, *The Fraudulent Gospel: Politics and the World Council of Churches* (London: Covenant, 1991), and compare Ernest Lefever, *Amsterdam to Nairobi: The World Council of Churches and the Third World* (Washington, D.C.: Georgetown University Ethics and Public Policy Center, 1979).

25. For discussion of what can and cannot properly be characterized as institutionalized racism and institutionalized violence, compare my *Thinking about Social Thinking*, rev. ed. (London: Harper-Collins, 1992), pp. 72ff.

26. *Multi-ethnic Education in Schools*, appendix A, p. 21. (See note 4 above.)

27. See, for instance, Dinesh D'Souza, *Illiberal Education: The Politics of Race and Sex on Campus* (New York: The Free Press, 1991), and compare

Belz, *Equality Transformed* (1992).

28. Recently, in his regular column for the *Washington Times,* the distinguished (and, as it happens, black) economist Walter Williams both reported and denounced the racially discriminatory pass marks in the written examinations for promotion to the rank of sergeant in the New York City Police Department (75 percent for whites, 69 percent for hispanics, and 65 percent for blacks). Apparently, and much to their credit, some black candidates have proudly and properly refused to accept such promotion until they could earn it on the more exacting standard demanded of whites.

14

Freedom and Human Nature

Our hope that freedom is not going to be ultimately destroyed by
the joint pressure of totalitarianism and the general bureaucratization
of the world, and indeed our very readiness to defend it, depends
crucially on our belief that the desire for freedom . . . is not an
accidental fancy of history, nor a result of peculiar social conditions
or a temporary by-product of specific economic life forms . . . but
that it is rooted in the very quality of being human.

Leszek Kolakowski[1]

Taking the words "freedom" and "liberty" to be for present purposes
substantially synonymous, this concluding chapter argues that
Kolakowski was right. The first necessity here is to distinguish two
fundamentally different yet intimately connected senses of these key
words. Kolakowski's concern was with what—so long as we do not
forget that liberties may also sometimes be guaranteed or limited by
institutions other than the state—we can conveniently call political
freedom. The other sense refers to what it is usual albeit, as has been
argued earlier,[2] extremely misleading to characterize as the freedom of
the will. The making of this preliminary distinction opens the way for
the contention that it must be very difficult, if not practically impossible,
to become and to remain committed to the extension of political liberties
and the defense of political freedom so long as you refuse to recognize

that such "freedom of the will" is indeed "rooted in the very quality of being human."

That it is in fact so rooted surely became clear in section 5 of chapter 5 above. For there, with the help of the great chapter "Of Power" in Locke's *Essay concerning Human Understanding,* we reminded ourselves that we are all members of a peculiar kind of creatures which can, and therefore cannot but,[3] make choices. Furthermore the very ideas of choice and of being able to do other than we actually do—to say nothing of the scientifically and practically essential ideas of physical necessity, physical impossibility, and contrary-to-fact conditionality—could, it was argued, only be acquired and employed by creatures capable of understanding and explaining them by reference to their own experience.

Once we have recognized that we are indeed agents, who as such can and cannot but make choices between alternative physically possible courses of action or inaction, and who, also as such, possess various kinds and amounts of power (personal), then it becomes obvious both that this complex fact is of enormous and quite fundamental importance for our understanding of the nature of man and that it must have substantial bearing upon questions about which of our choices ought properly to be subject to some external coercion or constraint, and how much and of what kinds.

1. A "science" of man without anthropomorphism

Some years ago now, under the sinister yet altogether fitting title *Beyond Freedom and Dignity,* the then doyen of behavioristic psychology, B. F. Skinner, made what his publishers described as his "definitive statement about man and society." This "definitive statement" provides abundant illustrative material under both heads.

Skinner's catastrophic, misguiding principle was that, to be genuinely scientific, any study of man must eschew all anthropomorphic notions. The explicit and authoritative statement of this grotesque general assumption is possibly more important than anything else in the entire book. For Skinner said outright what others more cautious leave implicit.

He began, "We have used the instruments of science; we have counted and measured and compared; but something essential to scientific practice is missing in almost all current discussions of human behavior."[4]

It appears that what is missing is, awkwardly, the absence of certain notions that Skinner insists can have no place in any truly scientific discourse. For, he continued, "although physics soon stopped personifying things . . . it continued for a long time to speak as if they had wills, impulses, feelings, purposes and other fragmentary attributes of an indwelling agent. . . . All this was eventually abandoned, and to good effect." Nevertheless, deplorably, what should be "the behavioral sciences still appeal to comparable internal states."[5]

We are, therefore, supposed to regret that "almost everyone who is concerned with human affairs—as political scientist, philosopher, man of letters, economist, psychologist, linguist, sociologist, theologian, educator, or psychotherapist—continues to talk about human behavior in this prescientific way."[6] We all of us, that is to say, continue to ask for and to offer explanations of the conduct of agents in terms of the plans and the purposes, the desires and decisions, of those agents themselves. But "a scientific analysis," we were told, "shifts both the responsibility and the achievement to the environment."[7]

So it is, it seems, unscientific to claim that anyone ever effected anything. Hence certain unnamed Freudians were rebuked for recklessly "assuring their patients that they are free to choose among different courses of action and are in the long run the architects of their own destinies."[8] For Skinner as a psychological scientist the true causes of all human behavior were, and could only be, both environmental and necessitating.

Certainly all such everyday discourse about the conduct of agents has to be prescientific in the obvious, purely temporal sense that it was going on long before there was anything that deserved to be called science. Yet Skinner clearly took it to be not only, innocuously, prescientific, but also, damagingly, unscientific. He took it that it must be just as much a superstitious mistake thus to try to explain the actions of an actual person by reference to his will, impulses, feelings, and purposes as it undoubtedly would be first to personify some inanimate object, and then to undertake to explain its movements in the same sort of way. However, the reason why the latter enterprise would be superstitious and a mistake is, of course, that inanimate objects are not people or even brutes, and hence do not and cannot have wills, impulses, feelings, purposes, or any other such human attributes. But the former undertaking is, by the same token, neither superstitious nor a mistake. So any psychological program committed to maintaining the contrary is, by that preposterous commitment alone, sufficiently discredited.

The first reason why Skinner believed that he had to embrace this absurdity is, as we have just seen, that he misconstrued the expulsion of such notions from physics as the repudiation of essentially superstitious ideas, rather than as the rejection of misapplications of ideas in themselves entirely proper, indeed indispensable.

Skinner's second reason is that he wants to ask and to answer questions other than those to which such prescientific explanations are relevant, and that he also believes that different explanations must always and necessarily be competing for the same logical space. Thus he writes: "If we ask someone, 'Why did you go to the theatre?' and he says, 'Because I felt like going,' we are apt to take his reply as a kind of explanation."[9]

We are indeed. For that "I wanted to go to the theatre" or that "I am determined to make it with Cyn," may fully explain conduct previously found puzzling. What these responses will not do is answer the additional questions: why I have a taste, and this particular taste, for the theatre; and why I find girls, and in particular Cynthia, so powerfully attractive. But these are the kind of questions Skinner wants to press: "It would be much more to the point to know what has happened when he has gone to the theatre in the past, what he has heard and read about the play he went to see, and what other things in his past or present environments induced him to go."[10]

The third reason is more particular. It is that Skinner saw all these ideas of will, feeling, purpose, intention, and so on as involving and involved in what was for him an utterly unacceptable concept, "autonomous man." This is something of which he had much to say in *Beyond Freedom and Dignity*. But the most revealing statement was put into the mouth of Frazier in chapter 29 of Skinner's earlier work, the utopian novel *Walden Two:* " 'I deny that freedom exists at all. I must deny it or my programme would be absurd. You can't have a science about a subject matter which hops capriciously about.' "[11]

On the contrary: it is Skinner's actual program that truly is absurd. It is a program for erecting a science of human behavior upon the false and perversely factitious assumption that all behavior is physically necessitated, and none of it the conduct of agents who always as such could do other than they in fact do do.

Skinner was wrong too in insisting that to admit the reality of agency must be to foreclose on the possibility of discovering causes and developing a science. The first essential here is to distinguish two crucially different senses of the word "cause." This distinction—as was noted in chapter 5 above—seems to have been introduced first by Hume. But, having earlier denied the legitimacy of any conception of physical necessity, he had disqualified himself from admitting what is for us the crux. In his essay "Of National Characters" he wrote, "By *moral* causes I mean all circumstances, which are fitted to work on the mind as motives or reasons. . . . By *physical* causes I mean those qualities of the air and climate, which are supposed to work insensibly on the temper, by altering the tone and habit of the body."[12]

This distinction between two senses of the word "cause" is at the same time a distinction between the different subject materials of the physical and the human sciences—what Hume would have called the moral sciences.[13] For there is an absolutely fundamental difference between, on the one hand, ensuring that people will act in one particular way by providing them with some overwhelmingly strong reason so to do, and on the other hand making some purely physical phenomenon happen by bringing about the causally sufficient conditions of its occurrence.

That absolutely fundamental difference is that, whereas such sufficient physical causes physically necessitate the occurrence of their effects, correspondingly sufficient moral causes do not. If, for instance, I convey to you some splendid news—news that if you decided to celebrate, you and everyone else would point to as the cause of that celebration, I do not by so doing ensure that you must, willy-nilly, celebrate. Actions thus caused by moral causes are neither uncaused nor necessarily capricious and inexplicable, although, inasmuch as they are indeed actions, it is impossible for them to be physically necessitated. It is equally mistaken to assume, as apparently Skinner did and many professing psychological and social scientists still do, that all environmental causes are, in the sense explained, physical. If indeed they were, then they would presumably be necessitating and hence excusing.

2. Possible applications of such supposed science

Since he outright denied the reality of agency and choice, Skinner was bound to make a shambles of all the crucial distinctions. And so he did. The previous section attended to what Skinner insisted must be the necessary presuppositions of a science of psychology. But his chief concern, not only in *Walden Two* but also in *Beyond Freedom and Dignity,* was the application of that science; and he came to write about it as if it was something we, or at any rate he, already had. Thus the later book begins with a review of "the terrifying problems that face us in the world today." It then proceeds to argue that to solve these problems "we need to make vast changes in human behavior," so that "what we need is a technology of behavior." He eventually concludes, "A scientific view of man offers exciting possibilities. We have not yet seen what man can make of man."[14]

We have to recognize, what is not immediately obvious from this latest statement, that Skinner's political program is designed for a totalitarian "party of the vanguard,"[15] although it is in our time unusual among such programs in owing nothing to Lenin. The crux is to appreciate that the words "we" and "man," upon which so much depends, are not always used to refer to exactly the same sets. Earlier, in chapter 31 of *Walden Two,* Frazier made exactly this point, with characteristic frankness: " 'When we ask what Man can make of Man, we don't mean the same thing by "Man" in both instances. We mean to ask what a few men can make of mankind. And that's the all-absorbing question of the twentieth century. What kind of world can we build—those of us who understand the science of behavior?' "

*   *   *

(i) Several elements in the answer to this key question are revealed in *Beyond Freedom and Dignity*. First, Skinner refused to recognize any real difference between a set-up in which abortion is illegal and one in which it is not. In the latter case, "The individual is 'permitted' to decide the issue for himself [sic], simply in the sense that he [sic] will act because of consequences to which legal punishment is no longer to be added."[16] It is, of course, about precisely this to Skinner entirely insubstantial difference that the legalization versus criminalization battles rage.

(ii) Second, Skinner considers "the practice of inviting prisoners to volunteer for possibly dangerous experiments—for example, on new drugs—in return for better living conditions or shorter sentences." He asks, rhetorically, "But are they really free when positively reinforced . . . ?"[17] Since positive reinforcement is Skinner's technical way of talking about the promised rewards, the correct answer is, clearly, "Yes." The crucial contrast is, for instance, with those prisoners in Belsen and Dachau who were forced to become subjects for medical experimentation with no alternative choice, and without promise of reward.

(iii) Third, "A person never becomes truly self-reliant. Even though he deals effectively with things, he is necessarily dependent upon those who have taught him to do so."[18] But what self-reliance excludes is present dependence, not having been so educated in the past that you have now become self-reliant. (It is disturbing to reflect that a great many of those employed to study and to teach educational psychology in the United States belong to this lamentably illiberal and preposterously blinkered Harvard school.)

(iv) Fourth, and finally, Skinner refuses to allow any important difference between persuasion by the giving of reasons and "persuasion" by forcible methods of mind-bending: " 'Brain-washing' is proscribed by those who otherwise condone the changing of minds, simply because the control is obvious."[19] But the issue—examined in chapter 12 above—does not concern what is overt as opposed to what is covert. It is, rather, a matter of giving or not giving what are, or are thought to be, good reasons, as well as of employing or not employing force and the threat of force. (No doubt the whole business of giving and considering reasons is out of place and unfamiliar in and around the rat cages and pigeon lofts of a Skinnerian psychology laboratory.)

Politically libertarian hopes perhaps rise a little when we read, "Permissive practices have many advantages." Any such hopes are soon dashed: "Permissiveness is not, however, a policy; it is the abandonment of policy, and its apparent advantages are illusory. To refuse to control is to leave control not to the person himself, but to other parts of the social and non-social environments."[20]

This statement is on two counts obnoxious. First, even if I have got to be controlled either by a person or by impersonal forces, still the difference between these alternatives matters enormously. If, for instance, I suffer something painful, I am much less upset if I believe this to be the result of blind forces than if I believe it to be someone's malign intention. (This is one reason why a moment's thought makes the ideal of a totally planned society so repellent to all but those who see themselves as the total planners, and, correspondingly, so endlessly enchanting to actual or aspiring members of such power elites.)

Second, Skinner's contention that leaving control to the person himself is an illusion is supported only by his insistence that the true and always necessitating causes of human behavior are, and can only be, environmental. This is a misconception, as crucial as it is fundamental. For, as we saw in section 1 above, the causes of most if not all of those of our behaviors that are actions are, because moral, non-necessitating, while the immediate moral cause of those same behaviors cannot be, because internal, environmental.

This crucial and fundamental Skinnerian misconception is peculiarly incongruous with the program proclaimed in *Walden Two*, the program, that is, under which the unenlightened, psychologically lay masses are to be controlled—for our own good, of course—by a psychologically initiated elite. For how, upon Skinner principles, can it be right to say that in Skinner's Utopia it would be Skinner's Controllers who would be controlling the lesser breeds, rather than the environment of the Controllers that would be ultimately controlling everybody?[21]

Notes

1. Author of a monumental three-volume study of the *Main Currents of Marxism: Its Rise, Growth and Dissolution* (Oxford: Clarendon, 1978), and, before his exile in 1968, professor of philosophy in the University of Warsaw.

2. In subsection 6 (iii) of chapter 2 above.

3. "For it is unavoidably necessary to prefer the doing, or forebearance, of an Action in a Man's power. . . . a Man must necessarily *will* the one, or the other, of them; upon which preference, or volition, the action, or its forebearance, certainly follows, and is truly voluntary: But the act of volition, or preferring one of the two, being that which he cannot avoid, a Man, in respect of that act of *willing,* is under a necessity, and so cannot be free." So Locke in section 23 of that chapter (pp. 246–47 of the standard Nidditch edition).

4. B. F. Skinner, *Beyond Freedom and Dignity* (New York: Knopf, 1971), p. 7. This work was also published in the United Kingdom, and later Pelicanned.

5. Ibid., p. 8.

6. Ibid., p. 9.

7. Ibid., p. 25.

8. Ibid., pp. 20–21.

9. Ibid., pp. 12–13.

10. Ibid., p. 13.

11. B. F. Skinner, *Walden Two* (New York: Macmillan, 1948).

12. David Hume, *Essays Moral, Political and Literary,* ed. E. F. Miller (Indianapolis, Ind.: Liberty, 1985), p. 198.

13. See Antony Flew, *David Hume: Philosopher of Moral Science* (Oxford: Blackwell, 1986), passim, and compare the same author's *Thinking about Social Thinking* (London: Harper-Collins, 1992), chapters 3, 6, and 7.

14. *Beyond Freedom and Dignity,* pp. 3, 4, 5, and 215.

15. Compare J. L. Talmon, *The Origins of Totalitarian Democracy* (London: Secker and Warburg, 1952), passim.

16. *Beyond Freedom and Dignity,* p. 97.

17. Ibid., p. 39.

18. Ibid., p. 91. This implicit insistence upon impossibly demanding criteria for self-reliance constitutes a paradigm case of what Paul Edwards in "Bertrand Russell's Doubts about Induction" in Antony Flew, ed., *Logic and Language* (Oxford: Blackwell, First Series, 1951), christened "high redefinition."

19. *Beyond Freedom and Dignity,* p. 96.

20. Ibid., p. 84.

21. Are they supposed to have escaped from the supposedly universal human condition, under which we are all completely creatures of our environments, and, if so, how? Skinner would appear to have been both a client of the self-destructive kind of naturalism considered in section 6 of chapter 5 above and a protagonist of what in his *The Plato Cult and Other Philosophical Follies* (Oxford: Blackwell, 1991) David Stove calls "the Ishmael effect." Skinner's general account of the human condition leaves no room for his own rational initiatives.